Michael White is the author of the internationally bestselling novel *Equinox*. He is the author of thirty-five books including the international best-sellers *Stephen Hawking: A Life in Science* (with John Gribbin), *Leonardo: The First Scientist*, *Tolkien: A Biography* and *The Science of the X-Files*. There are over 200 editions of Michael White's books published globally. He was awarded the Bookman Prize in the US for best popular science book of 1998 for his biography of Isaac Newton, *The Last Sorcerer*. In 2002 his book *Rivals* was short-listed for the prestigious Aventis Award and in 2006 his *Fruits of War* was long-listed for the prize. Michael White has been a newspaper columnist, science editor for *GQ* magazine and a series consultant for the Discovery Channel's *The Science of the Impossible*. In 2001 he was awarded a Distinguished Talent visa by the Australian government and now lives in Sydney with his wife and four children.

For more information visit Michael White's website at: www.michaelwhite.com.au

Also by Michael White

STEPHEN HAWKING: A LIFE IN SCIENCE
(with John Gribbin)

EINSTEIN: A LIFE IN SCIENCE
(with John Gribbin)

DARWIN: A LIFE IN SCIENCE
(with John Gribbin)

ASIMOV: THE UNAUTHORISED LIFE

BREAKTHROUGH: THE HUNT FOR THE BREAST CANCER GENE
(with Kevin Davies)

MOZART

LENNON

NEWTON

GALILEO

THE SCIENCE OF THE X-FILES

ISAAC NEWTON: THE LAST SORCERER

LIFE OUT THERE

ALIEN LIFE FORMS

MIND AND MATTER

SUPERSCIENCE

TOLKIEN

THE POPE AND THE HERETIC

MACHIAVELLI: A MAN MISUNDERSTOOD

C. S. LEWIS: THE BOY WHO CREATED NARNIA

LEONARDO DA VINCI

The First Scientist

Michael White

ABACUS

First published in Great Britain in 2000
by Little, Brown and Company
This paperback edition published in 2001 by Abacus
Reprinted 2001 (three times), 2003, 2004, 2005, 2007, 2009, 2010, 2012

A CIP catalogue record for this book
is available from the British Library.

ISBN 978-0-349-11274-9

Typeset in Perpetua by M Rules
Printed and bound in Great Britain by
Clays Ltd, St Ives plc

Papers used by Abacus are from well-managed forests
and other responsible sources.

MIX
Paper from
responsible sources
FSC® C104740

Abacus
An imprint of
Little, Brown Book Group
100 Victoria Embankment
London EC4Y 0DY

An Hachette UK Company
www.hachette.co.uk

www.littlebrown.co.uk

For our son, George, born 8 December 1998

CONTENTS

'*It seems that in him all science was born, and that he is passing it on to succeeding centuries as in a grandiose sketch.*'

FOREWORD

Leonardo da Vinci was my childhood hero, and he remains one of the few great geniuses of history (accompanied on my personal rostrum by Mozart, Egon Schiele and Charles Darwin) whose personality as well as his work still inspires me to value humanity. As a boy, I wanted to know everything I could about Leonardo. I tried to immerse myself in his world. In fact, it is no exaggeration to say that I wanted to *be* Leonardo.

Having now completed this biography (something I never dreamed as a child I would ever do), he is even more important to me, for I feel I have grown to know him just about as well as I could hope from my position in time almost half a millennium after his death.

When I began to research this account I had just stepped back from three years spent with a very different historical figure, Sir Isaac Newton, the subject of my most recent biography, *The Last Sorcerer*. It had not been easy living with Newton; a great intellect he undoubtedly had and revolutionary thinker he certainly was, but he was also a spiteful, twisted, often cruel individual. Leonardo was a man who, except for his brilliance, was the very opposite of Sir Isaac, and I have come away from this interpretation of his life in better spirits for it.

In beginning this book I did not want to simply produce yet another 'Life of Leonardo'. There have been far too many of those. I wanted instead to tackle an ignored aspect of the man. As well as telling the story of his life as we know it, I wanted to set into sharp relief what I believe to be a face of Leonardo every bit as impressive, glamorous and inspirational as the familiar one of Leonardo: the artist. My Leonardo is a colourful, untameable eccentric, a risk-taker, a man who strayed very close to the edge of heresy and necromancy, a man gifted in so many ways it was almost impossible for him to settle upon any one thing that fascinated him or any one skill above all others. But more than this, my Leonardo is Leonardo: the first scientist.

In this book, Leonardo's scientific ideas take priority. I'm not qualified to interpret his artistic contribution or to analyse individual paintings, although I do of course discuss his life as an artist; how could a biographer of Leonardo ignore it? But then, even Leonardo's art was infused with his understanding of science. Indeed, I argue that his last and greatest paintings were paeans to his paired skills as an artist and a scientist, celebrations of his twinned talents.

Overarching this life of Leonardo as the first scientist is a story of re-evaluation. In calling Leonardo a scientist at all I am courting controversy; with the inclusion of the word 'first' in my title I risk still further opprobrium. But it is my contention, and I hope I convey this here, that he really was the *first* scientist. Going still further, I could have used equally well the title, *The Lost Science of Leonardo*, or *The Ignored Importance of Leonardo the Scientist*, for these are also accurate descriptions. Leonardo's findings, we now know, predated many important scientific discoveries, but in this account I show how his thoughts were literally sealed off from society and tragically wasted, lost for two centuries while the world caught up and relearned lessons already taught.

All biographers set out to find 'another side' to their subject. This almost always involves revelations concerning darker aspects of the personality under the microscope. True to literary honesty, my senses were open to such negative aspects, for often they add depth and colour to our heroes. And indeed, Leonardo was no angel. In many ways he was a man like any other, but he was also an exceptionally tolerant and humane individual whose lifestyle and personal conduct were in almost all ways completely at variance with the character of the time during which he lived, a cruel, dark era in which human life was almost worthless.

But, beyond this, Leonardo's drives were entirely unusual, and this, I believe, is what made him unique. In Leonardo, ego appears to have been subsumed completely by an almost psychotic need to discover, to unravel the mystery of life; and the reasons for this became clear to me only towards the end of my time researching and writing, after I had immersed myself in his personality and drawn out his impulses, desires and fears.

It was because Leonardo could successfully channel these impulses and employ them to give form to his desires that he could achieve all that he did. And in so doing, Leonardo da Vinci lit up the world of the Renaissance.

Michael White
September 1999

INTRODUCTION:

THE TOTAL MAN

Man is unique not because he does science, and he is unique not because he does art, but because science and art equally are expressions of his marvellous plasticity of mind.

— J. Bronowski, *The Ascent of Man*

When Leonardo da Vinci died, on 23 April 1519, his constant companion, the aristocratic artist Francesco Melzi, became custodian of his material and intellectual legacy. Grief-stricken, Melzi did not leave Leonardo's final resting place, the home of King Francis I of France at Cloux, for several months, but when he did his servants packed a cart and burdened horses with box after box of papers, wooden and metal models, and paintings; a priceless treasure that would ensure the master's reputation for centuries to come.

For the purposes of our story, the most important part of this collection was some 13,000 pages of notes, many tied with string and ribbon, others gathered in leather-bound notebooks and folders. These Melzi took with him to his ancestral home at Vaprio near Milan with the intention of cataloguing Leonardo's life work, his thoughts on subjects ranging from the construction of siege towers to the flight of birds, from the internal workings of the kidney to observations of the Moon's craters. This was Leonardo's gift to the world, the researches of the first scientist.

A few years later Melzi married, and began to collate Leonardo's work, but the task seemed beyond him and, even with the assistance of two full-time scribes, little was done apart from an incomplete volume on painting, later known as *Trattato della Pittura*, Leonardo's *Treatise on Painting* which eventually reached the Vatican library, to be published in diluted and greatly altered form in 1651.

When Melzi died in 1570, his only son, Orazio, inherited the entire collection. But Orazio had absolutely no interest in Leonardo or his amazing works. He collected up his father's papers simply to clear space in the house, deposited them unceremoniously in a cupboard in an attic on the estate and forgot about them.

Others were more aware of the value of these papers and Orazio's astute tutor, Lelio Gavardi, easily persuaded Orazio Melzi to part with no fewer than thirteen volumes of notebooks which he then sold to the Grand Duke of Tuscany. A few years later, an altruistic Milanese monk named Mazenta persuaded the Grand Duke to allow him to return them to the Melzi family, but when the monk arrived with the collection, Orazio told him to keep them as they already had plenty.

Gradually, word seeped out that Orazio Melzi had a vast collection of notes and drawings from the hand of the great Leonardo da Vinci, and soon treasure-hunters were descending upon Vaprio, many of whom returned home with at least a few pages ripped from one notebook or another.

So, from Francesco's careful attentions, little was gained; the notebooks were dispersed. Some ended up in the collection of the British royal family at Windsor, others found their way through the hands of noblemen and pontiffs to storerooms in libraries in Italy, Spain and France. But along the way much was lost or destroyed. It has been estimated that of the original 13,000 pages Melzi took with him from Cloux in 1519, the whereabouts of little more than one half are known, some 7,000 pages in total. Most of these are today in public collections around the world and a few are in private collections. The most famous of these is the *Codex Hammer* purchased in 1994 by Bill Gates for $30 million.*

And without doubt this tale of loss and confusion has had an enormous impact upon all our lives, for because of it, Leonardo's work was effectively lost to civilisation for almost two hundred years; two hundred years in which others rediscovered many of the ideas Leonardo had revealed but never published.

Today, any scientific discovery is published as soon as it is verified and checked, usually in a scientific journal; and if the discovery is important enough it finds its way into the newspapers of the world the next day. This publicising of science only began in the nineteenth century. Before then, scientists around the world kept in touch via specialised publications created by organisations such as the Royal Society, but in Leonardo's time, two hundred years before Newton, the only way a scientific idea could be passed on was if the innovator wrote and published a book about it. In this way, Galileo changed the history of science with his collection of books, most notably *Dialogue on the Chief World Systems, Ptolemaic and Copernican* (1632) and *Discourses Concerning Two New Sciences* (1638). But Leonardo's writings describing a vast collection of experiments and the findings he derived from them were unknown to all but a tiny group of noblemen and art collectors who, to a man, knew nothing about science or engineering. Leonardo's insights lay hidden only to be discovered again by men such as Newton, Leibniz, Fermat, Huygens and many others some 250 years after

---

* A short time before beginning this book I interviewed Bill Gates and I asked him why he had bought the *Codex Hammer*. With a wry smile he replied, 'Because I wanted it.' Later he went on to explain how it was also a commercial move, because he planned to use the *Codex* to produce a Microsoft CD-ROM (which has now been published) and to use Leonardo's work in a 'virtual gallery' to be created on the Internet. It is also interesting to note that Leonardo notebooks are usually named after their owner, so *Codex Hammer* was so named when it was in the possession of the Hammer Institute in California. However, for his own reasons, Bill Gates has not renamed the *Codex* after himself but restored its original name, *Codex Leicester*.

Melzi's journey from Cloux to Vaprio. Leonardo had made startling discoveries in his studies of optics, mechanics, anatomy and geology. He had created a form of plastic, developed a sophisticated predecessor of the camera (the *camera obscura*), written of contact lenses and steam power, explained why the sky is blue and developed visual techniques for the representation of the body that would only be seen again with the invention of the CAT scan.

We can only wonder what would have happened to the history of science, and from that the development of technology, if Leonardo's work had been known about and read widely soon after his death. Where would we be today? What technological wonders would we now enjoy?

The term 'Renaissance man' has become a cliché, yet if ever there was a person in history who fitted this description it was Leonardo da Vinci. Born into an age in which only an elite few had ever even seen a book, he drew together many confused strands of human knowledge and lent a logic and cohesion to what he understood of the world; he then translated it into an encyclopaedia of information about an incredible range of subjects.

Leonardo was by no means the only great polymath of the era. A generation before him, Leon Alberti sought to unify all areas of knowledge, Filippo Brunelleschi created mechanical wonders and laid the foundations of modern architecture and structural engineering, and another fellow countryman, Pico della Mirandola, who was born a decade after Leonardo, is considered by many to have displayed a comparable polymathic genius but died so young he never realised his full potential. What makes Leonardo unique is that he worked for half a century bringing together vastly different areas of knowledge and uniting them with an intellect that could find expression equally well as an artist, experimenter, engineer and designer.

Leonardo da Vinci's contemporaries make up a veritable *Who's Who* of history. Many of these great figures knew him and some were friends, for the Renaissance world was a small place, communication and travel were extremely limited and the great Western minds of the era were concentrated in just a few capitals of Europe.

In the world of art, the older Botticelli became a colleague and friend of Leonardo's; Michelangelo grew to be a reviled enemy; while Raphael, thirty years Da Vinci's junior, drew inspiration from the older man's work and is known to have made sketches of the *Mona Lisa*. Hieronymus Bosch painted *The Garden of Earthly Delights* in 1485 when Leonardo was thirty-three and just beginning to make a name for himself as a painter, and Titian was born that year. Beyond this arena, Christopher Columbus was born a year before Leonardo and went on to discover the New World while Leonardo was working for the Duke of Milan; and Leonardo also knew the Italian scientist and geographer Toscanelli, who had inspired Columbus's travels. Fernando de Magellanes became the first to circumnavigate the globe on an expedition that began six months after Leonardo's death.

Dante's *Divine Comedy* was printed in 1472 at Foligno, north of Rome. Nicolaus Copernicus was born some quarter of a century after Da Vinci and arrived in Italy with the first draft of his heliocentric theory *De revolutionibus orbium coelestium*, *The Revolution of the Heavenly Spheres*, just as Leonardo was spending his last years in the country. Leonardo was befriended by the murderous Cesare Borgia and, for a year, worked for him as a military adviser. Through Borgia, Leonardo became a close friend of Niccolò Machiavelli when he was also working for the Borgias and gathering material for his masterpiece, *The Prince*, published in 1515, four years before Da Vinci's death.

Leonardo was quite aware his talents were exceptional, and this led him to an exaggerated sense of his own destiny, writing in his notebooks: '*Facil cosa e farsi universale*' – 'It's easy to make oneself universal.' However, in spite of the fact that he left us some 13,000 pages of notes, there is very little in these of a personal nature and almost nothing to indicate the way he perceived his own life. He refers occasionally to contemporary events, and once in a while he reveals his emotions with a succinct but telling comment, but these are mere glimpses. And, because he was an unconventional character and his achievements were so varied and so impressive, he has been the inevitable subject of hyperbole since the time of his earliest biographers.

The artist and writer Giorgio Vasari wrote the first biography of Leonardo, a short treatise included in his *Lives of the Painters, Sculptors and Architects*, completed in 1568, some half-century after Leonardo's death. Vasari is responsible for many legends about Leonardo's life, but, if we ignore the exaggeration and hagiographic aspects of his writing, we should be grateful to him for giving us some insight into Leonardo's character. 'He was so pleasing in conversation,' Vasari tells us,

. . . that he attracted to himself the hearts of men. And although he possessed, one might say, nothing, and worked little, he always kept servants and horses, in which latter he took much delight, and particularly in other animals, which he managed with the greatest love and patience; and this he showed when often passing by the places where birds were sold, for, taking them with his own hand out of their cages, and having paid to those who sold them the price that was asked, he let them fly away into the air, restoring to them their lost liberty. For which reason nature was pleased so to favour him that, wherever he turned his thought, brain and mind, he displayed such divine power in his works, that, in giving them their perfection, no one was ever his peer in readiness, vivacity, excellence, beauty and grace.[1]

Other, more recent historians have portrayed Leonardo in equally over-the-top fashion. The scholar Giorgio Nicodemi, writing during the 1930s, says:

Leonardo might well take a place among the perfect heroes of antiquity. Like them he was strong, possessed of a powerful will, and yet accessible to human emotion. Like them he could meet adversity with intelligence and continue on the road before him, conscious of a heroic mission . . . Leonardo's strength lay in his serene and accurate thinking. He accepted life's transient woes and its inevitable end with a stout heart. His feeling that existence had a social value was strong enough to alleviate all his sadness. He never expresses a trace of melancholy isolation so often found in vain personalities. Study of Leonardo's life yields us the same profound joy that we derive from following the destinies of epic figures like Ulysses or Aeneas, or of historical figures such as Dante or Napoleon.[2]

As a young man Leonardo was exceptionally beautiful, and in old age he had the face of a sage weighed down by the strain of what he had learned about the universe. He was a homosexual vegetarian born out of wedlock who received very little formal education and was excluded by birthright from almost all professions. He was a mass of contradictions and conflicts, a man who rarely completed a commission, travelled widely for the age during which he lived, a man who wanted to experience life to the full and to reach the root of all phenomena, explain all things, do as much as he possibly could and record everything he witnessed. He wrote disapprovingly of war, but designed military hardware for several different European warlords; he was a masterful painter, perhaps the greatest who ever lived, but tired of art. He was scornful of received wisdom but steeped himself in Classical learning, and while he believed the human form was the ultimate expression of the divine, he despised humanity. And although Leonardo was the ultimate polymath, we may break down his contributions into three main areas: art, engineering and science.

A forest of paper has been consumed over the centuries to interpret and reinterpret Leonardo as an artist. Much has been written about Leonardo the engineer, but almost nothing has been said of the man's important scientific ideas. This is, in part, because Leonardo has for so long been recognised as such an overwhelmingly great artist his scientific thoughts have been overshadowed and overlooked. It is also true that to many twentieth- and twenty-first century scientists, Leonardo was not truly of the same breed as them.

Einstein said of those who tried to elevate Leonardo as a scientist:

We are falsely led to regard slightly related beginnings, vague tracks, hazy indications, which are found, as evidences of a real insight, which disposes us to 'promote one above another'. Hence a mythological process results, comparable to that which, in former times, thrust all conceivable feats of strength on to one Hercules.[3]

He was quite correct in viewing with suspicion the mythology surrounding Leonardo and those who wished to credit him with almost every invention and discovery in science. Yet it cannot be ignored that Einstein was also a part of the scientific establishment and concerned to maintain the image of his profession. Furthermore, in this case he was not, as this book will show, in full possession of the facts concerning Leonardo's scientific legacy.

It has been said that compared to many of the great masters, Leonardo has left almost no art for us to admire. Indeed there are only a handful of surviving paintings by Leonardo and only one, the *Mona Lisa*, autographed and known to be by him alone; but we must never forget that Leonardo's notebooks contain drawings on almost every page. Many of these are rough sketches, but there are also some 1,500 exquisitely drawn diagrams and illustrations, some of which are every bit as beautiful as the few surviving examples of his work as a painter.

This story deals almost exclusively with Leonardo the man and Leonardo the scientist, a tale so far told only piecemeal. But it is also a story of the amalgamation of art and science, for in Leonardo the two were intimately entwined, perhaps more so than in any other person in history.

At the leading edge of science, the division between mathematics, art and imagination becomes blurred. Modern physicists speak of the 'beauty' of sub-atomic symmetry and the 'elegant' equations describing the interaction of waves and particles. Some pioneering scientists are beginning to look at non-mathematical expressions of human intellect to find fresh avenues through the maze they hope will lead to a fuller understanding of our Universe.

Although Leonardo knew nothing of nuclear physics or unified theories, he too sought to find answers to the great universal questions by blending art and science. At the same time as he was using his skills as an artist to represent his scientific findings, he was applying his scientific learning to improve his art. His knowledge of anatomy helped him better represent human and animal figures, he used his understanding of optics to improve his use of shadow, contrast and perspective, and he relied upon his studies as a geographer and geologist to improve the accuracy and realism of his landscapes.

In Leonardo we may see the marriage of what many consider the extremes of human intellect, and in him art and science reached a *Gestalt*, giving us both true art and true science, each energised and made better by the other.

1

SINS OF THE FATHER

A man who awoke too early, while it is still dark and all around are sleeping.
— D. Merezhkovslei, *The Forerunner: The Romance of Leonardo da Vinci*

If you follow a route west from the Tuscan city of Florence, you pass through a conurbation that stretches some ninety kilometres to the coast and Pisa. Along the way you will pass through the industrial town of Empoli. If you take a right turn here and travel ten kilometres north, the road takes you to a tree-lined boulevard with commercial units set back from the road. The people who work here today trade in all manner of goods, but as you pass along this road you cannot help noticing the same word appearing with increasing frequency in many of the business names emblazoned on hoardings and warehouse signs, whether those of printers or tyre-shops. This word is 'Leonardo', for at the end of this road, a kilometre or two beyond the row of business premises, lies the little town of Vinci, a short drive from Leonardo's birthplace.

Vinci itself is now something of a tourist haven, but it retains its picturesque character. In Vinci you will find a museum dedicated to Leonardo's engineering endeavours, but if you want to get closer to Leonardo, to the soil on which he played as a boy and the vistas,

Fig. 1.1: Leonardo da Vinci's birthplace.

untouched by time to which he awoke each morning, then travel on a little further.

A steep single-lane track with the rather grand name of Strada Verde takes you two kilometres on into the true Italian countryside. Leaving behind the noise and bustle of the cities, you arrive at the hamlet of Anchiano, a place that makes even the sleepy town of Vinci seem like a distant metropolis. Here among the olive groves is the house the locals believe to be Leonardo's birthplace, *Casa Natale di Leonardo*. No one is absolutely sure this was the actual house of the Vinci family more than half a millennium ago, but a proud plaque next to the front door gives a form of official sanction to the claim and few have tried to dispute it.

Casa Natale di Leonardo is a pretty, single-storey stone building with a tiled roof. Set in its own grounds and surrounded by vineyards and olive trees that sweep away into the distance and trail over nearby hills, it is a simple house of three rooms: an entrance hall and two large rooms leading off to left and right. But when Leonardo was born here or near here in 1452, it would have been considered a smart residence, the home of modestly successful landowners and farmers. It is a place of tranquillity where great age welcomes the casual visitor. In the summer the only sound is the buzz of insects, while in winter a calm silence is broken only by one's own footfalls.

Today the light that splashes across the vineyards and along the roofs illuminates a scene not so very different from that which greeted the people who lived here five hundred years ago. Very little changes in Anchiano, but Leonardo was fortunate enough to have been born when Tuscany (particularly the cities of Florence and Siena) was at its most influential in world affairs, a region that lay at the very epicentre of the Renaissance. And, although many of his most fundamental drives and personal characteristics were deeply rooted in the isolation of Anchiano, Leonardo da Vinci travelled widely and, for his time, became truly cosmopolitan. His work and thought have of course penetrated far, so that what he achieved is now perceived as part of the fabric of cultural history, a marker for human progress across a broad spectrum of subjects. Some believe he was a man who lived far outside of his own time.

For one born into a very close-knit community living in relative isolation, we know with surprising accuracy the exact date and time of Leonardo's birth: Saturday, 15 April 1452, at 10.30p.m. And we have Leonardo's proud grandfather Antonio to thank for this. He recorded the event in a notebook which was lost after his death and discovered by a Leonardo researcher in 1939. The entry reads:

1452: There was born to me a grandson, the child of Ser Piero my son on 15 April, a Saturday, at the third hour of the night. He bears the name Leonardo.[1]

Antonio may have been so precise from habit, because — although he

Fig. 1.2: The view from Vinci.

was not himself a lawyer – he came from a long line of lawyers, and it was perhaps a familial bent towards record-keeping and note-taking that provides us with such a clear surviving record of the happy event. Indeed, the notebook Antonio used for this record was his father's notary book.

The first in the line to have taken the name of the village of Vinci was a certain Ser Michele da Vinci, who lived there during the mid-1300s. The 'Ser' is an honorary title denoting his profession, and he was Leonardo's great-great-great-grandfather. Thus began a succession of three generations of Da Vinci notaries. Michele was succeeded in the family business by his son, Ser Guido, and then by his son, Ser Piero. Each lived and worked in Florence and each became more successful than his father. Third in the line, Ser Piero joined the bourgeoisie by marrying the daughter of another successful notary, Lucia di Ser Piero Zosi di Bacchereto, in Florence, before rising to the rank of chancellor of the Republic.

Then, as often happens, there was a severe break in the chain.

Leonardo's grandfather Antonio resisted parental pressure to join the 'family firm', and instead returned to the property owned by the Da Vincis close to the village in which his great-grandfather had been born. Antonio appears to have wanted nothing more than to live the life of a country squire content to manage his land, to be a landowner with no real interest in improving his lot. Displaying little in the way of ambition, he leased much of his property to local cropsharers. Like his father, he also married the daughter of a notary, another Lucia. But this was no bourgeois union; his father-in-law was a local notary of little celebrity and Antonio was almost fifty by the time he decided he ought to marry; he most probably did so simply out of a sense of duty. The couple's first child, Piero, Leonardo's father, was born a year or two later.*

The distinction between Antonio and three generations of his progenitors was repeated again with his son, but in reverse. Piero turned back to the traditional mould of the Da Vinci family and became a young, ambitious notary whose success almost matched that of his determined and acquisitive grandfather and namesake. And he maintained a lifestyle to match his success. He began his professional career in Pisa and Pistoia, but was drawn early to the bright lights of Florence. His career flourished and he soon established a list of private clients as well as conducting freelance business for the government. Perhaps believing close proximity would help guide him towards the centre of power, he rented lavish rooms overlooking the seat of Florentine government, the Palazzo della Signoria.

By his mid-twenties, Ser Piero had become an intense and ambitious man-about-town, a local playboy who revelled in his early success and blossoming career. He spent almost all his time in Florence, returning infrequently and merely out of duty to the family estate in Vinci. It was probably during one of these visits that he formed a brief liaison with

---

* No precise record of the marriage date has survived.

a local peasant girl named Caterina and sired his first son, the illegitimate Leonardo.

In many cultures and during many eras illegitimacy has been no great impediment to a successful establishment career. But for Leonardo da Vinci it most certainly was. In fifteenth-century Tuscany, young men conceived out of wedlock were untouched by social restrictions so long as they were born into either the nobility or the peasant class. Cosimo de' Medici, who was head of the Medici bank and first citizen of Florence at the time of Leonardo's birth, had himself sired at least one illegitimate son, Carlo. The boy's illegitimacy did not prevent him from being appointed as papal chief secretary and later Archpriest of Prato, a large town close to Florence. Indeed, during the fifteenth and sixteenth centuries it was common for popes not only to confer upon their illegitimate sons full rights and honours, but in many cases to make them cardinals. This relaxed attitude even extended to royalty. One story relates how, on a state visit to the northern Italian city of Ferrara in 1459, when Leonardo was seven, Pope Pius II was met by seven princes from the royal household and not one of them was legitimate.

Yet, within middle-class or bourgeois society illegitimacy was despised, and the children of these unions were effectively ostracised. Leonardo was barred from attending university and could not hope to enter any of the respected professions, such as medicine or the law, because it was strictly against the rules of the professional guilds to accept anyone with his background.

Naturally, this restriction had a major impact upon his feelings for his own society. We can only speculate upon what might have happened to him if he had been Ser Piero's legitimate son. Leonardo may have been persuaded to enter the same profession as his father, but then other facets of the young man's character might have borne an equal or greater influence and steered him away from such a career, as had happened with his own grandfather.

But choice of career was not the only aspect of Leonardo's life affected by his inauspicious birthright. Although he achieved wonders in a vast range of studies, Leonardo was never able to come fully to terms with the fact that he had been deprived of a formal university education. It was partly because of this that he later became an autodidact and approached learning with such energy and determination, a process that endowed him with a unique perspective. Yet at the same time, although his illegitimacy helped mould him, there is also little doubt it pained him greatly. He once wrote with barely disguised bitterness:

If indeed I have no power to quote from authors as they [establishment scholars in general] have, it is a far bigger and more worthy thing to read by the light of experience which is the instructress of their masters. They strut about puffed up and pompous, decked out and adorned not with their own labours but with those of others and they will not even allow me my own.[2]

His lineage altered his life in other ways. Most importantly, Leonardo never benefited from a stable, traditional family upbringing. He was raised by his ancient grandparents in the tiny hamlet in which he was born and he led a solitary childhood, a pattern broken only by occasional trips to Florence for short stays with his father.[*]

Leonardo's mother Caterina was a shadowy figure for most of his early life and this too must have confused and disturbed the boy. Within months of Leonardo's birth, Ser Piero again followed his grandfather's example by marrying into the Florentine bourgeoisie, his partner

---

[*] Although they had the great benefit of legitimacy, it is doubtful many of Ser Piero's other children were brought up in what might be considered 'normal' circumstances either. He married four times and sired fifteen children in all.

another notary's daughter, Albiera di Giovanni Amadori. Meanwhile, the newborn was given to Caterina to look after.

The Vincis were not a very rich family; their land was mostly given over to wheat and olive trees. Antonio had depleted the family coffers rather than enhancing them and Ser Piero was probably living well beyond his means, so the employment of a professional wet-nurse was probably not even considered. Caterina would have lived only a few hundred yards from the Vincis and it is probable she was given a home by them for the first year to eighteen months of Leonardo's life.

Although Antonio was clearly not embarrassed by his son's illegitimacy, and arranged the baptism which involved a priest, Piero di Bartolomeo di Pagneca, and five male and five female witnesses from the village, it is significant that Caterina's name does not appear on her son's birth certificate. In fact, much of her life story comes to us in little more than contradictory snatches.[3]

It has been documented frequently that Leonardo possessed great physical beauty, and there is a strong suggestion that this came from his mother. There are no portraits of her to confirm or refute this, but Leonardo clearly believed his mother had been beautiful when he wrote in later life: 'Have you not seen peasant girls in the mountains, clad in their poor rags, bereft of all ornament, yet surpassing in beauty women covered with adornments?'[4]

Of her character almost nothing is known. We can only speculate about the relationship she had with Ser Piero. It is possible the couple had known one another for some time before Leonardo was conceived but Ser Piero's ambitions prevented him marrying a peasant girl. Knowing what we do of Antonio's character, he would probably not have objected to such a marriage, but Piero had his heart and mind set upon greater things and the relationship, however beautiful Caterina may have been, was doomed from the start.

Instead of Piero settling down with Caterina, when she was no longer useful to them the Da Vincis arranged for her to be married off to someone they considered more suitable, a certain Antonio di Piero di Andrea di Giovanni Buti, nicknamed Accattabriga (the Quarreller), who was employed as a lime-burner near the village.

There is some confusion about the timing of this arrangement. Some historians have placed the marriage four years after Leonardo's birth, which would imply that Piero may have kept Caterina as a mistress in Vinci during the early years of his marriage. This would mean she stayed with Leonardo for that entire time. Others place the marriage at about eighteen months after the birth, towards the end of 1453.

Whenever it happened, Caterina did leave the Vincis' home to live with her new husband in a tiny, single-roomed hut in the nearby village of Campo Zeppi. This would have broken the ties with Leonardo to some degree. Caterina and the Quarreller soon started their own family, and within a dozen years they had four daughters and a son. Caterina was almost certainly allowed to see her first-born, but only rarely, either because of pressure from the family or perhaps more likely at the insistence of her husband. Naturally, this would have had a profound emotional effect upon young Leonardo.

Because the community was so small and the villages so close geographically, mother and child inevitably met on feast days and special occasions, and this must have further confused the boy, because by the time Leonardo was old enough to understand that Caterina was his mother he would have seen her with other slightly younger children at her apron and perhaps a baby in her arms. It is not difficult to imagine how the boy must have felt, witnessing the affection his half-siblings received from her, while he was ignored.

As an adult, Leonardo demonstrated resentment at his illegitimacy and lay the blame squarely with his mother. In one of his notebooks he writes: 'Tell me how things are back there, and you can tell me what la Caterina wishes to do . . .'[5] Although incomplete, from this strange single sentence we may discern that Leonardo saw his illegitimacy as solely his mother's doing and it is interesting to note that he almost always referred to his father respectfully as: 'Ser Piero, my father', yet he could not bring himself to call Caterina his mother, invariably referring to her disingenuously as: 'la Caterina'.

Such partisanship could have been seeded by Leonardo's father in order to deflect any blame attachable to him, or this evident bitterness could have grown from the pain and impotence Leonardo felt after seeing his mother bestowing her love elsewhere. Later in life he certainly displayed unorthodox emotions and sexual proclivities. He was particularly fond of young boys, he rarely bestowed his trust upon anyone and remained obsessively secretive throughout his life. Some of his work also displayed a markedly skewed view of women and their role (particularly in a sexual context), and in his anatomical drawings he displayed a peculiar fascination with female genitalia. There is hardly a single example of an entire female body anywhere in his vast catalogue of scientific notebooks.

When one of his half-brothers informed him he had fathered a son, Leonardo wrote back:

I learn from your letter that you have an heir, an event which I understand has given you great pleasure. To the extent that I had formerly judged you to be endowed with prudence, I am now convinced that I was as far from being a perspicacious observer as you from being prudent. For you are congratulating yourself on having engendered a vigilant enemy, all of whose energy will be directed toward achieving a freedom he will acquire only on your death.[6]

At other times he displayed what some may consider to be an unhealthy contempt for humans in general, once declaring: 'How many people there are who could be described as mere channels for food, producers of excrement, fillers of latrines, for they have no other purpose in this world; they practise no virtue whatsoever; all that remains after them is a full latrine.'[7]

Such intense feelings concerning his fellow human beings must bring into question his motives, and the seeds of such misanthropy. Did he feel this way because of some deep-rooted existential angst precipitated by his unhappiness as a child, or did he, through his later researches and discoveries, grow so analytical about Nature that he saw humans as little more than machines?

His many drawings (and occasional paintings) of grotesques are a further example of his darker drives, and some commentators have suggested that Leonardo's series of drawings in which he places gruesomely ugly male heads upon the shoulders of sumptuously dressed and bejewelled women demonstrates a misogynist streak quite at odds with other, gentler aspects of his character.

Clearly, the pain of loss in his childhood ran deep, and it stayed with him his entire life. In middle age, when Leonardo was living in Milan, he composed a collection of riddles which were designed for a fashionable game of the time, an amusing diversion to entertain the court and to fill the leisure time of the nobility. A selection illustrates again his obsession with his own birth and the circumstances surrounding his early life: 'Many children will be torn from the arms of their mother with pitiless blows,' one began, '. . . and thrown to the ground to be mutilated.' The answer to this riddle was 'walnuts, acorns, and olives'.[8] Another ran: 'A tender and kind mother to some of your children, you are a cruel and implacable stepmother to others . . . I see your sons sold into slavery and their lives serving the oppressor.' The answer: 'donkeys.'[9] Other striking examples include: 'We will see fathers and mothers take more care of their stepchildren than of their own son.' The solution to this is 'trees', which utilise their sap to nurture grafts from others.[10] But most telling perhaps is: 'The time of Herod will return, for innocent children will be snatched from nursing mothers and will die of great wounds inflicted by cruel men.' This time the answer is: 'baby goats.'[11]

Although too much may be read into what was little more than a

Fig. 1.3: Leonardo's grotesques.

parlour game for the idle rich, childhood experience often bubbles to the surface in seemingly innocent, apparently unconnected ways during adulthood, especially within the psyche of creative individuals; usually those, like Leonardo, who maintain close mental and emotional links with their childhood experiences.

There is a striking similarity between this childhood drama and the early years of another very different genius. Isaac Newton's mother, Hannah, was also absent for much of Isaac's early childhood because she remarried when her son was three. This separation certainly played a significant role in moulding Newton's character. He became an emotionally desiccated person, a loner who devoted himself to learning and for most of his life shunned company. Newton was also homosexual but, living in a very different social climate to Leonardo, his sexuality was suppressed and hidden throughout his life and the little we know of it has been gleaned only during recent years.[12]

Overall, the characters of the two men could hardly have been more different; Newton pursued a limited number of interests and developed great discoveries in just a few areas; Leonardo was the model for the 'Renaissance man', who studied anything that interested him. For the most part he enjoyed the comforts of life and was, at least as a young man, flamboyant and vain. Newton was puritanical, isolated and frugal. Yet they shared some of the same obsessions. Each was fanatically secretive about his work and terrified of plagiarism, each was driven by a deep-rooted need to learn and discover, and each exploited his extraordinary talents to the full after completing a carefully planned autodidactic course.

The influence of Leonardo's unhappy childhood upon his later life has been the subject of study for well over a hundred years, and was fully explored by Freud early in the twentieth century. In 1909 Freud was treating a patient he described as having 'the same constitution as Leonardo but without his genius'.[13] What he meant by this was that the patient found it almost impossible to complete any task he started, which Freud linked to the fact that Leonardo rarely succeeded in completing the commissions he was offered during his career. Freud made a detailed study of Da Vinci and collected his thoughts on the subject in a lengthy paper called *Ein Kindheitserinnerung des Leonardo da Vinci* (*A Childhood Memory of Leonardo da Vinci*), which he later referred to as 'the only pretty thing' he had ever written.[14]

Vasari has it that Leonardo could rarely complete a piece of work because he was an obsessive perfectionist who believed he could never capture the true essence of what he was trying to represent: 'It is clear that Leonardo, through his comprehension of art, began many things and never finished one of them,' he wrote, '. . . since it seemed to him that the hand was not able to attain to the perfection of art in carrying out the things which he imagined.'[15]

However, Freud concluded it was Leonardo's illegitimacy that lay at the root of this anomaly and coined the term 'Leonardo complex' to describe the phenomenon. Freud also claimed Da Vinci's illegitimacy affected his sexual predisposition towards beautiful teenage boys. He supposed that Leonardo harboured a deep-seated resentment towards his mother for 'letting him go' as a baby and that this not only 'turned him towards homosexuality' but, through a process of sublimation, created in him an 'instinct of investigation' which both eroded his artistic potential and bolstered his other intellectual drives.

There may be some truth in the assertion that Leonardo's illegitimacy and the loss of his natural mother at a very young age, along with the confused relationship that later developed between them, could have in some way affected his sexual relationships as an adult, and even perhaps influenced his attitudes to paid work. But in typical fashion, Freud went too far and made embarrassing errors in this study which damaged its credibility.

First, he suggested the trauma inflicted by his mother led Leonardo to diversify his intellectual pursuits or to spread himself too thin. To Freud, Da Vinci's scientific studies and his inventions were a distraction that damaged his artistic efforts, a curious conclusion considering the esteem with which Leonardo has always been regarded. However, more detrimental to the relevance of Freud's essay is his misinterpretation of one of the only self-contained memories of childhood that has come down to us from Leonardo himself.

On the back of a manuscript on the flight of birds, written around 1505, when he was in his early fifties, Leonardo recalled an incident from his childhood:

> I seem to have been destined to write in such a detailed manner on the subject of the kite [the species of bird] . . . for in one of my earliest childhood memories, it seems to me that when I was in my cradle, a kite flew down and opened my mouth with its tail and struck me many times with the tail on the inside of my lips.[16]

Freud was using a German translation of Leonardo's notebook containing this quote, but the translator had interpreted the word *nibbio* used by Leonardo for 'kite' to mean 'vulture'. Freud then devised an elaborate theory (partly based upon references to Egyptian mythology surrounding the vulture) and concluded that Leonardo had not remembered a bird's tail but the maternal breast. This then led him to bold assumptions linking Leonardo's childhood trauma with his inability to complete commissions. It was only years later, some time after Freud's death, that an observant linguist spotted that *nibbio* did not mean 'vulture' but a very different bird, a discovery that rather diminishes the credibility of Freud's argument.

It is easy to be too hard on Freud. Most of *A Childhood Memory of Leonardo da Vinci* is fanciful and convoluted to the point of absurdity, but at the time it did open paths into Da Vinci's personality along which no one else had before dared venture. The Victorians had oddly mixed feelings about Leonardo – perceiving his art to be wonderful but his science and engineering as little more than party tricks and gimmicks, and having almost no idea about his inner life.

Leonardo was certainly disturbed by his unconventional early life, but this should not be exaggerated. As is true for most people, there were many other influences during his childhood.

In his sprawling *History of Florence*, published in 1532, Machiavelli described a hurricane that ravaged the Val d'Arno in 1456 when Leonardo was four years old. Ten years later, in 1466, the Arno burst its banks and flooded the region. These cataclysms would almost certainly have had an enormous impact upon Leonardo's life in Anchiano, and may have played a significant role in producing one of his lifelong obsessions. We will see repeatedly how he devoted a great deal of time and energy to the study of water, including how water behaved in nature and how it could be utilised in the service of man. He was fascinated by water, finding it both awe-inspiring and terrifying. Later in life he produced hundreds of drawings of catastrophic deluges and wrote of how water was the most powerful of all elements and how it could overwhelm civilisation, seeing it as a great destroyer but also a force he wanted to tame and control.

Apart from the irregular and infrequent spells with his self-obsessed father and his half-siblings in Florence, Leonardo spent most of his time in the fields around Vinci and Anchiano. His grandparents were largely responsible for his upbringing, although Piero would have paid for his keep. Antonio and his wife Lucia certainly seem to have thrived on their relaxed, rural life, for Antonio was almost eighty when Leonardo was born, and according to the (admittedly unreliable) records of the time, he lived to the astonishing age of ninety-six. But despite the evident vigour of his grandparents, Leonardo's life in the home of the ancient Antonio and Lucia would have been incredibly dull if it had not been for his uncle Francesco (Antonio's younger son), only sixteen years Leonardo's senior, who lived for many years in the family home and was very close to the young boy.

In many respects, Francesco was similar to Antonio and the very opposite of his more ebullient elder brother, Piero. He loved the land and worked on his father's farm his entire life, planting and nurturing olive groves, tilling the soil and managing the animals. He appears to have had an innate empathy with Nature and it is believed with some justification that Leonardo gained his great interest in the country from his uncle, with whom he spent many hours on the farm and walking the hills.

Giorgio Vasari realised the importance of Francesco in Leonardo's life but rather confusingly, in the first edition of his biographical account he had Ser Piero, rather than Francesco, as the influential uncle. This was later rectified and may have been a rather feeble attempt to disguise Leonardo's illegitimacy for future generations. But, if he transposed the characters by mistake, Vasari may not have been too far from the truth, because Francesco was much more of a father-figure to Leonardo than his elder brother ever was. The writer Walter Pater describes Leonardo's earliest days on the Tuscan farm, 'watching the lizards and glow-worms and other strange small creatures which haunt an Italian vineyard'.[17] There is no doubt this prepared him for his later fascination with Nature and the rhythm of life so evident in his paintings and his choice of intellectual pursuits.

The bond between Leonardo and Francesco is evident from the fact that when the uncle died childless in 1506 he left all his possessions to his nephew. These did not amount to much, but his gesture is informative about the complex relationship between Leonardo and his half-siblings. Small as the inheritance was, they contested the will and fought a protracted court battle over it.

According to most historians, Leonardo did not even have the benefit of an education in Florence, where Piero's legitimate children were schooled. It is thought that he instead attended a village school and picked up the rudiments of reading and writing from his family, probably thanks again to Uncle Francesco and Antonio.

But others disagree. Osvald Sirén, writing in the early years of the twentieth century, claimed Leonardo attended the same *scuola dell'abbaco* as his half-brothers. This, though, seems unlikely for one very good reason: Leonardo's natural left-handedness was never corrected.

In common with many cultures during different eras of history, left-handedness in early Renaissance Italy was considered an undesirable anomaly, and children displaying this tendency were invariably forced to write using their right hand. Leonardo remained left-handed throughout his life and never showed any inclination to alter his ways. In fact, he took perverse pleasure in the fact that he was so wonderfully gifted yet 'anomalous'.

Little has come to us from the years between Leonardo's birth and his move to Florence, which is not surprising given that most of his early life was spent in rural seclusion and he was not a legitimate son of the hard-working, hard-playing Piero da Vinci. What little we have may be pieced together to give a picture of a childhood spent in an idyllic environment but overcast by shadows. On the positive side there was Leonardo's close relationship with his uncle, and the peace and serenity of life in the country far from the violent, disease-ridden cities. On the negative side we have the trauma presented by the manner of his birth, the fact that his natural mother was never far away but was also never his, and the social disadvantage his birthright had provided him.

Of the immense talent that blossomed later, little tangible evidence appears in Leonardo's childhood. All we have are apocryphal stories, exaggerated tales of Leonardo's early prowess and outstanding artistic ability told after he had become a famous artist. As one historian has pointed out: 'Almost from his youth Leonardo was a legendary figure, and some of the characteristics which we recognise as truest and most valuable in our picture of him are known only from legend.'[18]

We know Leonardo was living with his grandparents and uncle in Vinci in 1457, when he was five years old, because of a tax declaration to this effect made by Antonio da Vinci which lists him as 'Leonardo, son of said Ser Piero, illegitimate . . . five years old'. In early 1469, shortly after Antonio's death, his widow, Leonardo's grandmother Lucia, included Leonardo's name as a dependant or *bocca* (mouth to feed) on another tax return. But the following year his name appeared on Ser Piero's tax return, in which he is supposed to be living with his father in Florence. Although this seems confusing, the apparent discrepancy comes from the fact that the 1469 tax return submitted by Lucia required that all family members be listed; indeed Ser Piero himself appears on the record even though he was certainly living permanently with his second wife in Florence by that time.

Leonardo's grandparents died within months of each other towards the end of the 1460s; first, in 1468, his 96-year-old grandfather, Antonio, followed a year or two later by his much younger wife, then in her late seventies. But Leonardo was almost certainly living in Florence some time before then. Some historians place the beginning of Leonardo's apprenticeship around 1469. This was the year Piero gained the influential and lucrative post of notary to the Signoria of Florence, allowing him to provide for Leonardo more readily. It was also the year Antonio died, so perhaps, it is argued, Piero took over the upbringing of his son to relieve the elderly Lucia.

This is unlikely. Ser Piero was doing quite well as a notary long before he acquired his prestigious new job, and there is no reason to link Leonardo leaving Vinci with the passing of his grandfather; Ser Piero's second marriage in 1465, a year after the death of his first wife, or even Francesco's marriage sometime around the late 1460s, could equally well have precipitated the move. The usual age to begin an apprenticeship was twelve or thirteen, so we should place the beginning of his career as an artist in 1465 or 1466.

Piero had friends within the artistic community in Florence – he may even have acted on their behalf when they needed legal advice – and it is thought he knew the great Florentine artist Andrea del

Verrocchio personally, so that when it came time for him to find an apprenticeship for Leonardo, Verrocchio was his first choice.

Whether Piero had to pull strings, or because, as some recount, Verrocchio was so impressed with samples of Leonardo's work Piero showed him, a deal was struck between the two men. Leonardo had probably said goodbye to the rural life and the tranquillity of Vinci a year or two earlier and had been living in his father's house, but now he was to join the community of artists, a group at the epicentre of Renaissance culture.

It was from here Leonardo would eventually cast off the shackles of his inauspicious birth and start upon the road to recognition and the flowering of his unparalleled genius. But, before we follow the beginning of Leonardo's career as an artist and onward to his earliest dabbling in science and engineering, we shall take a brief look at the way scientific thought had evolved from the time of the Greeks to Leonardo's birth and the intellectual legacy Leonardo inherited from the texts he read and the philosophers and thinkers he was soon to meet.

2

LEONARDO'S INTELLECTUAL INHERITANCE

If you wish to gain knowledge of the forms of things, begin with the detail and only move from one detail to another when you have fixed the first firmly in your memory and become well acquainted with it.

— Leonardo, *Codex Trivulzianus*

The earliest foundations of science can be traced to the Greeks. And, although many of the ideas of the Hellenic tradition bear little relation to the way scientists think today, the influence of the Greeks upon the generations of scientific explorers up to the Age of Reason was huge. When considering the re-emergence of learning in Europe during the late fourteenth century, and the reintroduction of science, we must look closely at a handful of Greek philosophers and their contribution to this intellectual revolution.

Aristotle, possibly the most respected Hellenic figure, was born in 384 BC at Stagira in Chalcidice. His father was the court physician to Philip, King of Macedon, and through his father's connections he was taught by the greatest living philosopher of the time, Plato, then in middle age. Aristotle wrote a collection of tracts that were not only influential in his own era but became the foundation of almost all science until Newton's time, over two thousand years later. Aristotle's work was encyclopaedic in range, including treatises on philosophy, logic, astronomy, biology and physics. He was most able as a logician and, ironically, weakest as a 'natural philosopher' (or 'scientist') although his biology was stronger than his ideas about physics. His most significant work within the scope of natural philosophy (which, by the eighteenth century, had been renamed 'physics') were his books *On Generation and Corruption* and the *Physical Discourse*, which concentrated upon ideas concerning matter, form, motion, time and the heavenly and earthly realms.

Fundamental to Aristotle's vision of reality was the idea that the world in which we live is composed of a blend of four elements. If these are left to settle they arrange themselves into layers. Water, he reasoned, falls through air (or air moves up through water in the form of bubbles), earth falls through water and air, and fire exists in the top layer because it moves up through air. By this reasoning, rain falls downwards because it is trying to return to its rightful place, a layer beneath air; the flames of a fire rise upward to take up their proper position above the other three elements.

As well as formulating the idea of the four elements (a concept that lay at the heart of scientific reasoning for two millennia), Aristotle proposed the notion of the 'Unmoved Mover' – this was the name he gave to the omnipotent being who he imagined maintained the movement of the heavens, keeping the Sun and the planets travelling about the Earth.

Aristotle's reasoning was based upon a method of his own invention called syllogistic logic. This is the idea that a conclusion can be reached as a logical consequence of two preceding premises. An example of this would be: all politicians are animals; all animals live on Earth, therefore, all politicians live on Earth.

A syllogism is a powerful conceptual tool and was until recent decades an important technique employed by mathematicians, but the use of syllogistic logic in scientific reasoning is extremely limited. For example, it leads us to statements such as: all robots have two legs; humans have two legs, therefore, all robots are human. Syllogisms can be divorced from any form of experiment and consist merely of two statements and a conclusion all based upon superficial observation or deductive reasoning. Consequently, they can (and with Aristotle, did) lead to completely false conclusions quite at variance with reality.

Aristotle was not the only Greek to shun experimentation. His teacher, Plato, who established the School at the Academy in Athens which lasted nine centuries, actually viewed experimentation with distaste. According to one historian, he '. . . condemned [science] as either impious or a base mechanical art'.[1] And this was an approach which set the template for most Greek natural philosophy.

Instead of experiment, Plato placed inordinate importance upon pure mathematics. To him, number was everything. He even had written over the door of his Academy: 'Let no man enter who knows no geometry.' To which Leonardo himself later paid homage by writing in his notebooks: 'Let no man who is not a mathematician read my work.' He also formulated the idea that humanity could reach God through the study of Nature and a devotion to investigating the world in which we live.

Because of the status of Aristotle and Plato during their lifetimes and within the Classical tradition inherited by later generations, the concept of experiment gained little ground until the thirteenth century when Roger Bacon wrote of its value. Even then, what we now view as the 'scientific method' reached little further than the minds of a select group of pioneering thinkers, a situation that persisted until the work of Galileo during the early seventeenth century, almost one hundred years after Leonardo's death.

The modern scientific method is modelled upon both reasoning *and* experiment. During this process, an idea is first postulated (often after a 'flash of inspiration' or a sudden insight) and then developed into a tentative hypothesis employing reasoning, a process called the inductive method. Once the hypothesis is established, the scientist analyses its practical implications using mathematics before testing it with experiment. If the experimental results or observations conflict with the initial hypothesis, the scientist goes back to the hypothesis, alters it and conducts new experiments. This process is repeated until there is either agreement between reasoning and observation or the original idea is discarded. If reasoning and experiment eventually match, the hypothesis is viewed as a theory. Only then may the theory be used to try to explain more generalised situations or problems.

However, even then science does not see this as the only possible theory to fit the facts, and if new ideas come along that explain a situation or solve a problem more fully or more elegantly, then this will supersede the original theory.*

Aristotle and Plato had rivals, but they were overshadowed. Democritus, who was born seventy-five years before Aristotle, is now seen as a man who came much closer to the modern scientific viewpoint and has been dubbed 'the father of the atomic theory'. He believed that: 'According to convention there is a sweet and a bitter, a hot and a cold, and according to convention there is colour. In truth there are atoms and void.' Aristotle disagreed because it conflicted with his own world-view and he was unable to question his own dogma. This meant that the work of the early atomists was largely ignored until it was revived by thinkers of the early seventeenth

---

* An example of this is the way in which Einstein's theory of relativity explains how matter behaves under extreme conditions more successfully than Newtonian mechanics could. The theory of relativity does not need to be applied to everyday life (indeed, the computations for getting the Apollo spacecraft to the Moon used Newtonian mechanics) but it is a more powerful theory under certain circumstances. And upon verification of the theory of relativity early in the twentieth century, scientists were able, in very special circumstances, to supersede a theory that was then over 230 years old and apply the new one.

century, most especially Pierre Gassendi and, to a degree, René Descartes.

Much of the thinking of the Greeks was preserved in the great library in the city of Alexandria, and by the time of Aristotle's death in 322 BC, Alexandria was seen as the intellectual centre of the world. From the library containing an estimated 400,000 volumes and scrolls (said by contemporaries to be the repository of the sum total of human knowledge), learning spread east with the conquests of Alexander the Great and north-west into Europe, where Greek philosophy, science and literature formed the bedrock of Roman culture.

Yet many Roman and Alexandrian philosophers, men such as Pliny, who lived during the first century AD and authored a thirty-seven-volume treatise called *Naturalis Historia*, or the Alexandrian Ptolemy, a century earlier, did little original work themselves – almost everything they wrote about was a distillation of inherited Greek wisdom. Some Roman philosophers championed the rivals of Aristotle; for example Lucretius, in his poem *De Rerum Natura*, supported Democritus. But because Aristotle had dominated Greek science, his dogma, what Arthur Koestler called 'pure rubbish',[2] became almost a religion and his teachings were passed from generation to generation virtually unquestioned. This was a misguided development that led science along a partially blind alley for several hundred years without interruption. And it was this intransigence that was in part responsible for casting Europe into a time frozen in aspic, a dark age that lasted just a little under a millennium.

Meanwhile, the source of knowledge, the library of Alexandria, was devastated twice; firstly by the Christian Bishop Theophilus around AD 390 and then later by the Muslims during the seventh century. Fortunately, by the time of this second act of vandalism, much of the knowledge contained in Alexandria had been preserved by the Arabs.

Almost as potent a force as Aristotelian science were the ideas of Plato, which became especially popular during the era immediately following the fall of the Roman Empire. Interest in purely intellectual secular pursuits fell from favour, and in an age of religious fanaticism many of Aristotle's ideas were for a short time partially sidelined by Platonic philosophy.

The disciples of this new movement, those who believed in the supreme importance of pure spirit and pure mathematics over material existence, became known as Stoics. In terms of ideology, they were diametrically opposed to much of what Aristotle had to say and were quite uninterested in learning about the physical world. To them, Aristotle had been too concerned with material matters, his ideas were too mechanistic. Plato's notion of finding Truth through Nature, although appearing to some to veer close to the occult, was more conducive to their obsession with religious meaning.

Plato had followed an anthropocentric line, believing the Universe was created and controlled by a supreme being to whom humanity had a special importance. Plato took this concept so far he even held that the planets moved as they did simply to mark the pacing of time for humankind, and he viewed the cosmos as a single living organism with a body, a soul and reason.

Meanwhile, Arabic thinkers had made great strides in the understanding of alchemy, mathematics and astronomy, as Europe lay immersed in its age of intellectual darkness. Later, from about the ninth century onwards, some of the preserved knowledge of the Greeks and Romans filtered through them into the monasteries of Europe. But these islands of learning were few and isolated in an ocean of ignorance, and because those who acquired this ancient knowledge were working to a theological agenda, inherited Greek science soon became fused with theological dogma. This time, Platonic mysticism was dispensed with unceremoniously, and Aristotelian philosophy became dovetailed with Christian doctrine.

In some ways this was an improvement on the Stoics, but it brought with it new obsessions; this union of Aristotle and God meant that any attack upon Aristotle's science was also an attack upon Christianity. Together, these twinned beliefs produced a self-contained picture of the Universe: God created the world according to the Scriptures and guided all actions. All movement was not only set in motion by God, but was supervised by divine power. In this way, the Church's doctrine of divine omnipotence segued neatly with Aristotelian concepts such as the unmoved mover.

Popular understanding held that all matter consisted of the four elements as stated by Aristotle and these were not divisible into atoms as Democritus had proposed. To Aristotle, every material object was an individual and complete entity, created by God and composed of varying combinations of the four elements. Each object possessed certain distinct and observable qualities, such as heaviness, colour, smell, coolness. These were seen as *solely* intrinsic aspects or properties of the object and their observed nature had nothing to do with the perception of the observer.

Yet, despite the severe limitations this placed upon the development of scientific enquiry, the Middle Ages did produce a collection of notable and original thinkers who contributed to a gradual reawakening of rationality. These thinkers were also monks and have been called the Scholastics, men obsessed with the marriage of natural philosophy and theology but also able to rationalise and to allow a modest role for logic. The most famous of this group were St Thomas Aquinas, Albertus Magnus and Roger Bacon.

Thomas Aquinas and Albertus Magnus stuck to the traditional Aristotelian line and maintained a firm belief that man was the central object of the Creation and that the Universe was designed for him by God. But they were original enough and adventurous enough to contemplate the idea that the study of Nature and the physical realm could help humans to attain insights into theology.

The great Oxford scholar, Roger Bacon, took things further and may now be seen as one of the first to erode the restrictions inherent within the philosophy of the Scholastics. He was the first to see the usefulness of experiment and he composed three far-sighted tracts: *Opus Majus*, *Opus Minor* and *Opus Tertium*, which outlined his philosophy and his experimental techniques in a range of disciplines. Bacon's efforts have gained him an esteemed place in the history of science, but in his lifetime his work was viewed as heretical and its anti-Aristotelian elements subversive, leading Pope Nicolas IV to imprison him for life.

As the ideas of the Scholastics reached their peak, around the early thirteenth century, Aristotelian philosophy became an intrinsic element in the intellectual world of Europe and it was taught by rote almost unchallenged in every university in Europe for the next five centuries. But the Renaissance was to change the way Aristotle was understood and to prompt a re-evaluation of the ideas of other Greek and Roman thinkers. Following the Dark Ages, a reanimation of society towards learning meant science slowly emerged from the shadow of religion and gradually found its place as an intellectual and practical pursuit possessing an identity of its own.

There is no general agreement about the precise beginning or end of what historians have dubbed 'the Renaissance'. Those concerned with art and literature (by tradition the disciplines that define the period) would not apply the same dates as those more interested in politics, sociology, science or philosophy. Vasari was probably the first to coin a descriptive term for the time during which he lived, aptly calling it *rinascita*, or rebirth, and we may think of the era as the time during which Europe emerged from a particularly bleak and oppressive period in its history.

Fourteenth-century Europe was a profoundly unpleasant time and place in which to live. The continent was ravaged by one wave of plague after another, reaching its most virulent in the Black Death of the first quarter of the century. This catastrophe had left 75 million dead, about one-third of the population of Europe. The century had also been scarred by war. The Italian peninsula was the location for endless rivalry between city states, conflicts that drained the economy and depleted the population still further. And, at the other end of Europe, England and France fought what has since become known as the Hundred Years' War, a punctuated conflict that actually lasted longer than a century, beginning in 1337 and ending in 1453. By contrast, the era between Leonardo's birth and the last decade of the fifteenth century was one of relative peace in Europe, eventually broken by the reactivation of French expansionism in the 1490s.

Even so, during the slightly more enlightened late fifteenth century, the average life expectancy for a woman was just twenty-four, and only a tiny fraction of people could read or write. Peasants lived in extended family groups, often twenty to a tiny, single-roomed hut, sharing the straw floor with their goats and pigs. Their diet was plain and one in every four years saw a famine during which cannibalism was not uncommon. The nobility were insulated from some of the privations of the common folk, but not all: they too died of plague and their women in childbirth. They enjoyed a slightly better diet, but the wealthier members of this class over-indulged and suffered from gout, liver disease, obesity and syphilis; Catherine de' Medici, who married Henry II of France, lost both her parents to syphilis when she was only three weeks old.

It was only natural that during a stage in human development as fraught as the Dark Ages there would be little energy left for creativity and the advancement of culture. Indeed, during the millennium that stretched from the final gasp of Rome until the fourteenth century, very little had changed. Only a tiny percentage of people in the world had any idea in which year they lived. Beyond the walls of the monasteries innovation was actively shunned, and anyone who suggested a way to improve life in even the simplest way was often regarded with suspicion; some were excluded from communities as witches and wizards, a few met still worse fates. Legend has it that education became so bad in England that for a time during the eighth century the

Benedictine monk, the Venerable Bede, was the only literate person in the country.

It is no mere coincidence that as life very slowly improved and Europe dragged itself from the mire of the Dark Ages, painting, literature and the advancement of ideas started to gain importance. Because of this, within a hundred years a wave of change had swept across Europe transforming the intellectual landscape beyond the wildest dreams of those who had suffered grim recent history.

Almost all facets of culture were transformed during this period. As a point of reference to the enormous changes gripping Europe, it is startling to realise that when Leonardo was four years old, Gutenberg printed his first book and introduced it to a Europe in which there already existed only 30,000 volumes; yet by the time Da Vinci was middle-aged in 1500, there were an estimated 8 million books in print.

There were two important factors that dragged European culture from an era in which an often confused set of scientific ideas were held by a tiny group of monks to an age that could prepare the ground for Leonardo, Galileo, Newton and, later, the Industrial Revolution. First of these was the finding of ancient manuscripts that gave the intellectuals of the Renaissance direct access to Classical thought; the other was the almost contemporaneous invention of movable type.

The search for surviving Classical manuscripts was really inspired by the humanist scholar, Francesco Petrarch, who was born in 1304 in the little town of Arezzo, about fifty miles from Florence. From an early age he was obsessed with Classical literature. While still a child, he wrote:

> From my early youth, when the other boys were studying only in Prosper and in Aesop, I gave myself wholly to Cicero . . . At that stage I was incapable of understanding what I read, but I took so much delight in the harmonious disposition of the words that any other book I read or heard read seemed to me to give off a

graceless, discordant sound . . . That love for Cicero increased day by day, and my father, amazed, encouraged my immature propensity through parental affection. And I, dodging no labour that might aid my purpose, breaking the rind, began to savour the taste of the fruit, and could not be restrained from my study.[3]

Growing up to become the most celebrated intellectual of his age, Petrarch gathered about him a collection of like-minded adepts who shared their master's love of the Classical tradition. They believed there were perhaps hundreds of manuscripts and documents in the original Latin and Greek secreted away in private collections and in the monasteries of Europe. Many of these men made it their life's work to search them out.

Petrarch wrote several important tracts linked with the Classical knowledge he had acquired through decades of study. Most notable is his *Lives of Illustrious Men*, which is a collection of biographies of the most important figures from the Roman era. This he composed with the intention of stimulating his countrymen to follow the example set by their ancient ancestors and to build a new 'Latin culture'.

One of Petrarch's closest friends was Giovanni Boccaccio, who is credited with finding Tacitus' *Histories* and part of his *Annales*, and wrote several acclaimed books himself, including *On the Genealogy of the Gods*. In the style of his friend, he composed two biographical diction-aries, called *On the Fortunes of Great Men* and *On Famous Women*.*

Successive generations of scholars maintained the momentum of finding increasingly significant texts from the Roman era. Coluccio Salutati, born in 1330, and Giovanni Conversini, seventeen years his

---

* One of the consequences of the awakening of intellect during the early Renaissance was a slight improvement in the lives of noblewomen, who were in the most part better educated and, some argue, more likely to hold positions of responsibility than in any earlier age.

junior, were both active in this search. Salutati was particularly influential and from his prestigious post as principal secretary or chancellor of the governing Signoria of Florence he could begin to bring to life Petrarch's ideal of a Latin revival in Florence, and by blending political power and a cultural ethic he was able in some degree to direct the thinking of many wealthy and important citizens of the state.

A generation later some of the most significant finds in the area of ancient 'scientific' studies were made by those who succeeded Salutati and Conversini. Particularly important were Niccolò Niccoli and Poggio Bracciolini who, during the second decade of the fifteenth century, discovered *Astronomica* by the Roman writer Manilius, Lucretius' *De Rerum Natura* and several books about mining and agriculture including *Silvae* by Statius and *De Re Rustica* by Columella.

A few years later, Bracciolini found Cassio Frontinus' *On Aqueducts*, which had provided the cornerstone of Roman architectural technique, and Cicero's *Brutus*, a book that soon became politically controversial because of its portrayal of the virtues of a monarchical form of government. Other finds from these years included works on architecture by Vitruvius and medical texts by Celsus, both of which were to play an important role in moulding many of Leonardo's ideas on these subjects.

What was significant about these finds was that they were written in the original Latin and as close to being unadulterated as possible, so for the first time the Florentine elite of the late fourteenth and early fifteenth centuries could read the words of the great thinkers of the Classical era exactly as they had been written, rather than fragments crudely translated by semi-educated monks.

In itself this was a tremendous advance, but perhaps even more important is the fact that when these works were translated and interpreted it was soon realised just how much of what Roman scholars had said of science was actually based upon an older source — the ideas of the Greeks and in particular such figures as Archimedes, Aristotle,

Pythagoras and Plato from the golden era of Greek learning between 500 and 250 BC.

The inevitable result of this was a new and intensified search for the original Greek sources of scientific knowledge. Now primed in the virtues of ancient learning, many of the richest people in Florence began to send abroad emissaries to locate and to purchase on their behalf anything they could find in the original Greek.

Until this time, the only original Greek manuscripts in Western European hands consisted of a few fragments of Aristotle and scraps of Plato, along with some quite substantial tracts of Euclid, all of which were either jealously guarded by monks or in the hands of a few devotees. Petrarch himself was reputed to have owned an original manuscript of Homer, but could not read a word of it. On the authority of the Roman writers to whom he referred, he accepted that Homer was a great poet and would kiss the book every night before retiring.

During the first three decades of the fifteenth century, several hundred original manuscripts found their way to Florence, largely from the East: where once Crusaders fought for Christendom, Western emissaries now bartered for and purchased intellectual capital from the Turk. A single Florentine agent, Giovanni Aurispa, returned after one particularly fruitful voyage in 1423 with 238 complete manuscripts.

In this way, the intellectual community of Florence acquired complete versions of Aristotle's *Politics*, the histories of Herodotus, the dialogues of Plato, the *Iliad*, the *Odyssey* and the plays of Sophocles, and most importantly for our chronology, the medical writings of Hippocrates and Galen (especially the latter's *Spiritus Animalis*), as well as some of the most important books from the Greco-Roman tradition (the first centuries AD) which had found their way from the library of Alexandria to wealthy collectors in Asia. Alongside these was a clutch of books that became hugely influential in Renaissance Europe, including the geographical studies of Ptolemy and Strabo and the former's *Almagest*, written during the second century AD.

Ptolemy's *Geography* was brought to Italy in 1406 by a Florentine merchant named Palla Strozzi. It detailed cartographic techniques including the measurement of distances on the surface of the Earth, a skill that had been forgotten in the West during the miasma that was the Dark Ages.

The Florentines were now in possession of the greatest works of humankind in their original language, but one problem remained; no one could speak or read ancient Greek. As early as the 1360s Petrarch and Boccaccio had tried to introduce the language into intellectual circles in Florence, and although neither of them had understood Greek themselves, they tried to establish a seat of Greek at the university. They had failed, but two generations later and prompted by the stunning collection of original works now at their disposal, the heirs of the men who had financed the original search for books finally sanctioned a chair at the Studium. This was soon occupied by an eminent scholar, Emmanuel Chrysoloras of Constantinople.

And so the first of the great factors of change was set in place. With accurate translations of a growing collection of Greek texts came the startling realisation that everything the Florentines had so far achieved culturally had been surpassed almost two millennia earlier by the Greeks. Rather than this discovery acting as a destructive force, however, it inspired them to emulate and even to dare to consider improving upon what the ancients had achieved.

In 1428, a committee was organised to instigate a series of changes to the education system of Florence. One of the trustees of the Studium, which lay at the cultural heart of the city, was Cosimo de' Medici, then a young banker living in Rome. He persuaded the clerical institutions of Florence to provide an annual 1,500 florins to add two new chairs to the rostrum of subjects. The existing curricula consisted of medicine, astrology, logic, grammar and law, and to these were added moral philosophy and a professorship of rhetoric and poetry. This provided a new syllabus for every student in Florence, and formed the foundation of the system adopted throughout Europe that remained in place within the universities of England, France and Italy until the eighteenth century.

Contemporaneous with these sweeping advances, many promising young scholars were moving from other parts of Italy and beyond to study and to teach in Florence; most in demand were aspiring Greek-speaking professors. And in turn, the consequent change in thinking of many of the city's most wealthy and politically powerful citizens had a dramatic effect upon the social structure of Florence.

As we have seen, medieval Europe, ravaged by disease and war, was in most ways totally passive. Innovation and inventiveness had been suffocated. The Renaissance was the reverse side of this coin, a time for participation, an era of action. An awareness of what could be achieved and a belief that humanity could do better than it had already done was a tremendous spur, and led to the age of discovery and the beginnings of modern scientific thinking, as well as providing a fertile ground for the artistic endeavours we see as emblematic of the time.

The importance of this shift in perception cannot be exaggerated. With a few notable exceptions (such as Roger Bacon), people since the fall of Rome had been paralysed by a deep-rooted sense of unworthiness. Central to their thinking and encouraged by Christian dogma was the notion that humans were mere creatures of God, pawns in a world where the forces of Nature and the will of the Lord were everything, a world in which the individual was totally without significance. Such thinking could lead nowhere but to a stagnant society, and although the belief that God controlled the Universe and was directly involved in all aspects of human existence persisted until the Darwinian revolution, in many ways those in positions of influence in Renaissance Europe thought very differently from their counterparts who had lived only two or three generations earlier.

Far from feeling insignificant and powerless, the thinkers of the Renaissance believed whole-heartedly in the idea that human intellect should be treasured and nourished. In this shift, we can see the impact of Platonic philosophy evolving into what has been called 'human virtue', a central tenet of active humanism. At the heart of Platonic philosophy is the concept that humanity can find God through unravelling the secrets of Nature. For Plato this was the foundation of 'inspiration', and it became a crucial element in the thinking of many of the best minds of the Renaissance. Leonardo, although unorthodox in his religious beliefs, understood this Platonic ideal even though he disagreed with many other aspects of Platonic philosophy. And although many intellectuals of the period blended the notion of 'virtue' with orthodox Christian doctrine, its origins were purely Classical.

Leonardo appears to have subscribed to a very modern interpretation of active humanism. To him, virtue stood apart from conventional religion. He saw it as an entirely human quality that could bring the individual closer to the essence of Nature. Indeed, Leon Battista Alberti, whom Leonardo knew personally and admired greatly, said those who possessed virtue were 'capable of scaling and possessing every sublime and excellent peak'.

This route from acquisition of ancient knowledge to the development of wisdom as a human need we may picture as a path followed by pure intellect, but also a crucial if esoteric influence upon Florentine culture. It offered an opening to new ways of perceiving the world, prompted by a great rediscovery of human worth and a positive realigning of the role of humanity in God's Universe. But this alone would probably not have generated the enormous changes in the material world we associate with the Europe of the fifteenth century; this paradigm shift required the other cornerstone of change, something seemingly far more prosaic; the invention of movable type and the spread of printing.

Received wisdom holds that printing was invented sometime between 1445 and 1448 by Johann Gutenberg working in Mainz, but this is an over-simplification. Printing is an ancient technique and was certainly practised by the Chinese of the second millennium BC. Gutenberg is actually credited with the invention of *movable* type which enabled a printer to produce different layouts very quickly.

The exact details of how movable type was first used is a fascinating tale in itself, and has been the subject of many books. But for any history of scientific development, what is most significant about it is the way printing spread through Europe and made possible a new intellectual climate.

Gutenberg's famous forty-two-line Bible was produced around 1455. Within three years there was a press in Strasbourg, by 1480 there were more than a dozen printers working in Rome and by the end of the century there were an estimated hundred printers in Venice, by which time some forty thousand different titles had been printed by over one thousand printers in Europe.

And how did this revolution affect the understanding of science?

To some modern commentators, Renaissance science is an oxymoron, but this is more to do with the way we perceive modern-day science than any great failing of the people of the fifteenth century. Naturally, science during this era was comparatively unsophisticated and little was known or understood that had not been known or interpreted by the Greeks two millennia earlier. There is also little doubt that many ideas about science were muddled up with mystical and occult concepts and practices. That said, some of the blame for this should lie with the Greeks and Romans from whom intellectuals of the Renaissance acquired most of their scientific knowledge.

An example is the way astronomy and astrology had become intertwined. Unlike the Greeks, who appear to have had no knowledge of (or at least no interest in) astrology, the ancient Romans were fascinated with the subject. The standard Latin text was Manilius' *Astronomica*, which included a lengthy discourse on the way planetary positions influenced the lives of individuals.

The *Astronomica* and other ancient works had such an impact upon fifteenth-century physics that the job of astrologer and astronomer fell invariably to the same person. Toscanelli, one of the most respected astronomers of the century, was also court astrologer and gave advice to the Signoria based upon his reading of astrological charts. This information was commonly used to decide upon the most auspicious moment to make political decisions, to wage war, to broker peace or to hold public festivals. Even one of the great rationalists of the time, Leon Alberti, wrote in his *On Architecture* of the most auspicious time to lay a foundation stone of a building.

This amorphous occult approach had its opponents. Petrarch had disclaimed astrology in his discourses analysing the knowledge of the ancients deciphered during his time. But the destructive influence of astrology was only stemmed towards the end of the fifteenth century with a book called *De Astrologia*, written by the humanist intellectual Pico della Mirandola, in which he turned on the astrologers with a piercing and cogent examination of their faults and inconsistencies.

Leonardo too was highly critical of astrology and astrologers, once describing the art as 'that fallacious judgement by means of which (begging your pardon) a living is made from fools'.[4]

So much for astronomy and astrology, but other areas linked with science were also tarnished by confused thinking, and reliant upon a heady blend of lore and occult practice. This may be seen most clearly from a survey of the medical knowledge and practices of the Renaissance.

The two most important texts translated from the Classical originals were *On Medicine* and *Natural History*. *On Medicine*, by the first century AD Roman medic, Cornelius Celsus, was published in translation in 1478 when Leonardo was twenty-six and living in Florence. *Natural History* was a vast collection of treatises, thirty-seven volumes in all, describing everything then known about science. Both were studied closely by anyone interested in medicine during the last quarter of the fifteenth century, but because they were largely fanciful they led to some very peculiar practices. Take for example the standard treatment for an open wound: 'In one pound of olive oil cook ten green lizards and filter through linen, add one measure of marjoram and worm-wood; cook slowly and set for use.' Or the alternative: 'Take earthworms washed in wine and place them in a closed jar; cook in a double vessel for one day; when they are liquefied add either properly prepared balsam, or resin of the fir or larch tree. This quickly heals any new wound and especially the wounds of the head.'[5]

Second only to plague, gout (in which urates, particularly sodium biurate, are deposited in the tissues of joints) was the medical scourge of the period. Cosimo de' Medici suffered badly from it; his son Piero was crippled by it, and his son Lorenzo died from complications of the affliction: fibrosis of the kidneys and high blood pressure. And it is in attempts to treat gout among the wealthier citizens that we may see Renaissance quackery at its most confused.

Lorenzo's physician, one Petrus Bonus Avogarius, prescribed as a cure the wearing of a sapphire ring on the third finger of the left hand. 'The pains in the joints will then cease,' he wrote, 'because that stone has occult virtues, and the specific one of preventing evil humours going into the joints . . . Afterwards,' he goes on to assure Lorenzo, 'in the summer during August, I will find celandine, which is a red stone that grows in the stomach of the swallow. I will send it to your Magnificence to be tied in a piece of linen and sewn in your shirt under the left breast at the nipple. This will have the same effect as the sapphire.'[6]

Fifteenth-century translations of the Greek physician Galen improved matters a little, but Galen too was prone to errors. Borrowing from his hero Hippocrates, he believed for example that all physiology was based upon a balance of fluids within the body, sub-stances he called humours, and stated that blood pulsated through minute perforations in the heart.[*] Ironically, it was the artists of the

---

[*] Although, to give Galen credit, in his *On the Differences Between Pulses*, he gave a log-ical and learned appraisal of how the pulse could be used as a form of diagnosis.

period who made the greatest strides in the advancement of anatomy and physiology, and their discoveries slowly percolated into other areas of medicine.

During Leonardo's time the study of human and animal anatomy had become a recognised element in the training of any professional artist. It was perceived as an essential skill for the aspiring artist because, by knowing how animal bodies were constructed, the artist could better represent the human figure upon the canvas. Donatello's *Anatomy of the Miser's Heart* is testimony to this new approach, and a few years later Antonio Pollaiuolo made detailed studies of the musculature of humans from dissection before producing one of his most famous works: *The Battle of Nude Men*.

Leonardo is seen as the greatest Renaissance anatomist, and this perception is entirely justified: he is thought to have carried out at least thirty complete dissections of human bodies and produced thousands of sketches and detailed studies of animal physiology. But there were others who became interested in dissection before Leonardo, and these men acted as an inspiration for him and contributed greatly to an understanding of how the body functioned. Probably the most influential painter and anatomist in his own time, a contemporary of Leonardo and friend of Lorenzo de' Medici, was the Florentine, Antonio Benivieni, who dissected the bodies of executed criminals and wrote a treatise on his findings called *De Abditis Causis*. During the course of his investigations he conducted and documented more than twenty dissections and made attempts to find links between criminal behaviour and anomalous anatomy, and to explain the functions of the heart and other internal organs. However, he came away from this work with little that was tangible or truly important.

Even so, in his own small way Benivieni achieved more than all the professors of medicine in the universities of Italy up to that time, men who had been content to preach Galen and Pliny and did nothing to encourage hands-on investigation until they were embarrassed into change by the efforts of the artistic community. An illustration of how, in a relatively short time, the attitude towards investigating the workings of the body began to shift, may be seen by comparing Benivieni's noble efforts with a declaration from 1399 concerning anatomical investigations: '. . . and whatever diligent nature has no less curiously concealed than constructed, all which so far departs from humanity that one cannot even hear of it without a certain horror, and I do not see how the caverns of the human body can be viewed without effusion of tears'.[7]

But hear of dissection the adventurous did, and this shows clearly how we should not think too negatively about Renaissance science. Much of it was based upon false ideas and assumptions intermingled with hocus-pocus, but the spread of learning, precipitated by the discovery of Classical knowledge and the means to proliferate it, created an enormous change in the perception of the world, and with it came a clearer insight into how the Universe might operate. If nothing else, this laid the foundation for the scientific revolution of Newton's time two centuries on. It also provided for the self-education of Leonardo, later enabling him to make his own private scientific investigations.

A further illustration of this reawakening can be seen by contrasting the ideology of Petrarch, who was, we should recall, an acclaimed intellectual of the early Renaissance, with a man of equal stature, Aeneas Silvius Piccolomini (later Pope Pius II) who lived a century later.

While staying in Vaucluse, in 1335, Petrarch happened to read in Livy that King Philip of Macedon had climbed Mount Hemus and had been rewarded with an astonishing view of both the Black Sea and the Adriatic. The 6,000-foot Mount Venoux stood a few miles from where Petrarch was staying and so he decided, against the fashion of the time (medieval Europeans showed no interest in exploring mountains), to scale the peak. He set off, and upon reaching the summit with its splendid vistas he sat down to read. Opening at random a copy of St

Augustine's *Confessions* he found: 'Men go about to marvel at the heights of the mountains, at the huge waves of the sea, at the broad estuaries of the rivers, at the circuits of the oceans, and at the revolutions of the stars, and forsake their own souls.' Seeing this as an omen and a sign of his folly, Petrarch closed the book and immediately returned home, never to explore another mountain.

A century later, Aeneas Silvius Piccolomini was visiting the court of King James I of Scotland when he heard the fanciful tale that barnacle geese were produced from the fruit of a riverside tree and that they flew off into the air as the fruit fell and landed in the river. Intrigued, he headed off to the Scottish Highlands to discover whether or not the tale was true. After investigating the story as thoroughly as time would allow, he learned from the locals that this biological oddity was indeed true but that it only ever occurred in the Orkneys, many miles further north. Piccolomini was about to set sail for the Orkneys to witness the phenomenon for himself when he was recalled to James's court on business.

The difference between Petrarch and Piccolomini has little to do with their personalities or ages (Petrarch was only thirty-one at the time); instead, it demonstrates the gulf in the intellectual Zeitgeist of the two eras. Petrarch, although a consummate scholar and one of the instigators of the new learning, was in almost all ways a medieval character, whereas Piccolomini was a man of the Renaissance enthused with the new spirit of discovery and exploration.

The fifteenth century was filled with the great efforts of many special individuals. There were many important figures from the generations immediately before Leonardo who also made substantial contributions, and in some areas of research laid the foundations upon which Leonardo was able to build.

Best remembered for the fact that he pointed the way to the Americas for Christopher Columbus was the talented astronomer and geographer, Paolo Toscanelli. Born over half a century before

Leonardo, he came from a wealthy family who numbered Cosimo de' Medici as a friend. Thanks to a substantial inheritance, Toscanelli was lucky enough to be able to devote most of his adult life to scientific research. None of his writings have survived, but from the records of contemporaries, he is known to have followed and plotted the paths of numerous comets, including the 1456 visit of Halley's Comet. To do this he used a system in which he divided up a drawing of the night sky above Florence into regions and traced the trajectory of the comet from observations made over many successive nights.

By making these observations, it became clear to Toscanelli that comets lay beyond the orbit of the Moon and followed regular paths. Aristotle had declared two thousand years earlier that comets travelled irregular paths and were 'sublunary vapours'. How Toscanelli worded his conclusions, at complete odds with the cast-in-stone ideology of the ancients, has not come down to us, but it is significant to realise that in this pre-Copernican age there were already free thinkers who were beginning to doubt traditional inherited wisdom because experience and experiment clearly conflicted with dogma.

Toscanelli was aided by the fact that the Florentines then prided themselves on encouraging the uncensored exchange of ideas, and supported the intellectually adventurous, especially if they came from the nobility. An indication of this is illustrated by the way Toscanelli was assisted with his experiments. When he needed to determine the height of the Sun at noon and asked to set up a gnomon in the cathedral (because the higher he could place the device the more accurate would be the experiment), he was given permission without hesitation.

Another great thinker of the same era was Leon Alberti, who was, as we have seen, a character even more influential in Leonardo's education than Toscanelli. Born illegitimate ten years after Toscanelli, in 1407, Alberti, like Leonardo, may be seen as the embodiment of the Renaissance man. He was a master of all trades, at once architect, artist, writer, historian, linguist and engineer. In fact, he was so versatile and prolific, his talents prompted one contemporary to write of him: '*Dimmi che cosa ignorò mai quest'uomo?*' 'Is there anything this man does not know?'[8]

Like many of the figures surrounding Leonardo, Alberti deserves a modern biography of his own, but even if we concentrate only upon his scientific ideas and contributions he can be seen as a key figure in the development of Renaissance thought. Before he was thirty, he had written a famous treatise on painting which placed great emphasis upon its technical aspects and the application of scientific principles. At one point he declared, 'The painter ought to possess all the forms of knowledge useful to his art.'[9] There should be little surprise then that this book was a huge influence upon Leonardo, especially during the writing of his own treatise on painting, *Trattato della Pittura*.

Experiment was an approach that had been largely neglected since Bacon two centuries earlier, but, like his contemporary Toscanelli and his successor Leonardo, Alberti conducted his own experiments and documented what he observed.

And what of the practical approach to science? We must not ignore the primitive forms of technology gleaned from the Classical tradition then adapted and improved upon by the people of the Renaissance.

Then, as now, technological development revolved around the desire to make money and to accumulate worldly possessions.[10] Motivated by money, people of the fifteenth and early sixteenth centuries invented better navigational techniques to help them reach unexplored lands and to return with material rewards. This drive towards a fragmented form of pre-industrial technology extended far. In agriculture, drainage systems introduced by the Dutch were used and techniques developed by men such as the self-taught Georg Agricola were employed in tin and silver mining.* Meanwhile, in manufacturing, the spinning wheel,

---

* Georg Agricola later published a book on the subject called *De Re Metallica, On the Principles of Metals*.

which had been used for centuries, was improved with the introduction of the flyer, making it possible to spin and wind simultaneously.

Leonardo was influenced by both the theoretical and the practical strands of scientific evolution. On the one hand he was an eminently practical man, able to build and model. He was a man of the country at heart and his earliest education had come from his Uncle Francesco, whose knowledge of Nature and the practical considerations of the farmer would have made a lasting impression upon him. But Leonardo also encountered men such as Toscanelli and Alberti who infused him with an understanding of theoretical principles and technique.

This then may be seen as one of the pillars of Leonardo's genius. He was an amalgam of the influences that underpinned the Renaissance itself. In Leonardo, the practicality of invention and the distillation of intellect became one. Just as the roots of the Renaissance can be traced to a timely blend of the practical (such as printing) with the intellectual, encapsulated in the rediscovery of ancient knowledge, Leonardo may be seen as the epitome of what we understand by the term 'Renaissance'.

Leonardo soaked up the learning of his age and took many of the things he discovered far further than anyone before him. He also had the talent to represent his findings in exquisite drawings and using an innate literary flair, so that today we can see for ourselves the paths his mind followed.

But before we can see how he took the first steps towards his achievements as scientist, inventor and engineer, we must follow him to Florence and his formative years there.

3

A NEW BEGINNING

All our knowledge proceeds from what we feel.
— Leonardo, *Codex Trivulzianus*

The exact date on which Leonardo rode into Florence to begin his new life there is not known with certainty, but we do know that the city in which he was to spend at least the next sixteen years of his life was, during the 1460s, enjoying the most expansive and exciting period in its already long history.

Florence was the wellspring of the Renaissance, and one need only look at what came out of that city during a relatively short period to acquire the essence and the meaning of this great flowering of human endeavour – a period during which many aspects of human culture developed more rapidly than at any other time until the beginning of this century.

Brunelleschi's gorgeous dome for the Duomo was newly finished, the materials hauled almost three hundred and fifty feet above the ground by machines of the architect's own design. The Pitti Palace had been started by Luca Fancelli and would rise in fits and starts against the glorious backdrop of the Boboli Gardens. In dynamic contrast, on the Via Larga in the centre of the city stood Michelozzo's Medici

Palace. And crossing the Ponte Vecchio, which had already spanned the Arno for over a century and boasted butchers' shops where today jewellers and hawkers ply their trade, you would find Alberti's palace for the Rucellai family.

Beyond the tiny enclave into which Leonardo was born, the world was changing at a phenomenal rate, and with the benefit of five hundred years of hindsight we can see that his birth occurred on the crest of a wave, a moment in history that would sweep him up into the great torrent of cultural development, an era during which his unique talents would find nourishment. And although Leonardo was cast by chance into this maelstrom of human activity and progress, five hundred years later he can also be perceived as one of the key players of his time, a figure who not only represents the Renaissance, but a man who helped shape it.

Aside from the fact that the Renaissance brought forth so many wonders and acted as a spur for so many later developments, it is astonishing to consider how much came from such a tiny region of the world. Although some of the elements of change cast into the melting pot of the Renaissance came from other parts of Italy and beyond, from Venice, Milan, Rome, The Hague and even from London, the prime movers of the fabric of the Renaissance were the artists and thinkers, financiers and poets of Florence.

Stendhal dubbed the city 'the London of the Middle Ages', but we should remember that although it was large for the time, by today's standards its population of 125,000 was tiny. The Renaissance emerged from very few people; and for the most part they led short lives. Life expectancy had improved a little since the previous century, when a man in his thirties would have been considered old, but it still did not come close to the three score and ten promised in the Old Testament. Many of the great men responsible for moulding the Renaissance died young. One of the key figures of the era, Lorenzo de' Medici (known as Lorenzo the Magnificent), who was a great patron of the arts, died at the age of forty-three. The sculptor Desiderio da Settignano lived to the age of thirty-four and the painter Masaccio died before his thirtieth birthday.

Life may have been short, but at least in Florence those with talent and determination could find success, and during the fifteenth and early sixteenth centuries this city was probably the most exciting place in the world in which to live and work. It was extremely well located. Like Venice, Florence acted as a nexus for East and West, North and South. Through centuries of successful trade it had developed a strong mercantile base, which meant intellectuals and artists were attracted to the city, generating what may be thought of as an 'intellectual market'. This never appeared on a balance sheet but it did make a significant impact upon the material wealth of the city because a reputation for nurturing ideas, arts and architectural splendour inevitably attracted investment and foreign wealth.

For Leonardo, Florence at first provided the perfect atmosphere in which to flourish. His arrival there would be comparable to an artist moving to Paris in the 1890s or setting up home in Greenwich Village during the early 1960s; the city acted as a seedbed for talent and, for the most part, encouraged its young.

Florence was one of the most liberal and free-thinking places in the world during the second half of the fifteenth century. It exemplified the emerging ideas of humanism and a form of democracy which encouraged novelty and innovation. This was partially reflected in the city's political system, a sort of primitive democracy in which the wealthiest citizens controlled affairs using a form of election.[*]

Although their lot was improving rapidly, painters and other artists were accorded little respect as citizens, even though the wealthy relied upon them to enhance their lives and to decorate their homes. Like all other Italian cities of the period, Florence was run by the most

---

[*] Of course, these people constituted only a tiny percentage of the population.

successful merchants and bankers. Top of the pile were the Medici family who had been unofficial heads of government for three decades by the time Leonardo arrived there.

The first great administrator, banker and patron of the dynasty was Cosimo de' Medici, who in his youth had openly challenged the ruling oligarchy of the city and held power from the mid-1430s until his death in 1464, perhaps only a year before Leonardo began his apprenticeship. Although he rarely held the highest position in the government, Cosimo was known to have maintained an iron grip on all levels of the ruling establishment. Much loved by his people and seen favourably by most historians, upon his death he was given the title *Pater Patriae*, father of the country.

Cosimo was crucial to the evolution of the Renaissance in Florence because his patronage cradled the careers of many principal artists of the time, men such as Botticelli and Leonardo's master, Verrocchio. More than anyone, he and his family changed utterly the lives of the great Florentine artists and offered them previously unimagined opportunities. As a consequence, the patronage of the Medicis enormously expanded the canon of great art, literature and learning of the world of the fifteenth century. Yet, staggeringly, Cosimo's father, Giovanni, owned only three books.

Cosimo was succeeded as head of the family empire by his eldest son Piero, and Cosimo's grandson Lorenzo took over when Piero died in 1469 after only five years at the pinnacle of influence. Lorenzo was every bit as popular as his grandfather, and if anything he did more for the arts. Lorenzo was undeclared ruler of Florence for most of the time Leonardo lived in the city. He and Leonardo were certainly not friends, but the two men were well acquainted by the time Leonardo became a master and began working on state commissions.

But this lay in Leonardo's future. First he had to learn his trade. Natural ability he undoubtedly had, but he, like all artists, had to acquire a formal, traditional training before he could develop his own style and follow his artistic instincts. By good fortune, Piero da Vinci's choice of Verrocchio had been inspired. The great Florentine sculptor and painter was the perfect master for the young Leonardo.

Fig. 3.1: Via de Agnolo today.

Situated on the Via de Agnolo, Verrocchio's workshop was one of the two most important in the city. The other was that of Antonio and Piero Pollaiuolo, who enjoyed a reputation as innovators and consummate professionals comparable to Verrocchio. However, Verrocchio's workshop may have had a slight edge over the Pollaiuolos' studio when it came to the quality of apprenticeship offered to young artists.

The workshop system, in which young talent was apprenticed and the truly gifted trained to become masters, could be viewed as the original 'university of life'. The workshops bore little relation to the artists' studios of modern myth. They did not presage Monet's sun-splashed retreat or Picasso's Paris garret. Today, the Via de Agnolo is a busy, narrow Florentine street packed with cars and mopeds a short walk from the Duomo. On each side of the street you will find terraced houses and tiny shops and, on the narrow pavement, news-stands and sweets traders. Half a millennium ago it was even more cramped, the road a mere track bordered by wooden buildings built out into the road further as each storey was added, so that anyone leaning out of the window on the top (usually third) floor could almost shake hands with another doing the same in the house across the street. Like others in the city, the studio was on the ground floor and opened directly on to the street. Children and animals ran in and out unrestrained, and just beyond the front door the artist's work was displayed for passers-by to peruse and perhaps purchase. Those who worked there – the master, his close assistants and a small cadre of young apprentices – also lived on the premises, in cramped, often unhygienic conditions.

But the workshop, or *bottega*, was also an inspiring place, a meeting point for like-minded people and young students from around the city and beyond, and if the apprentice was of an easy-going temperament and had a good relationship with the master, there could be no better place for a talented young artist to live, to learn and to work. Verrocchio's workshop was also a place where the master's friends and fellow artists and thinkers would gather to exchange ideas. On one level, we might compare the leisure-time atmosphere of these work-shops to the student café scene of turn-of-the-century Prague, or perhaps even the folk-clubs and bars of downtown New York between the mid-1950s and early 1960s.

As well as having a reputation as a skilled craftsman and a man never short of commissions, Verrocchio was known as an inspired teacher. However, opinion is divided concerning his abilities as an artist. In his *Lives of the Painters, Sculptors and Architects*, Vasari has us believe that: 'In the arts of sculpture and painting, to tell the truth, he [Verrocchio] had a manner somewhat hard and crude, as one who acquired it rather by infinite study than by the facility of a natural gift.'[1] Others have been more complimentary. The art historian A. H. R. Martindale goes as far as to say that: 'In the large-scale works of his mature period, Verrocchio displays the mastery and sensitivity of Desiderio at his best.'[2]

Whatever Verrocchio's merit as an artist, there is little doubt his personal contribution to the Renaissance has been completely over-shadowed by the great figures with whom he was so closely associated. He is thought to have been taught by no less an artist than Donatello, and as well as guiding Leonardo through his apprenticeship, Verrocchio was the tutor of such legendary figures as Perugino and Botticelli. As the writer Ugolino Verino points out: 'Verrocchio had as disciples almost all those whose names now fly above the cities of Italy.'[3]

It is hard to imagine how Vasari came to his conclusions, and it seems improbable that an artist who was not himself first-rate could teach so well so many young men who went on to become some of the greatest artists of their era.

Verrocchio's life had been blighted early by misfortune. When he was thirteen he was charged with manslaughter after a prank went terribly wrong. A stone he had thrown over a wall without looking had killed a passer-by. He was lucky to serve a prison sentence of only a few weeks. Then, shortly after his release, his father died suddenly, leaving his family in debt. As the eldest son, he was responsible for the well-being of his mother and siblings, which forced him into a variety of poorly paid jobs to support his family. At the same time, he realised his only chance of acquiring any degree of social status was to educate himself. Working by day and studying by night, he gradually found his way into the goldsmith's trade. From there, through sheer hard work, determination and abundant talent he became a master craftsman and later developed his skills as a painter and sculptor. Obsessed with success, and by all accounts incredibly conscientious, he became a favourite of the Medicis, and was recognised by many of his contemporaries as a sculptor of great merit as well as being famed as an accomplished teacher. Verrocchio spent much of his time on decorations and banners for festivals and pageants, but perhaps his most important lasting contribution was his *Baptism of Christ*, now in the Uffizi, the execution of which involved assistance from Leonardo, who is known to have painted one of the angels to the left of the main figures. Although he was never without work, he seems to have spent most of his life scrambling after commissions and never became as rich as he would have liked.

When Leonardo arrived at the bottega, Verrocchio was only seventeen years older than his new apprentice. Leonardo was something of a country bumpkin, with rough manners and a pronounced rural accent; but Verrocchio was no snob. In many respects some of Leonardo's unconventionality may have derived from his teacher, a man who encouraged in his charges free-thinking and individuality. The two of them got on well, which was fortunate because, like the other apprentices, Leonardo spent twenty-four hours a day, seven days a week in his care, working twelve hours a day, eating all his meals in the bottega and sleeping on the straw-covered floor.

And the training process was gruelling. The painter Cennino Cennini described it as 'placing oneself in servitude'.[4] And in his influential book *Treatise on Painting*, written some thirty-five years before

Leonardo started working for Verrocchio, Cennini proposed a thirteen-year course which took the young apprentice through a succession of grades, the most important of which were *garzone* (journeyman) and, several years on, *maestro* (master craftsman), by which time a young artist had become a fully paid-up member of an artists' guild.

Leonardo's course certainly did not last thirteen years; his transition from apprentice to master could not have taken more than six, because by 1472 he was registered as a master, a member of the painters' guild, the Company of St Luke. Although Cennini's ideas may have only provided a guide to a painter's training, much of what he wrote about in the 1430s presages Leonardo's own memories of his time under Verrocchio's tutelage. Leonardo described various techniques for blending paints lifted almost directly from Cennini. 'Take oil of cypress, which you will then distil,' he notes. '. . . Have ready a large vase in which you put the distilled oil, with enough water to give it an amber colour. Cover it well, so that it does not evaporate . . .'[5] Elsewhere, Leonardo noted some less orthodox recipes, clearly of his own design: 'Salts can be made from human excrement,' he writes, '. . . burned, calcified, stored and dried over a low fire; any excrement will yield salt in this manner, and once distilled these salts are very caustic.'[6]

Life at the bottega was undoubtedly demanding, but Leonardo was totally absorbed in what he was doing. At this time he lived to paint and he took unsullied delight in learning. And it was not all hard work; the bottega was also a place where he learned much beside the rules of painting and the mechanics of mixing paints and preparing surfaces. In Verrocchio's studio, life came to the artist, and the true sense of exploration and adventurousness of thought, of imagination and desire to acquire knowledge that epitomises the Renaissance was there in abundance. Leonardo summed up the mood of the time when, years later, he wrote: 'The desire to know is natural to good men.'[7]

He may have first studied sculpture. He later noted in his *Treatise on*

Painting that he had worked '. . . no less in sculpture than in painting, being equally adept at the one and the other.'[8] And Vasari tells us he made 'heads of laughing women'.[9] As well as these clues, the Milanese painter Giovanni Lomazzo reported in the 1560s that he owned

a little head of Christ, as a child, from the hand of Leonardo Avinci himself [*sic*], in which are to be seen childish simplicity and purity accompanied by a certain something of wisdom, intellect, and majesty, and with an air which is that of a tender child, while seeming to have something of the age of judgement, a truly excellent thing.[10]

Those who worked and lived in the bottega discussed music, books, philosophy, science, the remnants of magic – still a factor that impacted on philosophy – and of course, natural science. They also played music; Verrocchio was an accomplished musician who taught Leonardo to play the *lira da braccio* (the lyre). Young artists from other botteghe dropped by after work and Leonardo frequented the workshop of the Pollaiuolo brothers and others. When Leonardo first arrived in Florence, Botticelli, eight years his senior, was still working there, employed as Verrocchio's closest assistant. And the botteghe were places travelling thinkers and peripatetic alchemists, mystics, writers and musicians would visit as they passed through the city. Sometimes these wanderers and the young apprentice painters would rub shoulders with famous intellectuals, friends of the master, some of whom had once been apprentices themselves.

One such figure was Leon Battista Alberti, whom we encountered in the previous chapter. Alberti died in 1472, so Leonardo knew him for only a short time, but the man's influence is clear to see in Leonardo's own life and work. Alongside another great figure of his generation, Verrocchio's teacher Donatello, Alberti was a founder member of the humanist movement, and he believed the most important and beautiful art (particularly architecture and sculpture) should derive from Classical simplicity. But as we have seen, Alberti was also a far-sighted man, an extraordinarily talented polymath who had little patience with officialdom and never allowed himself to be fettered by convention or authority; all attributes and characteristics that later became increasingly prominent in Leonardo's personality and behaviour.

Contemporaries commented upon Leonardo's beauty and his flamboyance, that he loved to dress in revealing short tunics and to grow his beard long. In fact, reports from Leonardo's time as well as those from writers of the following generation almost always make particular reference to his physical appearance as a preface to any description of his works and achievements. The *Anonimo Gaddiano* tells us he wore his beard 'combed and curled', and that he favoured 'rose-coloured tunics that reached only to the knee'.[11]

But how did Leonardo change so quickly from country lad to dandy? And more importantly, what were the influences that enabled him to develop his unique insights and to begin his intellectual endeavours? So many years after the event, this route is a difficult one to follow, but we can try to highlight some of the key moments in Leonardo's formative years.

For much of it, we have Verrocchio to thank; but there are other clues to Leonardo's internal renaissance. This began with Uncle Francesco, but accelerated rapidly after Leonardo moved to Piero's house and then the workshop.

Leonardo had enjoyed the outdoor life and the rustic freedom of Vinci and this had generated in him a love of simple, natural things; but Florence, with its bustle and energy, glamour and money, the buzz of commerce, noise and constant activity, offered a different kind of inspiration. For the young artist, the point where all these factors met was the bottega itself, but what probably influenced Leonardo's personality most during this impressionable time was the confidence he gained from the appreciation of others. Before his arrival in Florence he had only a small circle of family who may have understood his talent, but in Florence he thrived on attention. Gradually he must have started to believe in his own extraordinary abilities.

An illustration of his new-found confidence and the ease with which he startled others, even at this age, can be found in a tale that, like many anecdotes from Leonardo's early life, may or may not be true. The story recounts how, soon after Leonardo began his apprenticeship, a sharecropper from Piero's estate in Vinci asked Piero if he could help him find a suitable artist in Florence to paint a wooden shield he had just purchased. Piero naturally gave the job to his son, who took away the cheap, badly warped shield with promises that he would quickly return it painted.

Leonardo reasoned that a shield should carry a frightening image such as a dragon or some other mythical beast. So, to create as realistic an image as he could, he collected lizards and insects and dissected them, taking parts of each and amalgamating them into a hideous hybrid which he then depicted emerging from a cave and breathing flames. When he was finished, he placed the shield in the corner of a darkened room and invited his father to come and inspect it. According to Vasari, Piero entered the room, saw the shield and was so terrified he was about to flee, when his son emerged from the shadows smiling, satisfied, and declaring that that was the effect a shield should produce.[12] Piero was so impressed he switched the shield for a cheap one he found in a local market and sold his son's work to a merchant in Florence for one hundred ducats (about £1,500). According to legend, the merchant later sold it to the Duke of Milan for three times this price.

Although this sort of appreciation did not go too much to his head or in any way overwhelm his embryonic genius, it did give Leonardo the self-confidence to realise at a very early stage in his career that the only way to make a truly significant mark in the world was to go his own way, to absorb what others could offer and then to forge his path forward. This may have been a dramatic realisation for a boy who had up to this time been made to feel inferior due to the unfortunate circumstances of his birth and his rustic upbringing. But perhaps it was a reaction against this; Leonardo's way of proving to himself and the world that social convention could not hold him down.

This powerful individualism is quite clear in Leonardo's notebooks. Among the thousands of surviving pages, he never once mentions his master, Verrocchio. Because of this, historians have long claimed the two men parted under a cloud when Leonardo qualified as a master craftsman, but this does not stand up to close scrutiny. If nothing else, the fact that he remained at Verrocchio's workshop for some time after entering the Company of St Luke indicates the very opposite.

One possible explanation is that he wanted in some sense to dissociate himself from his teacher. Leonardo is brutal in his portrayal of those who merely copy their masters, and it is probably for this reason he makes no mention of his own. In one of his discourses on painting he claimed: 'How painting declines and is lost from age to age, when painters have as their only model the paintings of their predecessors.'[13] Later, he remarks: 'The painter will produce mediocre pictures if he is inspired by the work of others.'[14] And most controversially: 'Avoid [excessive] study,' he declares; 'it will give rise to a work destined to die with the workman.'[15]

Making his point as clearly as possible he added:

I well know that, not being a literary man, certain presumptuous persons will think that they may reasonably deride me with the allegation that I am a man without letters. Stupid fellows! Do they not know that I might reply as Marius did in answering the Roman patricians, by saying that they who adorn themselves with the labours of others, will not concede to me my very own: they will say that, not having learning, I will properly speak of that which

I wish to elucidate. But do they not know that my subjects are to be better illustrated from experience than by yet more words? Experience which has been the mistress of all those who wrote well, and thus, as mistress, I will cite her in all cases.[16]

Some years later, he remarked:

The adversary* says that in order to acquire practice and do a great deal of work, it is better that the first period of study should be employed in drawing various compositions executed on paper or on walls by diverse masters, and that in this way practice is rapidly gained, and good methods; to which I reply that the method will be good if it is based on works of good composition from the hands of skilled masters. But since such masters are so rare that there are but few of them to be found, it is a surer way to go to natural objects than to those which are imitated from nature with great deterioration, and so produce bad methods; for he who can go to the fountain does not go to the water jar.[17]

Whatever we may think of this disregard for those who helped shape him, such an approach is often to be seen in Leonardo's attitude towards his masters. It is almost as though he dare not invoke the names of those who guided and nurtured his talent for some perverse fear it would in some way demean his own achievements. It is also partly down to a desire on Leonardo's part to project fully the originality of his ideas, to show them as rootless or at least rooted only in ancient tradition.

However, looked at dispassionately, Leonardo was absolutely right to take the stance he did. The purpose of any creative individual,

---

* The 'adversary' mentioned here is probably Michelangelo, who was, as we will see later, a great rival of Leonardo's, and a man who disliked him intensely.

whether artist or scientist, is to forge new ideas, to till new ground. Perhaps Leonardo could not follow his own path and at the same time find room to praise the influence of his masters, most especially the one man to whom he owed the greatest artistic debt, Verrocchio.

For Leonardo the font of inspiration came in large part from within, from experience. In middle age, he wrote: 'Men wrongly complain of experience, which with great abuse they accuse of falsity, but let experience be, and turn such complaints against your own ignorance which causes you to be carried away by vain and foolish desires.'[18]

But Leonardo too had a hero. This was Giotto, who as a young man had deliberately turned away from copying his predecessors and followed his own path. Leonardo reminds us of this in his notebooks, commenting, 'Giotto was not satisfied with imitating the works of his master, Cimabue.'[19]

Interestingly, on the scrap of notes where this statement is to be found, it is crossed out, almost as though he felt he had gone too far, been too critical. However, it is not difficult to see from where this obsession for following an individualist path and degrading the importance of the master had come. Leonardo, the illegitimate son of a self-interested careerist, must have found it almost impossible to subsume his own personality to that of his master, no matter how strong their friendship or how much Leonardo respected him. Verrocchio was certainly a surrogate father as well as a guide and master. But, from necessity, Leonardo had maintained a detached, self-motivated energy throughout his childhood and adolescence; he could not now accept a second figurehead as anything but friend and respected instructor. Perhaps in the end the subconscious fear that he may lose another parental figure was too much for him to bear.

Tracing back even further, we have few clues to any inspirational or revelatory moments in Leonardo's early life. He wrote so little about what he thought about himself, gave us so little autobiographical detail, we are left with mere fragments that are all too tempting to elevate and exaggerate.

In the summer of 1473, when he was twenty-one, he spent some time in Vinci. Such trips may have been a regular feature of his life, or that summer might have been exceptionally hot in Florence, prompting him to leave the city for his home village. He travelled the countryside, we presume alone, and recorded what he saw in some of the earliest of his drawings to survive, two landscapes depicting the rugged and wild countryside of his boyhood. Unusually, he dated one of these – 5 August 1473 – and on the reverse he wrote: 'Stopped by at Antonio's, am content.'*

This fragment tells us a little about the Leonardo of 1473. It does not necessarily imply he was unhappy in Florence; in fact this is probably far from the truth, but it does reveal an attachment to his home and the tranquillity of the countryside, away from the hubbub, as well as the excitement and inspirational energy of the city. However, it suggests Leonardo was already showing signs of a fractured personality. On the outside, he was flamboyant and extrovert. On the inside, he yearned for solitude and peace, needed his own company and the quiet of the world in which he had grown up. And this schism can be seen most clearly in his attitudes towards sex.

He was almost certainly introduced to homosexuality in Verrocchio's bottega, probably as soon as he arrived there aged between thirteen and fifteen. But such a young initiation would have been far from unusual for the time, especially among artists.

An indication of how homosexuality was viewed in fifteenth-century Florence may be seen in the fact that in Germany during the 1470s the popular word for homosexual was *Florenzer*. Also, homosexuality was most readily acceptable to those with libertine attitudes: the artists,

---

* These drawings are thought to be the first landscapes in Western art.

writers and musicians who were then attracted in growing numbers to Florence. Verrocchio was known to be a practising homosexual and he lived under the same roof as his assistants and apprentices. In such an environment, and with as many as a dozen young men living in one small room, homosexuality would have been difficult to avoid.

It is safe then to assume that the young Leonardo was quite comfortable with the notion of homosexuality and had perhaps been naturally inclined towards it from an early age. However, shortly after beginning the life of the libertine artist, any sexual freedom he may have enjoyed became irrevocably tarnished by cruel circumstance. Aged just twenty-three, he was accused of sodomy.

In Florence at this time, there existed a strange system that allowed citizens to proclaim their feelings about anything they wished by posting their grievance in writing in specially designed boxes called *tamburi* (drums) or *buchi della verità* (mouths of truth) dotted around the city. Citizens could say what they liked about anything or anybody.

Early in 1476, in a letter deposited in one such *tamburo*, Leonardo was accused along with three other young men of committing sodomy on the person of one Jacopo Salterelli, and brought to the attention of the Officers of the Night and Monasteries, a night watch that attempted to monitor and control social behaviour. The case was heard on 9 April 1476, but no result was proclaimed. Instead the judge called for a further hearing to be held on 7 June.

This must have been an agonising experience for Leonardo. He had proclaimed his innocence but had to wait a further two months before a new hearing could be arranged to decide his fate. And although the general mood within Florence at this time was one of tolerance towards homosexuality, according to the strict letter of the law the offence carried the death sentence, to be carried out by burning at the stake.

In June, the case was re-appraised, but again it passed without a judgement being made. The judge discharged the four men on the condition that the case be heard again. This third hearing duly took place a few days later, and this time the case was dismissed altogether. None of the four was charged with any crime.

The details of this whole affair are sketchy, but it seems likely there was more to the matter than a simple accusation and trial for sodomy. One of the accused, Lionardo de' Tornabuoni, was mentioned on the charge sheet without any domestic details, not even an address. This was almost certainly because he was related to the Medicis. Lorenzo de' Medici's mother was a Tornabuoni.

This suspicious fact implies that the entire matter was fabricated for political reasons, and that Leonardo had somehow become unwittingly embroiled in a failed attempt to discredit the Medici family. The fact that he was an artist and that artists were known to have what some would consider 'loose morals' merely added spice to the plotters' plans.

Whatever the details, Leonardo was affected dramatically by the incident. Not only did he have the threat of the stake hanging over him for two months, but the events surrounding the trial were well publicised throughout the city and he and the others were marked as sexual deviants even after they had been acquitted unconditionally.

Leonardo was deeply shamed by this exposure. It is possible that up to this time he had felt no real guilt about his homosexuality, that it had either been natural to him, or else he accepted it as part of his self-image; after all, there were certainly plenty of role models for him. But his sense of dishonour was very real and stemmed principally from the damage he believed the trial could cause his father.

Sadly, we have no record of Ser Piero's reaction to his son's arrest. If we had, it might illuminate their shadowy relationship. Ser Piero may have tried to intervene in the case on a professional level, or indeed he may have realised early on that the whole affair was a fiction. There is little doubt that as a respected notary he would have been greatly angered by the publicity his son had attracted, but there is no record of how this affected his relationship with Leonardo.

In many respects, the Salterelli trial led Leonardo to an emotional and psychological crisis. During his first decade in Florence, he had already accomplished great things. By 1476, he had ascended through the echelons at Verrocchio's studio and had acquired the technical skills which, combined with his huge natural talent, were to make him the greatest artist of his age. But he had also experienced trauma and pain and these were in their own way just as important in shaping him.

We can pinpoint four over-riding influences upon his character as a young man. First, he had arrived in Florence displaying the manners and mores of a simple country lad and, despite having since then associated with the entire social spectrum in Florence, he never entirely left this image behind. The second influence to consider is the burden of his insalubrious birthright. Although he had no desire to adopt many of the pretensions of the Florentine middle classes, from his teenage years he was very aware that his lowly birth acted as a barrier to his aspirations, and this affected him emotionally. Which leads to the third influence upon his youth. We must remember that Leonardo's father lived and worked in the same city and had long since acquired a reputation as a womaniser.

Ser Piero was a driven and self-obsessed man who appears to have had little regard for family life. He met his financial responsibilities, for failing to do so would certainly have damaged his social standing. But by the time of the Salterelli trial he had buried two wives and fathered a second illegitimate child. His first wife, Albiera di Giovanni Amadori, whom he had married in 1452, died childless in 1464; his second, Francesca di Ser Giuliano Lanfredini, he married within a year of Albiera's death. She too died childless, in 1473, and he married for a third time in 1475. Ser Piero's first legitimate child, Antonio, was born in 1476, a few weeks before Leonardo was accused of sodomy.

By Ser Piero's vivid presence, Leonardo was reminded constantly that his father had sired him out of wedlock and that this was the source of the restrictions to his career and social life. This must have caused Leonardo distress, highlighting his sense of otherness and misanthropy and, as a reaction, shaping his unconventional and occasionally rebellious side. He had an abiding lack of respect for authority which, as we shall see, almost certainly cost him commissions and preferment and sometimes damaged what could have been fruitful relationships. But it is equally important to realise this unconventional bent steered him towards his achievements both as an artist and as a scientist. Throughout Leonardo's life, the pain produced by childhood trauma, fuelled by the emotional catastrophe of the Salterelli affair, caused him misery, but also drove him onward towards greatness.

The fourth factor to consider is Leonardo's sexuality. Homosexuality was no impediment to a career as an artist, but this does not eradicate the difficulties Leonardo may have had dealing with his own feelings and did nothing to help him during and after the trial.

Combined, the psychic impact of his illegitimacy, the presence of an overbearing and narcissistic father, his unfashionable upbringing as a country lad and his sexual persona all fused during the second half of the 1470s and moulded the adult Leonardo from the clay of naïve youth. It led him to become secretive, to have difficulty working for authority figures in whatever form they presented themselves, and most importantly for his future and the world of the Renaissance, it led him to an autodidactic path, for this, he reasoned, was the only way he could develop.

Without doubt, the Salterelli trial scarred Leonardo deeply. It threw him into a paroxysm of anxiety from which he never fully recovered his emotional or sexual equilibrium, and this can be seen in comments he made later in life. In a note written during his early thirties, he describes an experience probably from his walking holiday in 1473:

Driven by an ardent desire, and anxious to view the abundance of varied and strange forms created by nature the artificer, having travelled a certain distance through overhanging rocks, I came to the entrance to a large cave and stopped for a moment, struck with amazement, for I had not suspected its existence. Stooping down, my left hand around my knee, while with the right I shaded my frowning eyes to peer in, I leaned this way and that, trying to see if there was anything inside, despite the darkness that reigned there; after I had remained thus for a moment, two emotions suddenly awoke in me: fear and desire – fear of the dark, threatening cave and desire to see if it contained some miraculous thing.[20]

Freud made much of the sexual imagery of this passage, but it has to be judged in its context. Immediately before this excerpt, Leonardo wrote about hurricanes and storms and the cruel impact of Nature upon human civilisation and the individual. So perhaps Leonardo is telling us nothing more than the facts, a simple account of an adventure while walking alone through the Tuscan hills. It is also conceivable this story does indeed relate Leonardo's inner sexual feelings. Instead of it being, as Freud would claim, an account dragged from the subconscious depicting his sexual confusion, it could be a simple, conscious analogy. He could be saying here, 'I have experienced a relationship with a woman through desire, but was fearful at the same time . . .' *Two emotions awoke in me: fear and desire – fear of the dark, threatening cave and desire to see if it contained some miraculous thing.*

It is common for avid keepers of notebooks, and Leonardo took his notebooks with him everywhere, to slip into reveries, to sidetrack, to add little notes, to write in semi-coded fashion or to relate a cryptic message as a story for private re-reading many years later. Perhaps this was just such a passage.

However, Leonardo's sexuality was confused throughout his life and became further fractured as he grew older. A thread that runs through his writings and his drawings is what appears to be a distaste for the sexual act and a repugnance towards the sexual organs, in particular female genitalia. He very rarely painted the entire female form and concentrated almost exclusively on the hands and face. Even in his medical notebooks, he is far more concerned with the male reproductive system than the female, and the only surviving sketches of female genitalia are oddly distorted and grotesquely caricatured.

So, what do we know of Leonardo's sexual awareness as an adult? From what he wrote on the subject (beginning some years after the Salterelli affair) it would appear he found sex distasteful and certainly aesthetically displeasing. 'He who does not restrain his lustful appetites,' he admonishes, 'places himself on the same level as the beasts.'[21] And elsewhere he remarks acerbically that, 'The act of coupling and the members engaged in it are so ugly that if it were not for

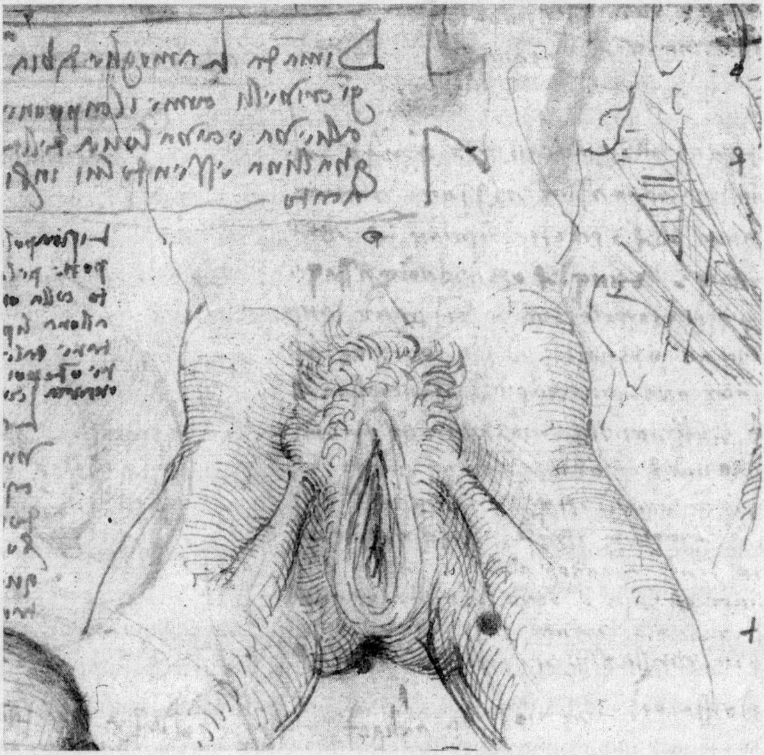

Fig. 3.2: Female genitalia.

the faces and adornments of the actors, and the impulses sustained, the human race would die out.'[22] As a scientist, he offered absolutely clinical comments concerning reproduction and the sexual act. An example is his observations about intercourse: 'In general, woman's desire is the opposite to man's. She wishes the size of the man's member to be as large as possible, while the man desires the opposite for the woman's genital parts.' But then he adds coldly, '. . . so that neither ever attains what is desired.'[23]

Such remarks seem even odder when we consider the general lasciviousness of the age during which Leonardo was writing. Fifteenth-century Italy saw popes fathering illegitimate children including, in the case of Pope Alexander VI, the child of his incestuous liaison with his daughter, Lucrezia Borgia, who was also sleeping with her older brother, Cesare. It was a time when venereal diseases were responsible for the deaths of thousands, when adultery was far more common than fidelity.

But it would seem the sodomy trial of 1476 had dug so deep it became a pivotal incident in Leonardo's life. In his notebooks years after these events he describes a parable which thinly disguises his feelings:

A stone of good size washed bare by the rain, once stood in a high place, surrounded by flowers of many colours, at the edge of a grove overlooking a rock-strewn road. After looking for so long on the stones on the path, it was overcome with desire to let fall down among them. 'What am I doing here among plants?' it asked itself. 'I ought to be down there, with my own kind.' So it rolled to the bottom of the slope and joined the others. But the wheels of carts, the hooves of horses, and the feet of passers-by had before long reduced it to a state of perpetual distress. Everything seemed to roll over it or kick it. Sometimes when it was soiled with mud or the dung of animals, it would look up a little – in vain – at the place it had left: that place of solitude and peaceful happiness. That is what happens to anyone who seeks to abandon the solitary and contemplative life to come to town, among people of infinite wickedness.[24]

Until the Salterelli trial, Leonardo had been an open, trusting individual, a young man who seemed confident and well-balanced, bursting with energy, still naïve and impressionable. After April 1476, the energy, the genius and the passion remained, but his personal life was now enshrouded by distrust, suspicion, defensiveness. And this was a change that was to have profound effects upon his attitude to work and the degree to which he revealed his creations and his ideas to the outside world. In turn this was to have an unparalleled effect upon our understanding of Leonardo da Vinci, the man, the artist and, later, the scientist. As we shall see, it also played a dramatic role in preventing later generations developing the insights Leonardo could have offered the world.

4

SHATTERED DREAMS,
NEW AWAKENINGS

When I thought I was learning to live I was learning to die.
— Leonardo, *Codex Atlanticus*

By the time of the Salterelli trial, Leonardo had been at Verrocchio's workshop for at least a decade and had risen to the position of chief assistant to the master, but he knew that soon he would need to cut himself adrift from Verrocchio's guidance and support and set up on his own.

During the summer of 1477, Verrocchio was commissioned to produce a marble monument to commemorate the life of one Cardinal Niccolò Forteguerri in the city of Pistoia, about twenty miles northwest of Florence. He took some members of the bottega with him, including Leonardo, and while they were there, the city authorities added another commission, a large altar painting, a Virgin and Child. These were both important commissions yet Leonardo appears to have had little to do with either of them, and already the job of master's assistant was passing to a young artist, Lorenzo di Credi, whom Leonardo himself had been preparing as his successor.

This excursion to Pistoia was his last with Verrocchio. Within a few months he had left the bottega altogether and Di Credi (who although a competent and dedicated painter was not in the same league as Leonardo) had taken on Leonardo's mantle.

Life outside the protective environment of Verrocchio's studio was not easy, and although the move was inevitable, indeed necessary, during his first years as an independent artist Leonardo was only rarely to experience the security offered by his earlier life on Via de Agnolo. Leonardo was many things, but efficient businessman he certainly was not, and he had only a sketchy sense of how to provide for himself in a world governed by commercial forces. He heeded little the value of money and let slip offers and commissions as though they meant almost nothing. Yet at the same time, he had no other means of supporting himself.

An offer to produce a painting to be placed upon the altar of St Bernard's chapel in the Signoria arrived from the government on New Year's Day 1478. The commission was for twenty-five florins, which the artist would have considered a worthwhile sum, especially for a first professional solo effort. Yet he never completed the job. According to the *Anonimo Gaddiano*, Leonardo produced only a sketch for the painting, and the piece was completed seven years later by Filippino Lippi, supposedly based upon Leonardo's original outline.[1]

January 1478 was in fact an inauspicious time to begin a new business venture, for Florence and much of the region stood at the opening of a traumatic year that witnessed not only floods and plague, but perhaps more significantly for the social fabric of Florence and for Leonardo's future career, one of the most dramatic political upheavals the city had ever witnessed.

Renaissance Italy was a cauldron of political intrigue and in-fighting. The peninsula was divided into more than a dozen independent states, all vying with one another in a confused power struggle that threatened at any moment to degenerate into all-out war. The key players were the five major powers of Rome, Milan, Venice, Naples and Florence, along with a set of smaller states that included Genoa, Siena and Mantua. At any one time, some of these states would form alliances against a group of others. It was a fluid arrangement in which allies became the bitterest of enemies only months after enjoying a friendly alliance, then to fall back into a different alliance shortly after. Add to this the ever-present threat of the Ottoman Empire to the east and French expansionism to the west and it is easy to see how any leader of an Italian state had a difficult job simply maintaining their position within the structure of European politics.

With the succession of Lorenzo de' Medici in 1469, the enemies of Florence saw an opportunity to cause trouble, and Lorenzo, who was to prove a master of political intrigue, quickly gained the respect of his people by taking a hard line against his rivals. In particular, Lorenzo stood up to Rome and the Pope, Sixtus IV. At the beginning of the 1470s the Turks had conquered Greece, an action that prompted the Pope to call for a holy war. Lorenzo had declined the invitation to join him and had immediately antagonised Rome. This was made worse when he quickly formed an alliance with Venice, which was then opposed to Naples, Milan and Rome.

Sixtus took swift reprisals against Lorenzo's decision: he terminated the exclusive Medici contract to manage Vatican finances and broke the family's monopoly of the crucially important alum trade, allowing it to pass to their great rivals, the Pazzi family. In retaliation, Lorenzo de' Medici accused one of the Pazzis of treason and had him arrested; he also destroyed another Pazzi's hopes of a substantial legacy.

When word of these countermeasures reached Rome the Pope was furious; his nephew, Cardinal Girolamo Riario, believed the time had come for passive grumbling to be superseded by action. On 26 April Lorenzo and his brother Giuliano were attending a service at the church of Santa Maria del Fiore when, as the bell rang for the end of the service, a group of men jumped up from the aisles and attacked them with knives and swords. With a sword through his heart, Giuliano died immediately. Lorenzo fought back, taking a knife wound to his throat, and escaped through the sacristy, bolting the brass doors behind him. Then, with the help of a few friends, he made his way back to the Medici palace on Via Larga.

The assassination attempt had been intended as a call to rebellion and the beginning of an uprising against the Medicis, but it backfired terribly. The conspiracy had been orchestrated in Florence by the Archbishop of Pisa, who bungled his role – he was meant to go to the Palazzo della Signoria and seize it in the name of liberty just as the murderers were completing their work.

But the major reason for the utter failure of the scheme was that Lorenzo de' Medici was actually a popular leader, opposed in the city by only a few malcontents who supported the aggrieved Pazzi family and were working treacherously with a foreign state, the Vatican. Instead of cries for revolution, the streets of Florence were soon ringing to the sound of the Medici rally cry, *Palle!*, and the common people were aiding the authorities in hunting down the criminals and dragging them to the Piazza della Signoria.

The assassins included a member of the Pazzi and two disaffected priests. They, along with the Archbishop, were hanged within hours of the attempted uprising and more executions followed in subsequent weeks.

It was soon discovered that the Vatican had been behind the plot, and so Florence declared war on the Pope, which meant that they were against Naples who had recently formed an alliance with Rome. Sixtus IV then took the melodramatic but ineffectual step of excommunicating the entire city of Florence and there began a series of military clashes which dragged on for the best part of two years. Finally, in a master-stroke of political innovation that secured his popularity for the rest of his life, Lorenzo travelled to Naples to face his enemy across a negotiating table and brokered a favourable deal that settled the conflict.

But how did all this affect Leonardo? He had almost no involvement in the events themselves, although he would certainly have attended the hangings and the political rallies that followed the astonishing events of 26 April. We also know he tried to acquire a commission worth forty gold florins to paint the hangings, but was passed over for his old friend Botticelli.

More than a year after the assassination attempt, one of the conspirators, Bernardo di Bandini Baroncelli, who had escaped to Turkey after the stabbing, was extradited and hanged. Leonardo was there to capture the event with a sketch we presume he intended as the basis of a full-scale painting for which he hoped to acquire a commission. The sketch, which includes notes describing the colours of the clothes worn by the condemned, is today in the Musée Bonnat in Bayonne, France, but that is all that was produced on the subject by Leonardo. Which sheds light upon his relationship with Lorenzo de' Medici.

Although Lorenzo knew of Leonardo, who had probably been recommended to him by Verrocchio, the first citizen of Florence did little to further Da Vinci's career and may have actively held him back. The *Anonimo Gaddiano* tells us Lorenzo de' Medici employed Leonardo in his garden of San Marco, where he repaired sculptures and fashioned new pieces, but this must be a fallacy because the gardens were not begun until 1480. More precise evidence shows that Lorenzo actually displayed a decidedly cool attitude towards Leonardo's great talents and it appears likely this was one of the major reasons for Da Vinci's decision to leave Florence within a few years of his setting up on his own.

In some respects, the two men had much in common. They were almost exact contemporaries and both were lovers of knowledge and art, but the differences in their characters, their way of perceiving the world, the disparity in the circumstances of birth and family, education and social standing far outweighed any similarities.

Lorenzo was heterosexual, later described by Machiavelli as 'incredibly given to the pleasures of Venus'. Leonardo was homosexual with a very public sodomy trial behind him. However, it is certain the different sexual tastes of the two men would not have been a major factor in the progress of their relationship. After all, Lorenzo actively encouraged at least one other homosexual artist, Michelangelo, giving him a string of commissions and even opening his homes to him, treating him almost as a social equal.

A more significant difference between Lorenzo and Leonardo lay in their personal style and tastes. Lorenzo was physically unattractive, even, some said, ugly, and he knew it. Surviving portraits represent a pale flat face, thick neck and broad, oft-broken nose. By contrast, all accounts agree Leonardo was exceptionally beautiful. Lorenzo shunned ostentation in his style of dress and although he enjoyed sex and hosted festivals and celebrations, he was austere in his personal tastes and fashion sense. As we have seen, prior to the sodomy trial (by which time Lorenzo would have known Leonardo well through the

Fig. 4.1: Lorenzo de' Medici.

commissions given to Verrocchio), Leonardo enjoyed a flamboyant lifestyle and wore revealing clothes on the limits of acceptable taste. Again, this incompatibility would not in itself have tarnished Leonardo's chances of work; many other artists were similarly extrovert and yet enjoyed lucrative professional relationships with the Medici family.

It seems the most pronounced barrier between the two men had little to do with the trappings of social life, style or personal tastes, but was to a large extent a matter of intellectual elitism on the part of Lorenzo de' Medici.

The head of the Medici family had received a Classical education, but unlike many sons of wealthy statesmen and bureaucrats, he had a genuine love for formal learning. He soaked up the knowledge of his teachers and was a model student – at one time he had four tutors, including a canon and a Platonic philosopher, all of whom instilled in him a love for traditional learning and the Classical tradition. As we have seen, the early life and education of the bastard Leonardo could not have been more different. He had little in the way of formal education and grew to resent the idea of trotting out inherited wisdom. To him, the only important contributors to the canon of human knowledge were the *inventori*, the truly original thinkers and innovators, men like Alberti and Giotto, whom he considered the only ones to have made genuine contributions to the advancement of civilisation.

The 'court' of the Medicis promoted what may be seen today as literary pretension. Lorenzo de' Medici was indeed a talented intellectual and he saw himself as a writer as well as a supreme diplomat, strategist and politician. His mother, Lucrezia Tornabuoni, was an amateur playwright who had started reading Greek to her son almost before he could walk, and he was quoting Virgil by the age of six. All of this was in stark contrast to Leonardo's formative years spent in the fields of Vinci with Uncle Francesco.

Leonardo called himself an: *uomo senza lettere*, a man without knowledge of literature, and for all his purported egalitarianism and humanist leanings, Lorenzo must have viewed him as a rough-tongued and rather crude man, and because of this he failed to appreciate his unique talents for what they were.

But then Leonardo had probably done little to help himself. He loathed intellectual pretension and openly mocked the social graces and falsities of the courtier. Even if he had been accepted by the Medicis he would have had little time for the social niceties expected of him. Although he treated Lorenzo de' Medici with the respect befitting their relative stations, Leonardo also knew his own value. It is also possible Leonardo's views had reached Medici ears.

The clash of personalities rested then upon an incompatibility in perception, an ideological clash. It was almost certainly never voiced by either party, but the combination of Lorenzo's intellectual elitism and Leonardo's sense of independence could have done little for his chances of preferment through the Medici family.

Time and again during the period between Leonardo's establishment as an independent artist in 1478 and his leaving Florence three years later, he was snubbed and passed over by the ruling family who chose other, lesser artists to decorate their palaces and to add colour to the many festivals and carnivals they organised.

Lorenzo was a keen believer in what the art historian André Chastel has called 'cultural propaganda'. He frequently offered the services of his favourite Florentine artists to his fellow heads of state, 'loaning' them as 'gifts'. Antonio Pollaiuolo, whom Lorenzo described as *principale maestro della città*, was sent to Rome for short periods; Botticelli followed him there; Verrocchio was posted to Pistoia, and later Venice, and the architect Giuliano da Maiano had worked for the King of Naples.

This apparent generosity actually served Lorenzo well. It boosted his ego by demonstrating his great knowledge of art, it was a cheap and visible sign of diplomacy and political goodwill and, perhaps most importantly, it showed how elevated the culture of Florence had become, thus helping the city establish itself as the engine of the Renaissance and the epicentre of European culture in the fifteenth century.

Significantly, Lorenzo showed almost no interest in sending Leonardo anywhere as his cultural representative, providing us with a clear impression of what he thought of him. He may have appreciated aspects of Leonardo's artistic talent (despite never giving him a single commission), but he could never have contemplated Leonardo da Vinci as a standard-bearer for Florentine culture. Quite simply, Lorenzo, beguiled by pretension and cultural ephemera, was embarrassed by Leonardo, the man.

The date Leonardo began his autodidactic course is not known but we can make some informed guesses. We know he was interested in engineering and practical mechanical problems during his early days at the bottega, but in the beginning much of this interest was unfocused and naïve. Vasari tells us that:

> . . . In architecture also, he made many drawings both of ground-plans and of other designs of buildings; and he was the first, although but a youth, who suggested the plan of reducing the river Arno to a navigable canal from Pisa to Florence. He made designs of flour-mills, fulling-mills and engines, which might be driven by the force of water.[2]

What Vasari means by 'but a youth' is misleading. Leonardo did not create plans to divert the Arno until he was almost fifty, but we should remember that he was born and raised in a rural setting and he would have been aware of irrigation systems and the constant problem of supplying water to parched summer fields, so he could have been thinking about these things during the earliest days at Verrocchio's studio.

Leonardo almost certainly picked up his earliest education in philosophy and science from the people who visited Verrocchio at the bottega. Unlike Lorenzo, Verrocchio was certainly not ashamed of Leonardo's peasant manner and lack of sophistication, and for his part Leonardo was ever hungry for knowledge and sought it out through direct contact with those older and wiser than himself. As a student he would have been every bit as able and as keen as Lorenzo de' Medici, but his education came from experience and conversation rather than the guidance of official tutors.

A scrap of manuscript dating from 1478, which is one of the oldest records of Leonardo's thinking, now kept in the Uffizi Museum, Florence, contains several drawings of mechanical devices showing that even this early in his career Leonardo had some elementary knowledge of contemporary engineering. These drawings tell us little about the direction of Leonardo's intellectual wanderings and are merely fragments, but they demonstrate that soon after leaving Verrocchio's studio, he was certainly thinking in terms of designing simple mechanical devices, and it suggests his plans for the river Arno, mentioned by Vasari, could indeed have come from his mid-twenties.

Whether or not these designs were actually ever employed and the results lost or destroyed is impossible to say, but many of the sketches represent machines that *could* have been built and they display an accurate understanding of mechanical principles. They include wonderful three-dimensional representations of a winch and an odd-looking device that appears to be for testing the breaking strain of a bow or used perhaps to reshape malleable objects. On a separate sheet we find a mass of miniature drawings, all beautifully rendered, providing an accurate design for a lathe, a die-stamping machine and what appears to be a cranking device for a crossbow.

From the same period, the late 1470s, Leonardo made a set of illustrations of war machines. This was the beginning of a lifelong fascination with mechanical devices for use in battle or to provide

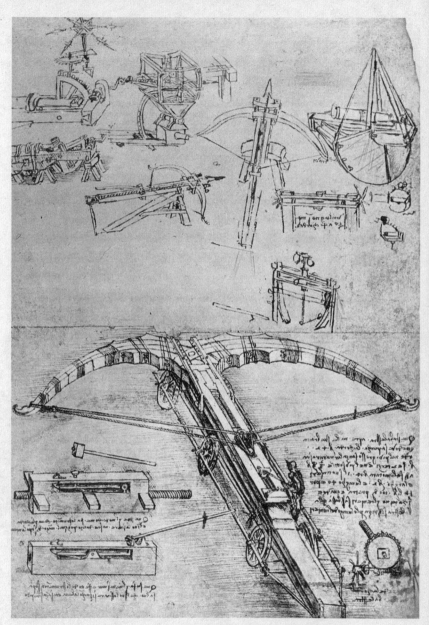

Fig. 4.2: Military engineering – sketches for crossbows and catapults.

defences, designs that could have appealed greatly to heads of state Leonardo had been weighing up as potential patrons. The earliest example is a 'design for a mechanism for repelling ladders' and is a neatly drawn illustration of how the ladders of attackers could be disabled during an attack. With a flourish typical of Leonardo, the illustration is completed with miniature figures hard at work operating the mechanisms. To one side of the page there are insets showing the details of how the system could work.

Elsewhere from the same final years of Leonardo's Florence period there are surviving sheets demonstrating another of Leonardo's obsessions – devices powered by water or used to transport water. These include a pen-and-ink drawing called *Devices for Raising Water* in the *Codex Atlanticus*, and beautifully rendered miniatures dealing with different systems in which water is the central feature. Along with these are drawings of a snorkel shown on the head of a user, a complex winch and machines for pumping water from subterranean sources, as well as illustrations of how water may be efficiently pumped through buildings.

With this final set of drawings Leonardo gives us a clue to his sources at this time. In the top right section of the sheet he produced a little drawing of a tower supplied by water from the ground using what every school science student knows to be an impractical hydraulic device, Archimedes' screw. Leonardo depicts the device as a tightly grooved spiral which allows the water to fall backwards under gravity as the mechanism moves it upward.

Archimedes was of course a key influence upon Renaissance scientific thinking and Roberto Valturio's *De Re Militari*, published in 1472, owed much to his mechanics. By the time Leonardo drew his representation, Archimedes' screw had become well known within intellectual circles. So although Leonardo was not then creating anything truly original, these drawings show that he was at least familiar with the latest thinking and cultural developments of the time.

By the late 1470s he was trying to structure an autodidactic course and he had made a note to himself, one of the *aides-mémoire* he often left in his notebooks, a list in the *Codex Atlanticus* of those he wanted to meet or had already met and whose brains he planned to pick:

The quadrant of Carlo Marmocchi [an astronomer and geographer]; Messer Francesco Araldo; Ser Benedetto Cieperello [a notary]; Benedetto on arithmetic [this may refer to a book Benedetto had written or a portable abacus he was known to have used]; Maestro Paolo, physician; Domenico di Michelino [painter]; el Calvo of the Alberti [possibly a relative of the polymathic Leon Battista Alberti]; Messer Giovanni Argiropolo [a Florentine scholar of Greek philosophy famous at the time].[3]

It is quite likely Leonardo's pursuit of knowledge was closely linked with his apparent lackadaisical approach to business; an attitude defined by one historian as: 'his constitutional inability to fulfil his obligations in a businesslike manner'.[4] And it could be argued he paid so little attention to business and was quite uninterested in making money because he was obsessed with discovery and learning, activities which at this stage gave him no financial return.

As well as being a time during which Leonardo immersed himself in understanding the fundamentals of science and engineering, later to form the bedrock of his own discoveries and innovations, his years of independence in Florence after leaving the bottega were tarnished by an increasing depression. Ironically this had little to do with his lack of material or financial success, but came instead from an intense feeling of claustrophobia and a gathering awareness of his own mortality and life's limitations.

This is evident in his writings of the time, in which he seems preoccupied with mortality, with human powerlessness in the face of the inexorable progress of time. 'We do not lack ways nor devices for dividing and measuring these *miserable* days of ours,' he writes solemnly, 'wherein it should be our pleasure that they be not frittered away or passed over in vain and without leaving behind any memory of ourselves in the mind of men.'[5]

At another point in his notebooks, in a passage written about 1480, he declares:

O time, devourer of all things and O envious age, you destroy all things and devour all things with the hard teeth of old age, little by little with lingering death. Helen, when looking in the mirror, seeing the shrivelled wrinkles of her face made by old age, wept and contemplated bitterly that she had twice been ravished.[6]

These comments indicate that Leonardo was raked by anxiety during those years, generating what has been described as 'harmonic tension',[7] a state in which he was feeling angst but also working furiously and with growing confidence as he probed the world of pure intellect. They also demonstrate the breadth of his reading at the time. The second excerpt is almost a direct translation of a passage from Ovid's *Metamorphoses*.[8] Made usually on the edge of a sheet of drawings or in the margin of other less personal writings, such notes provide us with a rare insight into his private thoughts and emotional concerns towards the end of the 1470s, a period during which the day-to-day events of his private life are otherwise obfuscated for the historian.[9]

We can safely assume that after leaving the bottega he met up with Verrocchio frequently, because they lived and worked within a few hundred metres of each other, and there is every reason to believe they had remained friends. Within a year of leaving, Leonardo had acquired his own lodgings (he probably lived with his father in the interim), and supported himself by producing a cartoon for a tapestry entitled *Adam and Eve in Paradise*, one of the few works he actually completed in this period. This was destined for Flanders, where the tapestry was to be completed in silks and gold thread, but for some unknown reason it never arrived and was presumably never made. Vasari apparently saw Leonardo's cartoon almost one hundred years after it was produced, describing it in his *Lives of the Painters, Sculptors and Architects*, and it is thought to have been in the possession of the Medicis between the 1470s and Vasari's time. Unfortunately, like so much of Leonardo's artistic output, the original cartoon has since been lost.

Living in his own rooms would have meant a major shift in lifestyle for Leonardo. At the age of twenty-seven he was living alone probably for the first time. It meant personal independence, freedom to do as he pleased, but this solitude may have also added to his sense of isolation and melancholy.

There was a small collection of men he considered close friends. Most important to him were two miniaturists, Gherardo di Giovanni and Attavante di Gabriello, who probably worked together in Via dei Librai (the street of booksellers) which today is called Via della Condotta. He was also friendly with Botticelli whom he had met in Verrocchio's studio during his first days in Florence. The older artist was known as a prankster and practical joker and within the fraternity of artists he was as famous for his sense of humour as he was for his work. Leonardo made several affectionate references to him in his notebooks, at one point calling him *il nostro Botticelli*,[10] although he was also candid about what he considered the older man's limited sense of perspective, declaring: 'Sandro, you do not say why the second things [objects or figures in the middle distance of a painting] appear lower than the third ones.'[11]

Leonardo's circle of friends was not restricted to other artists. He was known to have befriended one Tommaso di Giovanni Masini, the son of a gardener who claimed to be the bastard of a Florentine noble-man, one of the illustrious Rucellai family. Like Leonardo, Masini appears to have had a strong anti-establishment streak, but none of his friend's talent. He was said to have been involved with shady dealings and existed on the periphery of the criminal underclass of the day. He was fascinated with the occult and even adopted the title *Zoroastre de Peretola*, presumably in imitation of Zoroaster (or Zarathustra), the mystic who lived during the sixth century BC.

The memory of the Salterelli trial still loomed large for Leonardo, but he probably had at least one lover during his final two years in Florence. We have scant evidence to go by, but there are some occasional references and fragmentary notes in his manuscripts that lend us clues. Most prominent in Leonardo's private life during these years was a man named Fioravante di Domenico. We know almost nothing about him, except for a comment by Leonardo on a sheet of drawings dated 1478, which includes a portrait of a youth, beside which he has written 'Fioravante di Domenico . . . in Florence is my most cherished companion, as though he were my . . .'[12] The quote is difficult to read in the original and some linguists have translated it as: 'Fioravante di Domenico is my dearest friend in Florence . . . I love him like a young girl.'

Another ambiguous relationship from this time is that between Leonardo and a young falconer named Bernardo di Simone. On a piece of manuscript contemporaneous with the sheet upon which Fioravante is mentioned, Leonardo has doodled 'Bernardo di di di . . . Sim . . . di di di Simone.'[13] On the same page he wrote the name of his beloved uncle, Francesco, and added the word 'friends' in ornate script. Then at the bottom of the text he began toying with the words of his father's name, Di Ser Piero, altering the words to 'di.s.p.ero' or *dispero*, 'I despair'.

On a companion sheet is another set of personal writings, words from a contemporary poem written in another's hand to which Da Vinci has added: 'O Leonardo, why torment yourself with a vain love?'[14]

It is difficult to judge what these fragments mean. Even if we ignore the fact that they are badly damaged, faded and often only semi-legible and open to linguistic interpretation, so long after the events they may misguide us and represent a false image of Leonardo's private life and thoughts during this period. However, there is little doubt Leonardo remained a practising homosexual. We should not be surprised by the idea that he was in love with a nobleman such as Di Simone. Perhaps because of their difference in social position, or because Di Simone was heterosexual, this was probably an unrequited love and one that simply added to Leonardo's sense of angst. Nor should we be surprised that he may have had a more serious and fulfilling relationship with the young man Fioravante di Domenico. Although his sexual character was confused, it is important to remember he was also a healthy, fit young man, he was independent and an artist who lived and worked within a community dominated by homosexuals during an age and in a city in which it was usually quietly tolerated.

Yet there is no escaping the fact that, whether precipitated by sexual frustration or thwarted in his feelings, Leonardo was very unhappy at this time. A final comment on the sheet of notes referring to 'friends' tells us clearly how Leonardo felt about his life and hints at his hopes and aspirations. He writes, '*Dove mi poserò*', which some have translated as 'Where shall I settle?' This is then followed by 'You shall know this soon.'

Indeed he did. For Lorenzo de' Medici was about to make a decision which would affect Leonardo's plans dramatically.

In October 1481, and following Lorenzo's famous peace negotiations after the dispute with Naples and the Vatican, the states of Rome and Florence were once more on friendly terms, and Pope Sixtus IV asked Lorenzo if he would find him the best artists in the world to help decorate the newly constructed Sistine Chapel (which had been named after him).

Lorenzo no doubt saw this invitation as a great compliment and recognition of his famed knowledge and patronage of the arts, and he wanted to impress the Pope. Florence was buzzing with excitement throughout October, and in the botteghe dozens of artists waited anxiously for an invitation to the Medicis' palace on Via Larga. Earlier that year, Verrocchio had accepted a commission from the Doge of Venice, Giovanni Mocenigo, to produce a great equestrian statue of Bartolomeo Colleoni, the celebrated *condottiere* (leader of Venice's mercenary armed forces who had died six years earlier), effectively excluding him from Lorenzo's list.

But it would seem that Medici was anyway more inclined towards the younger generation of Florentine artists, a list which by any reckoning should have included Leonardo in the first rank. But as the graduates of the botteghe, including Sandro Botticelli, Domenico Ghirlandaio, Luca Signorelli and Perugino (Pietro di Cristoforo Vannucci) left for Rome, Leonardo was conspicuously ignored.

Early in 1481 he had received an important if rather odd commission, a painting to adorn the altar of the convent of the friars of San Donato at Scopeto, a few miles outside Florence. It had been important because it gave him an opportunity to bring together his many talents as a painter and to indulge himself in a painting almost two and a half metres wide. With this commission he also had the freedom to employ what is called the 'grand style', an extremely popular contemporary style in which a central set of figures is surrounded by dozens of minor characters.

Not least of the oddities of the commission was the fact that no money was to change hands. The friars of San Donato had inherited some land from a financially embarrassed merchant whose will had contained the condition that the monastery could take possession of the land so long as they provided the dowry for his daughter, Lisabetta. Leonardo was offered one-third of this estate, but only if he met three conditions: he had to complete the painting within twenty-four months of the commission, Lisabetta's dowry was to become his responsibility, and he had to supply all materials from his own pocket.

Rather surprisingly perhaps, Leonardo agreed to these terms (although he had to have the contract altered after two months so that the monks supplied his materials). We can only assume he was excited by the project and was willing to accept even these distinctly unattractive conditions. But what has exasperated art historians is not so much why Leonardo took on the project, but why he failed to complete it.

There are many theories. First, he may have decided to leave Florence and so deserted the friars and the incomplete painting. His employers may have been intolerant of his methods and his working practices; a result perhaps of a clash of attitudes and ideologies between artist and clergy, so that Leonardo became exasperated by the conditions imposed upon him. He may have felt rushed, or perhaps the monks wanted to direct him to paint something other than he had planned. Vasari suggests that Leonardo stopped for purely artistic reasons:

> . . . since it seemed to him that the hand was not able to attain to the perfection of art in carrying out the things which he imagined; for the reason that he conceived in idea difficulties so subtle and so marvellous, that they could never be expressed by the hands, be they ever so excellent.[15]

Others have intimated that the painting is actually a greater work of art *because* it is incomplete and that Leonardo was fully aware of this; that he stopped work on it when he thought it finished. In his definitive analysis of Leonardo as an artist, the late Kenneth Clark declared that the painting possesses an extra indefinable quality because it is unfinished. 'Finish is only of value when it is a true medium of expression,' he writes. 'To have carried the *Adoration* any further without depriving it of magic would have taxed even Leonardo's genius and would have taken him seven years instead of seven months.'[16] And the Italian art historian Nello Tarchiani goes as far as to say: 'The *Adoration* is indeed quite perfect just as it is, in its incomplete preparatory state . . . Amazingly enough, the painting offers in embryo the master's entire pictorial work: at thirty Leonardo had already created and defined his own almost superhuman imaginary world.'[17]

For our consideration of Leonardo as scientist and engineer, the painting contains a useful marker. On a sheet of sketches of figures he made in 1481 in preparation for the painting (since entitled *Studies of Figures in Conversation and Movement*), we find an incongruous item, a sketch of a hygrometer, a device for measuring the relative amount of moisture in the air. The simple sketch shows a sponge on the end of a lever attached to a scale, the idea being that as the sponge absorbs water from the air, the lever moves and indicates the level of moisture. Although this was not an original idea of Leonardo's – Alberti had described a similar mechanism at least two decades earlier – it again illustrates Leonardo's fascination with practical science, a preoccupation that was diverting his thoughts even as he prepared for his most important commission up to that time.

Whatever Leonardo's reasons for leaving the *Adoration of the Magi* incomplete, it is quite possible that at the very point when Lorenzo was selecting his representatives to travel to Rome, the friars of St Donato were complaining of Leonardo and word had reached as far as the Medici palace. Combined with the distinctly mixed feelings Lorenzo already had for Leonardo, it could have swayed his decision. The last person Lorenzo would have wanted in Rome was an artist who, despite his talent, might fail to perform for his masters.

The most convincing image of Leonardo's life towards the end of 1481 is that of a man weighed down with frustration and thwarted dreams. He was living in a city in which he had faced shame and huge disappointment. If Lorenzo had indeed passed him over through lack of faith, then his career was doomed there. He may also have been depressed by a recently ended love affair, for after this time we hear no more of Fioravante di Domenico, nor indeed Bernardo di Simone.

The last months of 1481 found Leonardo at the nadir of his life, and a move must have seemed the best chance for a fresh start. As he left behind the city of his youth and his earliest days as a professional artist, new opportunities opened up before him. Reversing the trend of the past few years, he was about to enter the happiest, most inspired and productive period of his life.

5

RECOGNITION

Nothing can be found in nature that is not a part of science.
— Leonardo, *Trattato della Pittura*

It might be argued that genius requires nurturing, that it needs an auspicious environment to fulfil promise. Perhaps another way of expressing this is to say that the thoughts of some geniuses will remain hidden and lost to time unless circumstances and luck play a role; others argue that genius will out whatever the vicissitudes. We will probably never know what sort of genius Leonardo possessed, but what is clear is that life in Florence did not provide nourishment for him; he did not flourish there, and the chances are, he knew it.

The manner of Leonardo's leaving Florence is shrouded in confusion and has generated many theories. Some suggest he merely walked away from the *Adoration of the Magi*, packed his bags and left soon after the embarrassment of rejection at the hands of the Medicis. Others believe Lorenzo de' Medici did not send Leonardo to Rome because he instead offered him the chance to move to Milan.

The Florentine statesman was known to have been a great lover of music. Undeterred by the fact that he could neither sing nor play, he often put self-penned verse to pieces produced for him by court composers. Leonardo was an accomplished musician and singer and so it is possible he had played publicly and may have been sent to Milan by Lorenzo as a musician.

Leonardo fondly referred to music as 'the representation of invisible things'.[1] He could read and write music and composed ditties, some of which have survived and may be found in his notebooks. An example is the lyric: '*Amore sol la mi fa remirare. La solmi fa sollecita*', which may be translated as: 'Only love makes me recall, it alone stirs my heart'.[2] He might even have been one of the composers Lorenzo used to accompany his words.

But Leonardo's interest in music went further. As a scientist, he later studied and wrote on the subject of acoustics and he is known to have designed unusual instruments, although most were probably never built, and as far as we know none have survived.[*]

On the manner of Leonardo's leaving Florence, the *Anonimo Gaddiano* informs us: 'It is said that when Leonardo was thirty years old, the Magnifico sent him to present a lyre to the Duke of Milan, with a certain Atalante Migliorotti, for he played upon this instrument exceptionally well.'[3]

We know with certainty that Leonardo arrived in Milan sometime early in 1482 and that he did indeed travel there in the company of a young musician named Atalante Migliorotti. Atalante is thought to have been about sixteen at the time. The link between him and Leonardo is well documented, but their personal relationship remains

---

[*] It is an indication of Leonardo's later international fame as a master of so many skills that his career as a musician is dogged by exaggeration and hyperbole. Legend has it he was not only a master player but invented the violin. This idea arose from a misinterpretation of events. Early in the sixteenth century, Leonardo recommended to King Francis I of France an instrument-maker with the odd name of Gasparo Diuffoprugcar, who most experts claim to be the inventor of the violin. Because he was made known to the world through Leonardo's introduction, it has been assumed that some years earlier Leonardo had commissioned Diuffoprugcar to produce a violin to his own design, but there is no evidence to support this.

vague. Leonardo had certainly drawn the boy in Florence, a sketch he titled and annotated with the words 'with head held high'.[4] However, we know little of Migliorotti's life or career apart from this period in Leonardo's company, and it seems most likely Leonardo had once been his music teacher.

Although his precise role in Atalante's journey to Milan remains unclear, several clues connecting Leonardo with music, and in particular the story of a lyre presented to the ruler of Milan, Ludovico Sforza, have come down to us. First is a drawing of a strange stringed instrument in Leonardo's notebooks. The instrument appears to consist of a soundboard with three strings attached to a headpiece resembling a composite of various animal heads. This may have been a preliminary sketch for a working instrument Leonardo was planning. Whether or not the instrument was ever made is unknown.

According to Vasari:

Leonardo was summoned to the Duke of Milan who took much delight in the sound of the lyre, to the end that he might play it: and Leonardo took with him that instrument which he had made with his own hands, in great part of silver, in the form of a horse's skull – a thing bizarre and new – in order that the harmony might be of greater volume and more sonorous in tone, with which he surpassed all the musicians who had come together there to play.[5]

All this may be based upon fact, yet some lingering doubt remains. Considering what we know of Lorenzo's feelings towards Leonardo, combined with the fact that, as far as we are aware, he was never offered a single commission by the Medicis and, perhaps most significantly, that Leonardo was never invited back to Florence by Lorenzo after a brief period in Milan, we must doubt the theory that he was sent there as a musician. It therefore remains a possibility that Leonardo made up his own mind to leave Florence and to start afresh in a foreign state that might offer him greater opportunities.[6*]

Whatever lay behind the move, Leonardo had no intention of wasting any opportunities that might come his way. Despite often displaying a staggering disregard for financial propriety, it is likely Leonardo had his own agenda of ambitions and at least knew how to sell himself and to get where he wanted to be. Once in Milan, he took advantage of the situation and decided to stay because he believed he could find there patronage for his many talents.

And what exactly did Leonardo want to do in 1482? Rather idealistically perhaps, he sought a position at court or in the service of a wealthy patron who would allow him to express himself in his multitudinous ways. The perfect position would have been as court engineer or architect, requiring him to act primarily as a consultant and providing him with plenty of free time to get on with his private interests. In this, as with so many things, he modelled himself on Giotto who had been employed as an architect and had designed the campanile of Santa Maria del Fiore (the Duomo) in Florence. And it can be no coincidence that Leonardo arrived in Milan shortly before the Duke's chief engineer, Bartolomeo Gadio, was due to retire.

Naturally, at this stage he could no more walk into such a position in Milan than he could have acquired a similar post in Florence. But with

---

* Another theory (but one now largely discredited) suggests that Leonardo had been inspired to leave Florence for Milan because of ideology. Working upon the rather vague principle that Florentine philosophers followed Platonic doctrine while their counterparts in Milan followed an Aristotelian line, some historians have supposed this influenced Leonardo's choice of home. Leonardo was certainly still greatly enamoured with Aristotelian philosophy at this time, but the idea he moved to Milan because of this is now perceived as an extreme over-simplification, for he was also deeply interested in Platonic thought. Furthermore, it is now seen as doubtful that Florentine and Milanese thinkers were as clearly partisan in their ideologies as was once believed. Leonardo's reasons for emigrating were almost certainly far more prosaic.

Gadio's position vacant there would be a reshuffle of important posts at court and perhaps a useful opening for him. He was being over-optimistic, however, and not surprisingly such an opportunity did not come his way. It was to take years of determined effort before Leonardo could work his way into the Milanese court.

When Leonardo arrived in Milan in 1482, the city was comparable in size to Florence. It was an immensely wealthy city state ruled by the dictatorial Sforzas, who had been masters of Milan since 1450 when they had succeeded the Visconti family. Yet despite its great wealth and its proud banking, commercial and military dominance, as a home for the fine arts it was perceived as a pale shadow of Florence or Rome.

The ruling Sforzas were in no sense charlatans or philistines, but Florence attracted the great master painters of the age and engendered elitism. Because of this, Milan could boast many fine musicians, poets, engineers and scientists lured there by financial incentives, but no great painters or sculptors. Among the illuminati of the city were the renowned musician and composer Franchino Gaffurio, and the widely praised poets Antonio Fregoso and Gaspare Visconti. Milan could also offer great intellectual resources. It had a fine university in Pavia which boasted one of the best libraries in Italy, a repository that later provided Leonardo with many of the materials for his studies, and no fewer than ninety distinguished professors, especially masters of law, mathematics and medicine.[*]

Milan and Florence were very different cities in many other ways. The ubiquitous Romanesque architecture of Milan was considered by many of Leonardo's contemporaries to be vulgar, and the few elegant buildings in the city were all designed by Florentine architects. The

---

[*] In 1488 Ludovico financed the building of the Lazzaretto, a hospital that specialised in treating and in endeavouring to find ways to prevent the scourge of the age, the plague.

great centre of medical studies, the Ospedale Maggiore, designed by Antonio Filarete, and the Medici bank with an entrance hall modelled by the great Michelozzo, were the finest examples of Florentine architectural influence. Even the cathedral, today considered an architectural splendour, was perceived as uncouth by the aesthetes of the period because it was designed in the 'barbaric' Germanic style.

Dominated by the Duke's residence, the gigantic Castello Sforzesco, Milan had more in common with the traditions of northern Europe than the more sophisticated style of Tuscany. Crowded and cramped, stifling in summer and freezing in winter, polluted and violent, its undoubted vibrancy attracted Leonardo immediately and he appears to have settled there without any trace of homesickness. In fact the two decades he spent in the city were the happiest and most productive of his life.

As the Medicis were synonymous with fifteenth-century Florence, the character of Milan at this time was moulded and shaped by the indomitable presence of its ruler, Ludovico Sforza.

Nicknamed *Il Moro* (the Moor) because of his dark skin tone, Ludovico Sforza was absolute ruler of Milan from 1476 until the French occupation of 1499. The Sforza name had been adopted by Ludovico's grandfather, Muzzo Attendolo: *sforzare* means 'to force' and Attendolo was an accomplished and respected soldier, a much honoured *condottiere*. His natural son, Francesco, was renowned for his amorous adventures and is said to have had a special secretary whose sole duty was to deal with his romantic correspondence. Francesco fathered many children, legitimate and illegitimate, and the oldest, Galeazzo Maria, became the Duke of Milan on his father's death.

Galeazzo Maria gained a far worse reputation than his amorous father. More inclined towards violence than romance, he became known throughout Italy as a bloodthirsty tyrant who derived pleasure from torturing anyone who crossed him. Under the threat of torture and execution, he separated wives from husbands in order to satisfy his lust. He was murdered in his early thirties leaving a sole heir, Gian Galeazzo, who had only just passed his eighth birthday.

Galeazzo Maria's wife became regent for a short time but made the mistake of becoming involved with a palace steward, bringing shame upon herself and giving Francesco's fourth son, Ludovico, the opportunity to seize power. He soon became *de facto* ruler and took the official title Duke of Barirather rather than the one he really wanted (held by the boy), the Duke of Milan.[*]

Ludovico was a multi-faceted man. Relatively well educated, he placed great value upon using culture as a political tool but never developed any real aesthetic sense. To Ludovico, everything revolved around politics; and culture, like diplomacy or military power, was there to play its role. He realised that in the rapidly changing world of the late fifteenth century a leader needed to be respected for his intellect as well as more traditional qualities.

Opinion differs over his precise political character. Leonardo said of him: 'The justice of the Moor [was] as black as himself.'[7] But in relative terms he might be considered a rather 'liberal-minded tyrant'. Unlike his bloodthirsty older brother, he took no pleasure in having criminals tortured and went in for simple executions, frequently imprisoning rather than having his enemies hung or publicly mutilated.

The Moor was only a few months older than Leonardo and was possessed of an almost overbearing dynamism, a belief that his life would be short, and that in spite of his importance on earth, his career would be fleeting.[†] He had a burning wish to leave his mark and threw himself into big plans, diverting funds into great architectural projects and commissioning large-scale works of art. When later Leonardo enjoyed Sforza's patronage, this attitude was to cause him serious

---

[*] Barirather is a small province on the Adriatic close to Brindisi and now part of south-east Italy.

[†] In fact, he lived to the respectable age of fifty-eight.

problems. He hated to be rushed or pushed into creating works of art to order, once declaring in his notebooks that 'To give orders is a gentleman's work; to carry them out is the act of a servant.'[8]

As much as Leonardo hated the idea that he might be seen merely as a ducal servant, when he arrived in Milan he was not even that; his name was almost unknown at Sforza's court. If he had not been ordered to Milan by Lorenzo as a pawn in the game of cultural propaganda, Leonardo may at best have been perceived as a free-living artist with a local reputation; either way, he would have meant very little to Ludovico.

But although Leonardo would have known this, he also understood his true worth and was ambitious. Whatever had drawn him there, he arrived in the city prepared for the opportunity of an introduction to the Milanese court. This is clear from a now famous letter amongst his notes in which he outlines a set of claimed skills and a concise description of what he could offer the great Ludovico Sforza. It reads:

Most Illustrious Lord, having by now sufficiently considered the experience of those men who claim to be skilled inventors of machines of war, and having realised that the said machines in no way differ from those commonly employed, I shall endeavour, without prejudice to anyone else, to reveal my secrets to Your Excellency, for whom I offer to execute, at your convenience, all the items briefly noted below.

I have a model of very strong but light bridges, extremely easy to carry, by means of which you will be able to pursue or if necessary flee an enemy; I have others which are sturdy and will resist fire as well as attack, and are easy to lay down and to take up. I also know ways to burn and destroy those of the enemy.

During a siege I know how to dry up the water of the moats and how to construct an infinite number of bridges, covered ways, scaling ladders, and other machines of this type of enterprise. If because of the height of the embankment, and the strength of the place or its size, it should be impossible to reduce it by bombardment, I know methods of destroying any citadel or fortress, even if it is built on rock.

I also have models of mortars that are very practical and easy to transport, with which I can project stones so that they seem to be raining down, and their smoke will plunge the enemy into terror, to his great hurt and confusion.

And if battle is to be joined at sea, I have many very efficient machines for both attack and defence; and vessels that will resist even the heaviest cannon fire, fumes and gunpowder.

I know how to use paths and secret underground tunnels, dug without noise and following tortuous routes, to reach a given place, even if it means passing below a moat or a river.

I will make covered vehicles, safe and unassailable, which will penetrate enemy ranks with their artillery and destroy the most powerful troops; the infantry may follow them without meeting obstacles or suffering damage.

In case of need, I will make large bombards, mortars, and flame-throwing engines, of beautiful and practical design, which will be different from those presently in use.

Where bombardment would fail, I can make catapults, man-gonels [a machine for throwing stones], *trabocchi** or other unusual machines of marvellous efficiency, not in common use. In short, whatever the situation, I can invent an infinite variety of machines for both attack and defence.

In peacetime, I think I can give perfect satisfaction and be the equal of any man in architecture, in the design of buildings public and private, or to conduct water from one place to

---

* The meaning of this is not entirely clear, the closest translation would be *traboccheto* or 'trap'.

another. I can carry out sculpture in marble, bronze, and clay; and in painting can do any kind of work as well as any man, whoever he be. Moreover, the bronze horse can be made that will be to the immortal glory and eternal honour of the lord your father of blessed memory and of the illustrious house of Sforza.

And, if any of the items mentioned above appears to anyone impossible or impractical, I am ready to give demonstration in your park or in any place that should please Your Excellency – to whom I recommend myself in all humility, etc.[9]

On another page of the same Codex Leonardo produces an inventory of the things he has made and brought with him from Florence along with the subjects he has studied:

Many flowers drawn from nature. A head, full face with curly hair. Certain figures of St Jerome. Measurements of a figure. Drawings of furnaces. A head of Christ made with the pen. Some bodies seen in perspective. Many throats of old women. A Madonna, finished. Some machines for ships and some machines of waterworks.[10]

This letter was almost certainly never sent, but it is clear Leonardo took great care over its composition. We may think of it as a form of CV or portfolio of abilities he hopes will sufficiently impress a prospective employer, one who will solve all his career problems.

The letter contains several prominent features worthy of close analysis. The first is what appears to be an over-riding dependence upon the military applications of his skills. And most striking is Leonardo's apparent enthusiasm for machines of mass destruction; his mortars which 'can project stones so that they seem to be raining down; and their smoke will plunge the enemy into terror, to his great hurt and confusion', and vehicles that could 'destroy the most powerful troops'. All of this seems rather at odds with the image of Leonardo the vegetarian bird-freer.

But to appreciate this apparent disparity we must look at both Leonardo's personal circumstances and the climate of the time, as well as the ethical framework of the era. Like all other states in fifteenth-century Europe, Milan lived by the sword. As a wealthy city, it could only keep its position by maintaining a well-equipped army that employed the latest military technology. In fact, by the 1470s Milan had grown into the most important arms manufacturer in Italy. Leonardo was naturally aware of this and knew it might provide him with a lever into the Milanese court.

He would have been aware of the latest arms developments, had certainly seen first-hand the armouries in Florence, and had read the standard texts including Roberto Valturio's *De Re Militari*. As well as this, he may have found some interesting ideas in the 1476 edition of Pliny's *Natural History*. However, the designs he had brought with him to Milan were actually not terribly original and a comparison between these and the designs of his contemporaries who specialised in this form of engineering, like Valturio, show that Leonardo was following rather than leading.

As for his personal involvement with such schemes, we must remember Leonardo lived during an age in which life was cheap and daily closeness to death moulded the opinions and attitudes of everyone. Plague, war and famine meant everyone was intimately aware of the fragility of human existence. To people of this age, pain and violent death were no strangers. Furthermore, Leonardo knew the skills he claimed as a designer of military hardware would be his best way of attracting attention. There is no doubt he abhorred war, and later in his notebooks he drew sketches of puny men overwhelmed by military machinery annotated with comments such as '*pazzia bestialissima*', 'bestial folly'. Yet, in spite of this, he knew that to gain a foothold in the

Milanese court he would have to prostitute his talents, at least until he could impress the Moor with his other skills.

And of course, these other talents were not insubstantial, a fact Leonardo makes clear in the final paragraph of the letter. On this ground he would have felt more confident. Boasts that he could sculpt, paint and draw as well as anyone he knew were rooted in undeniable fact and experience. Ironically, because painters were considered to be on the lowest rung of the artistic and cultural ladder, he was least inclined to offer his services in these disciplines. Frustratingly for Leonardo, he was most interested in an appointment as an engineer or an architect for the Milanese court, but had the greatest experience as a painter, sculptor and musician.

But his ambitions may have been more focused than a simple desire to gain a lucrative position in a profession that he had not already made his own and to forge a living while pursuing his independent interests. There was another reason for his emigration to Milan whether prompted by Medici or by his own volition.

Sometime during 1472 or 1473, Galeazzo Maria had decided to have cast in bronze an equestrian statue of his father, Muzio Attendolo. This was no philanthropic gesture to honour his dead father, but was intended to extol further the power of the Sforza family. Their reputation had been built and maintained on military prowess, so what better way of recognising the might of the family and the city as well as the cultural awareness of Galeazzo Maria than to represent the founder of the dynasty atop his favourite mare?

The problem with the scheme lay in the sheer size of the planned statue. The general feeling among experts of the time was that the skills involved in casting bronze statues to compare favourably with surviving examples from the Classical age had been lost during the Dark Ages. The standard against which all attempts were measured was the statue of Marcus Aurelius on the Capitol in Rome, which stood 4.24 metres (approximately fourteen feet) high. Almost three decades earlier, in 1453, Donatello had succeeded in producing the 3.2-metre-tall *Gattamelata*, and Verrocchio was even then occupied with the construction of his own *Colleoni* in Venice, which was only slightly larger than Donatello's famed work.

The challenge and the kudos that would have accompanied the successful construction of a statue to compare with the Marcus Aurelius, a bronze statue over four metres high, attracted many artists from all over Europe, and after Galeazzo Maria's death in 1476 the Sforza family continued the search for the right man. They probably approached the famous Mantegazza brothers and the Pollaiuolo family, both esteemed in the art of producing large statues, and Leonardo certainly would have heard of the project while he was still living in Florence.

Leonardo had been fascinated with equestrian drawing and painting since the early days of his apprenticeship, and from the time he began keeping notebooks, during the mid-1480s, until the end of his time in Milan, he filled page after page with sketches and plans for constructing a massive bronze equestrian statue. According to one commentator, Leonardo devoted sixteen years of his life to the idea.[11]

If anyone living during the fifteenth century could have designed and built an Attendolo statue to rival the Classical ideal, it would have been Leonardo. He probably first considered such an attempt through his contact with Verrocchio, who by 1481 had filled much of his studio floor space with a full-scale wooden model of his equestrian statue. By the end of his decade and a half of study and preparation, Leonardo would have had all the skills required – an instinctive understanding of form and composition, a mastery of anatomy and the necessary engineering knowledge. His boast to Ludovico Sforza – 'Moreover the bronze horse could be made that will be to the immortal glory and eternal honour of the lord your father of blessed memory and of the illustrious house of Sforza' – may have been an exaggerated claim at the time, but later, when the opportunity became a reality (during the 1490s), it would certainly not have been so.

> He proposed to the Duke to make a horse in bronze, of a mar-
> vellous greatness, in order to place upon it, as a memorial, the
> image of the Duke [Vasari tells us]. And on so vast a scale did he
> begin it and continue it, that it could never be completed. And
> there are those who have been of the opinion (so various and so
> often malign out of envy are the judgements of men) that he
> began it with no intention of finishing it, because being of so
> great a size, an incredible difficulty was encountered in seeking to
> cast it in one piece; and it might also be believed that, from the
> result, many may have formed such a judgement, since many of
> his works have remained unfinished. But in truth one can believe
> that his vast and most excellent mind was hampered through
> being too full of desire, and that his wish ever to seek out excel-
> lence upon excellence, and perfection upon perfection was the
> reason of it . . . And indeed those who saw the great model that
> Leonardo made in clay vow that they have never seen a more
> beautiful thing, or a more superb.[12]

In this account, Vasari implies the idea of the bronze horse came from Leonardo, but this is almost certainly untrue. As would be expected from hagiographic accounts, early biographical sketches such as the *Anonimo Gaddiano* and Vasari's *Lives of the Painters, Sculptors and Architects* create the impression that Leonardo's transition from itinerant artist to acclaimed and valued member of Ludovico's court was an easy one. We hear from Vasari: 'The Duke, hearing the marvellous discourse of Leonardo, became so enamoured of his genius, that it was something incredible: and he prevailed upon him by entreaties to paint an altar-panel containing a Nativity which was sent by the Duke to the Emperor.'[13]

Sadly for Leonardo, things did not run quite so smoothly. Ludovico was indeed won over by Leonardo's talents eventually, but it took more than a little 'discourse'. For at least his first two years in Milan, Leonardo was obliged to make a living from the profession that had sustained him in Florence, but which he was trying to leave behind.

Even then he needed to work his way into the Milanese art scene in order to establish himself. He joined forces with a group of comparatively mediocre artists, the Preda (or Predis) family, with whom he shared a home and studio. It was a symbiotic relationship. The six Preda brothers, all artists specialising in different forms, realised that in Leonardo they had found a talent far more refined and prodigious than their own, but they had the contacts in Milan and were already widely respected in the city. They could each learn and gain from the other.

Their first and most significant collaboration was an altarpiece for the Confraternity of the Immaculate Conception of the Blessed Virgin Mary, in the church of San Francisco Grande.

Accepted as the superior artist, Leonardo was given responsibility for the most important section of the altarpiece, the central panel of the triptych. He completed the task, but the result was far from the orthodox format expected by the monks who had commissioned the work, today known as *Virgin of the Rocks*.

Never conventional in his approach and probably secretly humiliated by the obligation to take on work he must have considered beneath him, Leonardo ignored the detailed remit provided by the friars, a document that dictated such things as the colours for the robes of the figures, the nature of the background and the arrangement of the figures. Instead of producing a painting using brocade and gold leaf for the main characters as requested, Leonardo painted a dark brooding landscape peopled with saintly figures who did not even have the traditional haloes and gathered in a decidedly unorthodox group.

If the painting provoked controversy at the time, it continues to do so today. Among art historians there is some dispute about whether or not this painting was started when Leonardo was still living in Florence and whether he incorporated an earlier version into the commissioned piece. More excitingly perhaps, questions have been raised recently concerning the composition and character of the painting, and what Leonardo is trying to depict with it, and whether he was working to a hidden private agenda.

The central figure in the painting is the Virgin Mary. Beside her sits St Elizabeth and in the foreground are Jesus and St John. It is an unsettling and strangely oppressive picture, and is as much a depiction of Nature as it is a religious representation. Mary sits at the mouth of a cave and much of the painting is taken up with rocks, plants and water. But most striking is that St John is a more dominant figure than the infant Christ.

Although no record of what precisely the monks of the Confraternity of the Immaculate Conception thought of the painting has survived, its unorthodox execution left them very ill at ease.[*] More importantly, the painting did cause a stir within the fraternity of artists in Milan, and most significantly for Leonardo's future prospects, the interest of the botteghe soon spread to the court, bringing with it a commission from Ludovico. This was a portrait of the Moor's latest mistress, the beautiful Cecilia Gallerani, the subject of one of the few surviving paintings produced by Leonardo, *Lady With an Ermine*.

Such work certainly helped to heighten Leonardo's profile, but the arc of his career was still rather flat and his acceptance by the Milanese ruler was tortuously slow. As with many creative individuals throughout history, his climb was dependent upon knowing the right people at

---

[*] However, as we shall see, the friars pursued Leonardo and the Predis family through the courts for compensation over the painting because they believed it was not what they had commissioned.

the right time and building upon a network of contacts within Milanese society and circumstance, but these contacts came only slowly.

In the summer of 1484 Milan was struck by plague. Almost nothing was understood of the disease except that it was horribly contagious and cut through the human population indiscriminately. To the people of the city this was divine retribution for some unknown crime and the only precautions taken to slow its course were those learned from earlier plagues such as the Black Death: the victims had to be isolated, and after they had died their clothing and bedding were burned. But in spite of a vague awareness of contagion, corpses were sometimes left for days in town squares, piled up and rotting, and the level of personal hygiene was so bad little could be done to stop the spread of disease within densely populated cities like Milan.

Leonardo had already lived through plague, in Florence in 1479, but the suffering in Milan was far worse. The disease lingered in the city for a full two years, killing upwards of ten thousand citizens.

Unfortunately we know almost nothing about how Leonardo may have lived and worked during those years. In his notebooks there are references to perfumes he produced to cover the stench of death but these could have been devised in Florence to use during his first brush with the plague. 'Take some fresh rose water and moisten your hands with it,' he wrote. 'It will be agreeable.'[14] Yet it is odd that Leonardo leaves us no direct account of the plague years and nothing of the unfolding events in the city, because one of the few things we know about those years is that by 1485 he had begun his notebooks, in which he recorded his experiences alongside his observations on a multitude of things. The fact that we have no record of his life in a plague-ravaged city is perplexing, and unless such an account has been lost, his failure to report such an experience, even if only from a detached medical standpoint, is an inconsistency difficult to explain.

Although we have no personalised account of this period his

experiences during the middle years of the 1480s appear to have had a profound effect upon his thoughts. We do not know if he lost friends or loved ones to the plague (the likelihood is that he did), but the effects of the disease clearly impressed themselves upon him. He came to the conclusion that human folly had exacerbated the effects of the disease in Milan and throughout Europe, and he realised, as few others seemed to, that the spread of the plague was aided by the cramped and insanitary conditions of city life. Why else, he reasoned, did the plague have far less impact upon rural communities? In his notebooks he commented pointedly: 'If the dwelling is dirty and neglected, the body will be kept by its soul in the same condition, dirty and neglected.'[15]

And if we are to assume Leonardo remained in Milan as others fled, we may link his experiences and observations of how the disease spread with a vast collection of notes and drawings in which he tackles the problems of planning cities for the future. Whether or not he submitted these designs to the Milanese court at any time after the plague years had passed is not known, but he was certainly serious about

Fig. 5.1: One of Leonardo's designs for cities and new buildings.

them and believed they provided practical solutions to many of the problems that had made Milan susceptible to disease in the first place. These included plans for automated street washers (which used a system of water wheels) to clean the city of refuse and the piles of human excrement tipped daily into the road and left to fester.

Leonardo was serious about these ideas and keen to realise his plans. He even outlined a detailed letter to Ludovico carefully arguing through each element of his complex schemes, but it was almost certainly never sent.

Leonardo's plans were utilitarian in the extreme. He envisaged a city divided into regions for the different strata of society and based upon an infrastructure that would not have been out of place in sketches for the sets of Fritz Lang's *Metropolis*. He drew road systems and street designs, providing for plumbing, drainage, as well as the transportation and housing of animals and people. 'In this way,' he wrote, 'you will disperse the mass of people who are now herded together like a flock of goats, filling every corner with their stench and spreading pestilential death'.[16]

In this statement we see again Leonardo's misanthropic side, the element of his personality that harboured a suppressed hatred for humanity, a state of mind that bursts out in occasional statements and in passages in which humanity *en masse* becomes depersonalised and viewed with repugnance. Then again, perhaps here we see Leonardo's personal feelings of pain during the plague years, sentiments missing in any direct form elsewhere in his notes. It is conceivable he was simply too close to the anguish to tell us about it plainly. Or is this coldness another example of the oft-times chilling acceptance of death and human mortality that was such a major component in the world-view of people who suffered far more than most of us could imagine from our twenty-first century perspective?

In his city plans, Leonardo divided the Milan of the future into regions in which different groups of people would live and work. There was an area for the poorest which was little more than a subterranean catacomb, a place that would have only rarely seen the light of day. And the rich, those who orbited the celestial Duke, were to reside in parklands and enjoy the open space. All of which is a strange echo of Leonardo's uncharacteristic interest in military hardware and the potential of weaponry. Are we seeing in these designs an uncaring, materialistic Leonardo, a man who spares little thought for human suffering?

Perhaps, but again this view is warped by the way we supplant our world-view on to others living in very different times. These ideas may seem totalitarian, but they are actually a clean and efficient version of the fifteenth-century world as it already was. The lowliest of Milan did live in almost subterranean squalor while the rich enjoyed the cool open spaces. Leonardo's drawings merely superimposed upon this a technocratic or scientifically-contrived veneer. Great thinker and innovator Leonardo undoubtedly was, but in many mundane ways he was a person of his time.

These plague years represent another blank time in Leonardo's life, but we do have one window into his frame of mind at the time, for as he was facing trauma and scheming his schemes, Leonardo was also escaping into a fantasy world in which he embarked upon an exotic journey that took him far from home and its stench of death.

The result is a singular work of fiction written in the form of letters to one Kait-Bai, a fictitious governor of Cairo, through which he relates tales from a lengthy sojourn in the Orient, a scientific mission for the Sultan of Egypt.

Leonardo's account tells us that after facing a frightening journey through storms and treacherous seas, he began his mission in Asia Minor where he collected information and sent dispatches to his temporary employer in Egypt:

> Finding myself in that region of Armenia to carry out with love
> and zeal the mission which you have assigned me, and to begin by

those parts which seem the best suited to your purposes, I came to the city of Claindra, which adjoins our borders. . . . This city is located on the coast, in the part of the Taurus that is separated from the Euphrates, and faces the great Taurus mountain to the west. These peaks are so high that they seem to touch the sky, for there is no other place on Earth so lofty as their summits, which the sun always strikes first at daybreak, four hours before rising. The extreme whiteness of the rock makes it blaze with matchless brilliance, and for the Armenians in this country it is like the light of the full moon when all else is wrapped in darkness. Its great altitude rises above the highest clouds, up to a distance of four miles as the crow flies . . . Why does the mountain, whose peak glows so splendidly during half or a third of the night, give the impression of a comet after sundown to those in the east? Why does the shape of this comet seem to vary, being at times round, at others long, and sometimes split into two or three parts, or all in one piece, alternately disappearing and becoming visible again?[17]

Leonardo's attention to detail never falters. In a further passage describing Mount Taurus, he recounts:

When I saw it, the shadow of the summit of the Taurus was so long that, in mid-June, when the sun is on the meridian, it reached the border of Sarmatia, a twelve-day journey away; and in mid-December it stretches all the way to the arctic mountains, a journey of one month to the north. Clouds and snow perpetually cover the slope in the path of the wind, which is split in two by the rocks it strikes; once past them it joins again, driving the clouds in all directions, leaving them behind only in those places that it strikes, and since it is always being struck by lightning because of the large number of clouds, the rock is full of crevices and ruins.[18]

At another point, he launches into an eccentric and dramatic account of a struggle with some form of monster or giant: 'I do not know what to say or do; I have the impression of swimming, plunging head down, in the enormous mouth, and that, deformed beyond recognition by death, I am swallowed into its giant belly.'[19]

Leonardo's descriptions and detailed accounts of this fantasy journey are quite remarkable. He lived during an age in which knowledge of places even a few days' journey from one's home was sketchy. Tales of strange distant lands were told by the fireside and over meals and a few descriptions could be gleaned from rare books. Most talk of foreign lands was founded upon inner vision rather than genuine exploration. And this is most probably the case with Leonardo's accounts. Perhaps this work was a form of escape from the hardships of life in Milan during the plague years, a dramatic romantic narrative, Leonardo's fascinating attempt at fiction, a novel.

Of course he had some wonderful resources to draw upon, accounts picked up from travellers he met as they passed through Milan as well as his conversations in Florence years earlier with the great geographer Paolo Toscanelli. Indeed, throughout his life Leonardo showed a keen interest in 'virtual' rather than actual travel, gathering information about distant countries and strange continents, deciphering rustic tales, trying to model a clear world-geography and expending great efforts studying cartography. He is also thought to have owned at one time a very rare *mappamondo*.

When we meet again the historically verifiable Leonardo, time has clearly changed him. Before the plague, Leonardo was just beginning to emerge as a creative force among the elite and the intelligentsia of the city. But from the mid-1480s his name is linked with some of the most respected figures in a variety of disciplines in Milan and many of these were to become close friends, leading him to the very heart of the Milanese court. Of great use to him were Galeazzo Sanseverino,

Marchesino Stanga and Bergonzo Botta, all high-ranking administrators close to the Moor himself.

Even more important to Leonardo, both as a close friend and as a man whose own career was in a steep ascendant, was Donato di Angelo, known to posterity as Bramante. The two men had a great deal in common. Both were trained as painters, both came from relatively modest backgrounds, both were interested in mathematics and engineering and they were in similar positions, each determined to make a name for himself at court and to receive patronage from the Moor.

For Leonardo, architecture was the noblest profession and he was fortunate to become friends with Bramante, who helped him develop his architectural ideas. Unlike Leonardo, who was concerned with the entire breadth of human knowledge and had an inherent need to explore the complete range of the intellectual and the practical, Bramante was most actively concerned with steering his career away from painting and into architecture alone. And he was amazingly successful, reaching the very highest level of his profession, eventually becoming the designer of St Peter's in Rome. And, as Bramante made advances, he naturally championed his friend, Leonardo da Vinci.

The painfully gradual acceptance of Leonardo as a great polymath by the court of the Sforzas was really a process of osmosis in which his many skills and achievements filtered through a critical barrier, bringing slow appreciation and then acclaim. He first made a minor impression with his musicianship; but there were many skilled musicians and poets in Milan and so this would have made little impact. Gradually, through his controversial painting, the *Virgin of the Rocks*, and then the coolly accomplished *Lady With an Ermine*, he began to be recognised as a first-class painter, and later acknowledged as the city's one great master of the medium. Only after this, and partly through the influence of Bramante and others, did Leonardo achieve what he had been chasing all along, recognition as an accomplished engineer and architect.

In the final years of the 1480s Leonardo became deeply interested in architecture. His fascination harked back to his days in Verrocchio's workshop, but was stimulated and focused by his friend Bramante.

Alongside drawings of armaments, human figures and sketches of strange ethereal landscapes, Leonardo's notebooks of this period are filled with spires and towers, buttresses and elevations. The architect was greatly respected in the Milan of the 1480s and the position of ducal architect was probably the highest to which Leonardo could ever hope to aspire, a goal he committed himself to for a while. Although he never achieved this ambition, he did become involved in the latest development of Milan cathedral, then the most important building-site in northern Italy and a project that had been in development almost since it was begun late in the previous century.

Soon he was helping to complete the apse of the cathedral and designing a way to rebuild a cupola that had eroded badly. He was never chosen to be one of the key architects for this work, but many of his drawings and models were used during the deliberations of the committee appointed by Sforza to implement the work, and it is certain he gained kudos from the Duke and the court for his contribution. In 1487, Leonardo received the finance to construct a model for repairing what he later referred to as 'a sick cathedral', but this design was not accepted by those managing the reconstruction even after he had written to them: 'Do not allow yourselves to be influenced by any passion, but choose either me or someone who has succeeded better than I in demonstrating what a building is and what the rules of correct building are.'[20]

One of the reasons Leonardo may have been used as a consultant but not actually assigned a leading role in this project was because (like so many of his ideas) his concept of architecture was esoteric and controversial. Following the lead of some of those who greatly influenced his intellectual framework, men such as Leon Alberti and Antonio Filarete, Leonardo subscribed to the radical view that architecture and human anatomy were linked.*

Fifteen centuries earlier, Vitruvius had, as part of an anthropo-morphising of fundamental architectural forms, correlated the ribbing of a building to the ribcage of the human body, the apse to the head, the transepts to the arms. In other words, the principles lying at the root of architectural design and used in all forms of buildings could, he claimed, be related to the structures found in Nature and in particular the human form.

Not surprisingly, this period of intense interest in architecture was (as we shall see in Chapter 7) also the time during which Leonardo was most heavily involved with his studies of human anatomy. His note-books contain page after page in which drawings of Milan cathedral appear alongside a venous limb or a torso.

In the *Codex Atlanticus*, Leonardo wrote:

Doctors, teachers and those who nurse the sick should be aware what sort of thing is man, what is life, what is health and in what manner a parity and concordance of the elements maintains it; while a discordance of these elements ruins and destroys it; and one with a good knowledge of the nature of things mentioned above will be better also to repair it than one who lacks know-ledge of them . . . the same is necessary for the ailing cathedral, in that a doctor-architect understands what kind of thing is a building and from what rules a correct building derives and whence these rules originate and into how many parts they may be divided and what are the causes which hold the building

---

* Alberti and Filarete had themselves been moulded by principles handed down by the Roman, Marcus Vitruvius Pollio, who, during the first century BC, wrote the classic *De Architectura*.

together and make it permanent, and what is the nature of weight and what is the potential of force, and in what manner they may be conjoined and interrelated, and what effect they will produce combined. He who has true knowledge of the things listed above will present the work satisfactorily to your understanding.[21]

This homogenising of disciplines was very important to Leonardo. He did not believe in compartmentalising concepts or even segregating whole areas of endeavour. To him geography, human anatomy, architecture, even pure mathematics were intimately linked and each could be viewed with the perception of one schooled in any of them. And, although this is diametrically opposed to the way in which any intellectual pursuit is followed today, such a principle of unification lies at the heart of Leonardo's approach to learning and research. It is a cliché that 'Renaissance man' is a term impossible to apply today because the amount of available information is vastly greater. This is of course true, but this line of thought takes into account only one aspect of what it means to apply the epithet to a person like Leonardo. It misses the fact that the label also derived from his exceptional ability to cross-fertilise ideas from different disciplines. Uniquely, he was able to see science from the perspective of an artist, to visualise art with the mind-set of a scientist and architecture from the viewpoint of the artist-scientist. If there is one simple defining skill that distinguishes Leonardo, it is this most useful of talents.

Leonardo's versatility could not fail to generate the interest of the rich and the powerful eventually. He was simply too talented and too energetic to be ignored or underrated for long. But, as I considered at the start of this chapter, it is possible that even the greatest genius may wither unless the time is right for them and the setting appropriate for their abilities to be nurtured. And in the years immediately following the plague of 1484–85, Milan underwent a complete transformation as it was swept up by an optimism and new-found vigour, a sense of excitement and hope for the future. And this reversal of fortune took Leonardo with it.

Suddenly, with the return of the court, new work was commissioned by the wealthy patrons of the city, led of course by the house of Sforza. Money was poured into designing and building new squares and avenues, whole sections of the city were remodelled, a competition to find the best plans for the improvements to be made to the cathedral produced a team of architects and decorators, and pageants, festivals and masques were organised.

In February 1489, at the height of this boom, Ludovico's nephew, Gian Galeazzo Sforza, was married to Isabella of Aragon. Gian Galeazzo was the rightful heir to the dukedom, but Ludovico had for years cunningly distracted the twenty-year-old with the scent of glamour and the opportunity to enjoy the fruits of power without the responsibility. As with much of his adult life, the festival marking Gian's marriage was dominated by the figure of the Moor, and Gian was encouraged to over-indulge but fooled into believing he was really masterminding the occasion.

Surprisingly perhaps, the wedding went without a hitch, but trouble was soon to follow. A year after the marriage, Isabella was still without child, and within the courts of Italy tongues began to wag. To deflect attention from this unhappy situation, in January 1490 Sforza decided to host a magnificent gala, the Feast of Paradise, to which he would invite diplomats and state leaders from across Italy.*

By this time, Leonardo had become a valued member of Sforza's court, referred to in official documents variously as 'ingeniarius ducalis' or 'ingeniarius camerarius'.† But it seems Leonardo's role was defined

---

* The court astrologers actually believed this ceremony would in a very real sense resolve the crisis.

† There were thirteen ingeniarii ducali in Milan at the time, four of whom had 'senior' status. Bramante and Leonardo were two of these, with subtitles of 'painter and engineer'.

only vaguely. Officially, he was one of the court engineers, but Sforza probably saw him as a 'master of all trades', so that he might find himself ordered to produce a painting here, a sculpture there or instructed to mastermind great works of engineering and to entertain the court as a musician when required. Sometimes Leonardo's duties relied upon a blend of his skills, which of course made him all the more useful to the Moor.

Ludovico's feast was to be a grand occasion and Leonardo was instructed to devise the climax of the evening, a masque, to be called *The Masque of the Planets*, requiring artistry, inventive engineering and a sense of showmanship, all qualities that met in Leonardo.

The Feast of Paradise was held in the Castello Sforzesco on 13 January 1490. Nothing of the evening has survived except for the recorded recollections of a few of those present and some sketches and designs in Leonardo's notebooks. The timing of the event was meticulously planned by the court astrologer, Ambrogio da Varese, and involved hundreds of designers, painters, actors and workmen. It began with dancing and a masked procession, and at midnight Ludovico, dressed in oriental costume, took centre stage, the music stopped, and at a wave a curtain was raised on Leonardo's offering, *The Masque of the Planets*, a giant model of the planets in their respective positions, each moving in its course with the signs of the zodiac illuminated by torches placed behind coloured glass.

One envoy, the ambassador from Ferrara, described the model as 'a sort of half-egg', with the planets represented by actors 'costumed according to poetic descriptions', and musicians playing 'marvellous melodies and soft and harmonic songs'.

'And it is called Paradise,' wrote the poet Bernardo Bellincione, who penned the libretto for the performance, 'because in it was made, with the great ingenuity and art of the Master Leonardo da Vinci the Florentine, Paradise, with all the seven planets which turned; and the planets were represented by men who looked and were dressed like poets, and each of these planets spoke in praise of the Duchess Isabella.'[22]

Drawings in the notebooks show a revolving stage, and designs for the layout of the model, but how much of these creations was original at the time and how much was taken from within the creative world of theatre design is impossible to say. Entirely original or not, the *Masque* made Leonardo famous throughout Italy. The impressed guests returned home not merely extolling the splendour and opulence of the Milanese court and the wealth of the city's rulers, but singing the praises of the singular genius who had created the evening's splendid finale.

Leonardo had at last arrived. *The Masque of the Planets* was merely the first of many such performances during the years he was to spend in Milan. And this, more than anything he had attempted before, consolidated his relationship with a delighted Ludovico who was now convinced he had in his court the greatest creative genius in Italy, if not the world.

Leonardo had come far indeed. He had succeeded in finding patronage so that he could pursue his abiding interests. His thirst for knowledge and his desire to understand the inner workings of everything and how all things relate to all things remained as active and as vital as ever. We will look at his ideas and writings in detail in Chapter 7, but before we do this, we should follow Leonardo into his final decade in Milan and the consolidation of his success.

6

TRIUMPH AND TURMOIL

May the creator grant that I be capable of revealing the nature and customs of man, just as I can describe his figure.

— Leonardo, *Quaderni, I*

In 1490, Leonardo was thirty-eight years old and entering his prime as a creative force. Encountering him in the street, we would find a man bearing little resemblance to the sage of his early sixteenth-century self-portrait and certainly not the exuberant dandy of Verrocchio's studio. If we were to head for a workshop near the centre of Milan, or perhaps to the court of Ludovico Sforza, we would discover a stylishly dressed man whose face retained some of the beguiling beauty of his boyhood but with the angelic features and the flawless skin hardened now by the weariness of leading an individualistic life. He had remained undeniably handsome, with a finely chiselled face, but it would now be lined with experience and worldliness. This Leonardo da Vinci was a man enjoying rapid ascent through the social strata of Milan, respected by the elite of Italy and a favourite of the Duke.

Leonardo was seen now as a cultured man, not only because of the breadth and depth of his knowledge, but because he had carefully modelled this image while surrounding himself with an air of mystery. But what attracted people to him most was the flexibility of his mind and his character of many layers. He may have had a liking for fine clothes, he undoubtedly enjoyed the company of attractive young men, and he may have been unreserved in his ambition, but to counter-balance this was a huge reservoir of mental activity. Leonardo was a ceaseless wanderer along the avenues and byways of knowledge. He wanted to soak it all up and to turn what he learned into something meaningful.

He was said to possess not only an indefinable elegance and poise but also the quality of grace. He was charismatic and charming, enjoyed company, but was also contemplative and needed to escape frequently, taking days off to wander the countryside or to sit alone in his studio. With his explorations he appears to have reached a strange crossroads in the way he viewed his fellow humans and his vision of our place in the Universe. On the one hand, he had little feeling for the grandiloquence of humans, the egocentric belief in our own importance. Having studied the beautiful intricacy of the human body, he was able to write brutally: 'I do not think that rough men, of bad habits and little intelligence, deserve such a fine instrument [as the body] and such a variety of mechanisms.'[1] And we have seen elsewhere how he referred to his fellow humans as 'latrine fillers'. But at the same time, he was a man imbued with an uncommon compassion for all living things, who bought caged birds in the marketplace merely to set them free. He was a vegetarian five hundred years before such a lifestyle became commonplace. And, during an age in which animals were seen as nothing but food, he wrote of their role in the cycle of life and placed them high in the hierarchy of living things.

He believed that anything capable of movement was also capable of pain and came to the conclusion that he would therefore eat only plants because they did not move,[2] writing: 'He who does not attach value to life does not deserve it.'[3]

Elsewhere in his notebooks he commented upon the ignorant misuse of animals, declaring: 'The practice of clipping horses' nostrils should be laughed to scorn. Imbeciles observe this custom as if they thought nature had not done its job properly and needed to be corrected by men'.[4]

He would not allow himself to become, as he put it, 'a tomb for other animals, an inn of the dead . . . a container of corruption'.[5] And on one page of his notebooks he composed a verse describing his ideas about hygiene:

> If you would be healthy, observe this advice:
> Eat only when hungry, and let light fare suffice.
> Chew all your food well, and this rule always follow:
> Well cooked and simple be all that you swallow.
> On leaving the table, a good posture keep,
> And after your luncheon do not yield to sleep.
> Let little and often be your rule for wine,
> But not between meals or when waiting to dine.
> Visits to the privy should not be postponed . . .[6]

These are interesting rules and make us wonder about their origin. They are certainly not conventional ideas for the time, an era in which large quantities of meat and wine were the usual fare for the wealthy; but then Leonardo's approach to life was invariably away from the well-trodden path. The emphasis upon vegetarianism and his attention to hygiene (which he had made much of in his plans for a new Milan) could have come from a fascination with Indian and Far Eastern cultures picked up from those he knew who travelled widely.

But Leonardo also had a less attractive side to his character, a dark cloud that hung over what otherwise seems an almost too-perfect image. He was paranoid, constantly afraid his ideas would be stolen and his work plagiarised. For this reason, he wrote all his notes in left-handed mirror writing and often employed codes and ciphers to disguise his ideas further. It seems likely this sense of anxiety, this lack of faith in his fellow man, arose from his bitter years in Florence. We have already seen how the Salterelli trial had tarnished his life there and turned him inward from the exuberant and extravagant lifestyle he had enjoyed before 1476, but this experience played long on his mind, hardening with time. As an old man, fearful of one of his hired assistants, he confessed to his notebooks: 'I cannot make anything secretly because of him . . . And if I should set him there to make my model, he would publish it.'[7] He constantly refers to the false actions of others, to fears of having his ideas stolen, and the ever-present threat of someone looking over his shoulder, someone unidentified ready to take credit for his efforts. At times his comments are obtuse, such as: 'The memory of benefits is fragile compared to ingratitude.'[8] At others, without offering us an identity, he is more blunt. 'All the evils that exist or have ever existed,' he declares, 'if he could bring them about, would still not satisfy the desires of his treacherous soul. And I could not, however long I tried, paint his true nature to you . . .'[9]

In a draft of a letter he planned to send to Ludovico Sforza, but probably never sent, he declares:

> There is a man who was expecting to receive from me more than his due, and being disappointed in his presumptuous desire, he has tried to turn all my friends against me, but since he found them forewarned and proof against his will, he has threatened to make accusations that would deprive me of my benefactors. (I am informing Your Lordship of this, so that this individual who wishes to create scandal will find no soil on which to sow the seeds of his wickedness) and that if this man should try to make Your Lordship the tool of his iniquitous and malicious nature, he will be thwarted in his desire.[10]

We have no evidence of Leonardo's work ever being stolen or copied during his lifetime, but perhaps this was because he protected his writings successfully. We shall see later how his trust was abused by a pair of treacherous assistants during his years in Rome, but we have no clues to help identify a mysterious interlocutor or series of enemies at this time. Nevertheless, this person or persons became something of an obsession for Leonardo during the early part of the 1490s. How much these suspicions and fears were grounded in fact is impossible to say, but there is clearly a real passion behind his feelings and it made him distrustful and permanently on his guard. For later generations this was a tragedy because, although Leonardo only produced one readable treatise in his lifetime, his collection of uncollated notes remained strictly private and, as we saw in the Introduction, these remained hidden for two centuries after his death. Perhaps if he had not been so fearful of plagiarism, these notebooks could have found their way into the public domain far sooner.

At the very point where he seems to have found acceptance at the Milanese court and acclaim beyond the city walls, Leonardo began to take on greater responsibilities, employing assistants for his workshop and instructing a small group of pupils. And in the summer of 1490 he began what was probably the most lasting and intimate relationship of his entire life, when he took under his wing a ten-year-old boy named Giacomo, whom the master quickly nicknamed 'Salai', meaning 'demon'.

Leonardo marks the boy's arrival in his life with the comment in his notebooks: 'Giacomo came to live with me on the feast of St Mary Magdalene of the year 1490. He is ten years old.'[11]

Much has been written about this relationship, and an exploration of its nature depends upon the perspective and mores of the investigator. Vasari makes little reference to Salai. His only real comment is to mention that:

In Milan he took for his assistant the Milanese Salai, who was most comely in grace and beauty, having fine locks, curling in ringlets, in which Leonardo greatly delighted; and he taught him many things of art; and certain works in Milan, which are said to be by Salai, were retouched by Leonardo.[12]

Almost everything about this brief comment is fabrication. There is no evidence to suggest the boy was Leonardo's assistant and he appears to have had little artistic ability. The surviving paintings accredited to him are poor, sentimental and show little in the way of inspiration or originality. Leonardo did have assistants at this time, pupils who paid for the privilege of working with the renowned master, and they acted as his assistants only after graduating in the traditional workshop programme Leonardo had himself endured in Florence. At the time, Leonardo's most promising student was the talented young painter Marco d'Oggione and there are very clear distinctions between what we know of Salai and, say, the apprenticeship of Marco d'Oggione in the master's studio.

Leonardo was said to have stumbled upon Salai one day in a marketplace. From other accounts, he first saw the boy sketching goats in a field. Either way, he was immediately struck by the boy's beauty. Salai's father was a peasant or *contadino* named Giovan Pietro Caprotti of Oreno who probably sold his son into Leonardo's service as a model-servant, where he was sure to lead a better life than anything his own family could have offered.

However, for Leonardo the burden of responsibility he now shouldered was not easy to bear. He was just beginning to find financial stability, and the drain on his purse of a young mouth to feed and body to clothe must have been a strain. He moans constantly in his notebooks about the material costs of keeping Salai and lists all the items he has to provide. But these problems paled into insignificance when matched with the trauma Salai's personality, that of a 'little demon', created for the otherworldly Leonardo.

Within days of his arrival Giacomo had begun to earn his nickname.

> The second day [Leonardo writes], I had tailored for him two
> shirts, a pair of hose, and a jerkin; but when I had put aside the
> money to pay for them, he stole this money (4 lire) from the
> purse. Although I have not been able to get him to admit it, I am
> absolutely sure that he did. The day after, I went to sup with
> Giacomo and the said Giacomo supped for two and did mischief
> for four, for he broke three cruets and spilled the wine.

And so it went on. Leonardo describes Salai stealing a pen from one
of his assistants (probably d'Oggione). He went on to steal a purse
during preparations for a tournament, pilfered the leather put aside for
a pair of boots and sold it to buy sweets, and behaved so badly at table
that he embarrassed Leonardo in front of important guests. In the
margin of his notes Leonardo scrawls comments such as, 'Thief, liar,
obstinate, greedy,' yet only a short time later he prepares a list of the
items he has lavished on the boy: '1 cloak: 2 lire; 6 shirts: 4 lire; 3
jerkins: 6 lire, 4 pairs of hose: 7 lire 8 soldi; a lined suit: 5 lire; 4 pairs
of shoes: 6 lire 5 soldi; a cap: 1 lire; thongs for belts: 1 lire.'[13]

This pattern of Leonardo spoiling Salai and receiving only bad behaviour in return continued, it seems, for long after the boy had grown
into a youth. A quarter of a century later, in 1505, Leonardo listed the
purchases and the favours. 'Tunic laced in the French fashion, belonging to Salai; a cape in the French mode, once owned by the Duke of
Valentinois [Cesare Borgia], belonging to Salai; a tunic of grey Flanders
cloth, belonging to Salai.'[14] Elsewhere there are lists of gifts that
include a chain, jewellery, bows and arrows, and silver brocade.[15] On
another occasion, he records contributing thirteen crowns towards
the dowry of Salai's sister.[16] Yet in 1496, when Salai was sixteen and
had lived with Leonardo for the best part of six years, Leonardo
records the not-so-little devil stealing 'a few soldi'[17] and how 'two

towels were lost.'[18] According to some accounts, Leonardo had difficulty keeping the youth from prison.*[19]

This all points to the fact that Giacomo, or Salai, was certainly no assistant or pupil. Leonardo would not have lavished money on a pupil; indeed, he was paid to teach. By this time he was in great demand as a master in Milan. A certain Galeazzo paid a monthly sum of five lire for his son's tutelage and accommodation in Leonardo's workshop. Pupils came and went, but few stayed close to Leonardo after they had qualified. Although the very best later became disciples of Leonardo's style, they did not become lifelong companions like Giacomo.

So, what can we say about the relationship between the middle-aged Leonardo and the ten-year-old Giacomo? It may have been a father–son relationship. Leonardo the homosexual free spirit never contemplated marriage, but perhaps he wanted a son. It is quite conceivable he felt a need to do the very opposite of his father, to nurture a child through life, to provide for him and support him, to take him from the gutter and give him a chance. In the constant references to Salai's misdemeanours and demands, it is easy to detect a sense of resignation rather than outrage; there is even a certain suppressed amusement just discernible, almost as though he saw a spark of rebelliousness in the boy that reminded him of himself. Where Leonardo had challenged the limits of artistic interpretation and walked away from contracted work, Salai stole and disrupted dinner parties.

Then again their relationship may have contained a physical element. Whispered rumours had hinted at a sexual relationship between Leonardo and the young singer Atalante Migliorotti eight years earlier. And he certainly had an eye for a pretty face. Salai, we

---

* Here the reader may wonder if Salai was in fact the person Leonardo feared would steal his ideas. I think this is improbable. First, if this were true, Leonardo would not have tolerated him, and second, although he was a petty thief and a spoilt brat, Salai probably would not have gone so far as to steal his master's notebooks or models.

are constantly reminded by biographers of Leonardo, was exceptionally beautiful.

Yet it is difficult for us to accept the notion of Leonardo keeping the boy as a sexual partner. To us, such behaviour is nothing but sanctioned paedophilia and quite abhorrent, but again we must accept that our moral framework should not be superimposed upon the social structure of Leonardo's day.

Biographers have skirted the issue of Leonardo's relationship with Salai because it has been a subject too sensitive to investigate candidly. Kenneth Clark, writing in the1930s, simply refers to the relationship by saying: 'These facts [in connection with Leonardo spoiling the boy] and the character of the drawings of Salai, inevitably suggest that his relationship with the master was of a kind honoured in classical times, and partly tolerated in the Renaissance, in spite of the censure of the Church.'[20] And of course Vasari, not wishing to tarnish the image of his hero in any way, especially in countries where attitudes towards homosexuality were less liberal than in Italy, merely makes clear the fact that Giacomo was 'most comely in grace and beauty'.

Whatever led Leonardo to take this peasant boy into his household, Giacomo soon became a fixture in his life and was hardly to leave his side for the next three decades. From his actions and the way Leonardo treated him, Salai played the role of son, friend, helper and, quite possibly, lover.

For the elite of such cities as Milan, the early 1490s were exciting times. New trade routes to Asia were opening up during the decade, bringing with them huge wealth and prosperity. For Leonardo it was a period of tremendous productivity, and as he forged ahead with new proposals for buildings and designs for machines and court entertainments, old projects were not forgotten.

Plans for the Sforza horse, the proposed statue of Attendolo, once so important to the Milanese nobility as well as the artistic community, had been shelved. It had been accepted almost universally that a bronze horse and rider on the desired scale was impossible. But by 1489 Ludovico had once more begun to entertain the idea. A letter written by a Florentine envoy to Milan revealing this renewed enthusiasm is an odd relic in which the Moor appears to betray Leonardo while casting his net wide in the hope of acquiring the talents of other artists.

The letter was addressed to Lorenzo de' Medici, and begins:

> Prince Ludovico is planning to provide a worthy tomb for his father, and he has given orders that Leonardo da Vinci should produce a model for it, that is to say an enormous bronze horse carrying Duke Francesco clad in armour. And since his excellency wishes to make a work that will be extraordinarily fine and something wonderful, he asks me to tell you that he would like you to send him one or two Florentine artists who specialise in this kind of work; although he has entrusted the task to Leonardo, he is not confident the latter is capable of bringing it safely to completion.[21]

This is a strange missive, which on the surface appears to be a straightforward request, but the Moor almost certainly took this action in order to spur Leonardo on. If this is true, it worked; because from this point on we find Leonardo immersed once more in the logistics of producing a gargantuan statue and again filling scores of pages of his notebooks with drawings of horses and designs for plinths and figures.

Ludovico's ploy, if that is what it was, was auspiciously timed because Leonardo was almost certainly just beginning to regain enthusiasm for the equestrian project after a spell during which he had completely lost interest in the idea. His loss of enthusiasm had been precipitated by the death in 1488 of his teacher, friend and one-time surrogate father Verrocchio. Verrocchio had been racing to complete his own vast equestrian statue, the *Colleoni* in Venice, and had caught a chill after working for a long period at the furnace during casting. Quite naturally this tragedy not only upset Leonardo, it made him uneasy about his own ideas for casting a vast statue. But then, by 1489, at about the time of Ludovico's own renewed interest, Leonardo appears to have overcome his anxieties and in his mind to have turned Verrocchio's death into a positive thing, almost as though he had decided he could step into the master's shoes and triumph against the odds, honouring Verrocchio in the process. Whether this or Ludovico's cunning gave Leonardo the push needed, he set about the daunting task with renewed vigour.

But even with the best intentions it was not easy for Leonardo to concentrate on the project. Following the success of *The Masque of the Planets* he was now in great demand at court preparing decorations and organising special events. These included a series of court weddings that followed each other in quick succession during the early 1490s. After seeing his nephew, Gian Galeazzo, married and siring an heir, in 1493 Ludovico arranged for his illegitimate daughter Bianca to wed his commander-in-chief. Next, he arranged his own wedding, a union with Beatrice d'Este, the younger daughter of the Duke of Ferrara, to whom he had been engaged since she was five years old. Finally, with great diplomatic stealth he contrived the marriage of his niece, another Bianca (the daughter of his brother Gian Galeazzo), to no less a figure than the Emperor Maximilian himself.

Ludovico's young bride Beatrice was a keen patron of the arts and employed Leonardo for a range of projects. He also helped create Ludovico's theatre, which opened for its first performance in 1493, and was called upon to design sets and decoration for almost every new play performed there during the 1490s, including *De Paulo e Daria Amanti* presented by the nobleman Gaspare Visconti in 1495. A year later, he directed a play on the theme of Danae's seduction by Jupiter, written by Ludovico's own chancellor, Baldassare Taccone. As well as this, Leonardo was sent by Ludovico for an extended stay in Pavia twenty miles south of Milan to inspect and draw plans and elevations of the work being done on the city's cathedral. All of which left little time for the horse.

But he pressed on, and for the next three years he spent as much time as he could spare studying equine anatomy and drawing and modelling parts of the bodies of horses. Alongside drawings of buttresses and set designs for Ludovico's theatre, we find the fetlocks of stallions and the musculature of horse necks, the fall of a mane and the geometry involved in positioning a rearing horse on a plinth. He also studied the work of other great sculptors, making a note about the *Regisole*, a bronze of the king of the Goths, Odoacer, commenting: 'It is above all admirable for its movement . . . It almost seems to be trotting like a freely moving animal.'[22]

Finally, in November 1493, Leonardo was ready to present a full-size clay model of his equine statue, and chose to do so at the occasion of the marriage of Bianca Maria Sforza. The clay model, as large as a building (the horse alone standing over twenty feet high), was placed directly in front of Ludovico's castello and is said to have created a stir rivalled only by the hyperbole of contemporary poets and chroniclers who documented the event. 'Neither Greece nor Rome saw anything greater,' Leonardo's friend, the chancellor and playwright Baldassare Taccone declared, and playing on the similarity between the words 'Vinci' and 'vincere' (to conquer), Bramante wrote: '*Vittoria vince e vinci tu vittore*', 'Victory to the victor, and you Vinci [victor] have the victory.'[23]

But although the materials for the bronze horse had been acquired and Leonardo spent the winter of 1493 and spring 1494 preparing for the casting of the huge metal statue, the glorious conclusion to this effort was never to be realised. In the end the arguments over whether or not the statue was feasible were made redundant. The horse was never cast, not because of anything Leonardo may or may not have done, but because his hopes and plans became entangled within the labyrinthine complexities of power politics in 1490s Europe.

To see how this came about we must turn back the clock to early 1493 when court jealousies and internal rivalries between the ruling Italian families first began to precipitate serious problems for Sforza's court and beyond. Isabella of Aragon, whom the Moor's nephew, Gian Galeazzo, had married in 1489, was becoming increasingly jealous of Ludovico's wife, Beatrice, who had begun to make a great show of her position, dubbing herself 'First Lady'. Beatrice spent a fortune on clothes and jewellery and indulging herself organising parties and pursuing her interest in the arts. Meanwhile, Isabella had grown to loathe her weak husband Gian for allowing his uncle to 'steal his kingdom', as well as for making a public show of his interest in a young boy known as *Il Bozzone*, the Rustic. Soon she began to complain of her situation to her powerful father, Alfonso of Calabria, and to her grandfather, Ferrante of Naples.

Ludovico knew of Isabella's protests but is said to have treated her wails with contempt and accused her of failing her husband. Believing he was comfortably placed within the power structure of Italy and protected by his armies, he did nothing about the growing tension in his own family. But soon, the flow of events began to move inexorably towards crisis.

Ludovico had enjoyed both the friendship of Lorenzo de' Medici and the support of Pope Innocent VIII, but Lorenzo died suddenly in 1492 and only a few months later Innocent followed him to the grave. Lorenzo was succeeded by his son Piero, who had none of his father's talent nor his political awareness, and within months had allowed Florence to became an ally of Naples, who in her turn was a traditional enemy of Milan. Meanwhile, in the same year, the papal succession had fallen to Cardinal Rodrigo Borgia (father of the infamous Cesare), who became Pope Alexander VI.

Borgia had no liking for the Moor. Despite Ludovico's rather pathetic attempts to buy the new Pope with emissaries travelling to the Vatican with trunks of gold, he reversed all agreements and treaties established with Milan by his predecessor, preferring instead to give moral support to Naples.

Even with this shift in the balance of power, Ludovico's confidence was barely dented. He deigned to form a verbal alliance with Venice and then took the extraordinary step of openly encouraging the French to become involved with Italian politics and simultaneously tried to draw in the Holy Roman Emperor, Maximilian, as a military counter-balance, thinking he could pull the strings of the major European powers and reap the rewards from the inevitable struggle.

The plan might conceivably have worked, but the political scene kept shifting faster than any one player, even a man as skilled as Sforza, could adjust or create new strategies. In January 1494 the seventy-year-old King of Naples, Ferrante, died. This motivated the young King of France, Charles VIII (who was actively encouraged by Ludovico), to reclaim his fiefdom of Naples which had once been occupied by the Normans during the twelfth century.

Charles was driven by a lust for imperial expansion as well as an evangelical faith, seeing Italy as a stepping stone to the advancement of a European army that would one day destroy the Turk. With such determination at the top it was not long before the French began to sweep through Italy, taking Florence and driving the Borgia Pope to hide in the Castel Sant'Angelo while Charles's troops ransacked Rome. All the while, Ludovico played the role of cautious guide and ally to Charles, helping him occupy Turin in autumn 1494, before realising that his kingdom and indeed his own life were in danger as French troops moved on towards Vigevano and then Pavia.

Late in 1494, just as Leonardo was making final preparations for the casting of his horse, Ludovico woke up to the fact that Charles would soon decide to attack Milan, switched sides overnight and helped pull together a temporary alliance between Milan, the Spanish, the Holy Roman Empire, Venice and Rome. Suddenly, Milan had a real enemy on its doorstep, the very soldiers Ludovico had invited in, and this new call to arms became a struggle for the survival of the Milanese state. And Leonardo had to play his part. He had stockpiled over seventy tons of bronze for the casting of the *gran cavallo*, and it was now needed for cannon and sword.

He faced this sudden change in fortune philosophically. He had no interest in politics, and it appears from the lack of comment in his notebooks that until war had almost befallen the Milanese he had little awareness of trouble brewing. When it came time to hand over the bronze, Leonardo simply commented, 'About the horse I will say nothing, for I know what times these are.'[24]

The alliance succeeded in repelling the French and drove them from Italy; at least for the time being. The decisive battle took place at Fornovo in 1495 when Charles's forces were soundly defeated.

As these events were unfolding, Leonardo's personal life was becoming increasingly complex. Most historians have long assumed he had completely lost contact with his mother when he moved to Florence to live with Piero. But this must be an over-simplification; Caterina may have been forbidden by Leonardo's family to see her first-born, but we don't know this for certain. Leonardo visited Vinci on many occasions after establishing himself in Verrocchio's studio, so it is not inconceivable he called in on his mother during at least one of these excursions. Whatever their relationship became during Leonardo's youth, there is evidence to suppose Caterina made a brief reappearance in his life shortly before her death.

In July 1493, as Leonardo was preparing his clay model of the horse, a woman named Caterina arrived at his workshop and stayed with him for about two years until she died sometime in 1495 or 1496. We know this because, unusually for Leonardo, he made detailed personal references to her appearance in his notebooks. They begin with: 'Caterina came, 16 July 1493.'[25] This in itself is an unusual comment because of the inclusion of a date. Leonardo frequently noted when pupils came to stay or left, but he never dated these entries and only once, a decade later, did he give a time – the time of day when his father Piero died in 1504.[26]

There may be no real significance to this, but it is just one piece in the puzzle concerning this woman and her relationship with Leonardo. Was this Caterina really his mother? It is possible she was merely a servant who happened to have the same name, and that Leonardo employed her because of a subliminal connection. Caterina was an unusual name at that time and at least one psychoanalysis of Leonardo posits the idea he was drawn to this woman because, as a servant who washed and cleaned, she would be performing the role of a mother in his household.[27] In 1493, Caterina would have been in her mid-sixties, an astonishing age for a peasant woman, but some people did live this long.

It should be remembered Leonardo was doing rather well for himself at this time and had a comfortable home and workshop, so perhaps his mother had been drawn to Milan in the hope she might live out her final days with him. Sadly, community records tell us almost nothing of Caterina's life after she married the Quarreller. It is conceivable he died during the early 1490s and that Caterina then turned to her son for help. Or perhaps Leonardo had heard of her situation and sent for her. It is worth noting a comment Leonardo made in his notebooks some two years before she turned up, in which he declares: 'Can you tell me what la Caterina wishes to do?'[28]

From tax registers, we know that Leonardo's mother was living in Vinci until 1490. She had four daughters and a son, but there is only a vague reference to her family in a census of 1504 in which it is reported that two of her daughters were still living in Vinci with children of their own; and in an addendum to the 1490 census we learn her son had died in a battle in Pisa.[29]

The strongest evidence that the Caterina of the notebooks and his mother were one and the same comes from Leonardo's record of domestic bills. These show he did not just provide a roof and food for

Caterina; they suggest he actively indulged her. In one list, he records what he had so far spent on the woman:

(29 JANUARY 1494)

Material for hose	4 lire 3 soldi
Lining	4s.
Making up	8s.
For Salai	3s.
Jasper ring	13s.
Stones for brilliants	11s.
For Caterina	10s.
For Caterina	10s.[30]

Clearly, Caterina was no servant. Leonardo did not lavish money on her but he appears to have included her in his 'family', something he certainly did not do with any of his pupils or staff. Then, when some two years after her arrival Caterina fell ill, he paid for doctor's expenses, and provided the costs of a funeral when she died.

'Expenses of Caterina's burial', he wrote in his notebook, and listed the details:

For 3 pounds of wax	27 soldi.
For the bier	8s.
Pall for the bier	12s.
Carriage and erection of cross	4s.
For the bearers	8s.
For 4 priests and 4 clerks	20s.
Bell, book, sponge	2s.
For the gravediggers	16s.
For the dean	8s.
For official permission	1s.
	——
	106s.

(EARLIER EXPENSES)

Doctor	5s.
Sugar and candles	12s.

———————

123s.[31]

These expenses are certainly more than would be spent on a servant, but perhaps less than expected for a beloved close relative. But then, Leonardo may have had his reasons for keeping the funeral a modest affair. If Caterina was indeed his mother, he would not have wanted to draw attention to the fact because it might have started damaging rumours concerning his inauspicious background as well as casting aspersions upon his mother's reputation.

Although we must not let wishful thinking sway us, it is pleasing to imagine that this Caterina was indeed Leonardo's mother. Like most women of her class, she would have led a tough life in Vinci, surviving on the borders of poverty while raising five children in a tiny, filthy hovel, working a full day on the land, merely subsisting until her husband's death. Then, hearing from her famous and successful son, and with her younger offspring now independent, she would have at least enjoyed the last two or three years of her life under Leonardo's roof. She would have seen her son rewarded for his genius and courted by the rich and the noble of Milan. She would have been there to see his triumphant unveiling of the clay horse and his invitation to decorate the rooms of Beatrice, the Duchess of Milan, and to create sets for performances at the city's new theatre. Her life had been tarnished by the illegitimate birth of her first son, and as Leonardo's father Ser Piero grew old and drifted into the background within the social fabric of Florence, perhaps Caterina had the last laugh.

Despite the ever-present threat of war and possible occupation, the Milanese carried on with their lives as usual and Leonardo never stopped working. He was now responsible for the welfare of both his mother and Salai and kept a household and studio in which perhaps a dozen pupils and apprentices worked. For a short time after the battle of Fornovo, the sense of impending doom hanging over most of the Italian peninsula dissipated, and for a while Ludovico returned (albeit with diminished authority) to being the grand propagandist and image-builder, a change in mood from which Leonardo benefited enormously.

Yet it was also a stressful time for Leonardo. He seemed to want responsibility and even courted it, but at the same time it weighed heavily upon him. The aspect of his character that led him to innovation also leaned him towards the rejection of conformity and mundane demands. He was still overworked, and indeed *Il Moro* was now making even greater demands upon his time and talents. Yet as much as the Duke obviously treasured his *ingeniarius ducalis*, he often failed to match his enthusiasm with hard cash. And sometimes the pressure became too much. Leonardo was almost always a level-headed and patient man, but there were occasions when even he was pushed beyond endurance and his patience snapped. One such clash came in June 1496 when Leonardo stormed out of Beatrice's rooms soon after he had begun to decorate them. The exact cause of the dispute is not known, but the rift between him and Ludovico must have cut deep because the Duke threatened to replace him on the project with Perugino. There survives a draft of a letter Leonardo intended for his patron in which he complains:

I regret being in need and I regret even more that this prevents me from conforming to my desire, which has always been to obey Your Lordship. I regret very much that having called upon me, you find me in need and that the necessity of providing for my subsistence has prevented me from . . . [Here the text is broken, but then he goes on:] I much regret that the need to provide for my subsistence obliges me to occupy myself with trifles, instead of continuing the task Your Lordship asked of me; but I hope I shall soon have earned enough money to be able, with peace of mind, to satisfy the wishes of Your Excellency, to whom I recommend myself; and if Your Majesty thought I had money, Your Lordship is mistaken: I have had to feed 6 persons for 56 months and have received only 50 ducats.[32]

It is difficult to interpret what Leonardo was trying to achieve with this letter. On the one hand it is a standard plea for consideration, but on the other it could be interpreted as heavily sarcastic, a letter in which Leonardo is saying, I'm terribly sorry for being poor, but there it is. If you want me, you'll have to pay me. And for this reason, we may safely assume it was never sent.

There is also some confusion over just how genuine were Leonardo's grievances. It is certainly true the coffers of the Duke, once thought to be bottomless, were now severely depleted by the demands of his army as well as the cost of bribes sent to his reluctant allies, but Leonardo was allowed to work on other commissions if he could squeeze them in. Furthermore, a contemporary writer, Matteo Bandello, suggests Ludovico actually paid Leonardo rather generously and lavished him with gifts.[33]

It would seem the most likely point of contention arose over the simple fact that Leonardo was being torn between important (and presumably well-paid) projects and the demands of Beatrice and others close to *Il Moro* who wanted to use his skills for trivial purposes. This not only broke his concentration and made it difficult for him to meet the demands of those commissioning large-scale works, it also meant he had a number of sources of income almost all of whom were reluctant to pay in full or punctually, leaving him financially embarrassed.

As this clash shows, the problem came to a head in 1496 when, as Leonardo puts it, he was prevented from 'conforming to my desire'; which was most likely a reference to a project that meant a great deal to him as well as to those who had commissioned it. And in the same letter he refers to what may be construed as a forthcoming payment he hopes will alleviate his financial problems and enable him to put aside enough money to support himself and his 'family' for some time to come. By this, Leonardo almost certainly meant he was due another interim payment for what has since become known as probably his greatest artistic work, the fresco depicting the Last Supper for the refectory of a Milanese monastery, Santa Maria delle Grazie, which he had begun the previous year.

The conventional form of fresco painting, *buonfresco*, was a speedy process in which the artist covered the walls before the plaster dried, but Leonardo wanted to spend a significantly longer time on this project than such a technique would allow and he decided to produce his own pigments and materials for sealing the paint to the wall. Sadly, his concoction was not as successful as he had hoped and the giant painting, measuring almost 9 metres (30 feet) in length, began to deteriorate even during his own lifetime.

But the degeneration of *The Last Supper* cannot be blamed upon Leonardo alone. The wall upon which the masterpiece was painted was exposed to the rain and the wind, and there is an underground stream passing directly beneath it which makes it permanently damp. However, a combination of bad luck, the elements and mistakes in the preparation of Leonardo's materials mean the painting is now a mere shadow of its former beauty.*

Leonardo was at the peak of his powers when he began working on

---

* *The Last Supper* has had a chequered history. In 1620, occupying Spanish troops punched a door in the painting, and two hundred years later Napoleon's soldiers tied horses to it. There have been many attempts to restore *The Last Supper* to its original glory but these have just mutilated it further. The most recent and enormously more sympathetic attempt by the Italian restorer, Signora Pinin Brambilla, is now complete and has returned Leonardo's great work to some semblance of its original beauty.

this magnificent painting and was by then certainly recognised beyond Milan as perhaps the greatest living Italian artist. He would often work on the painting in front of an audience whom he allowed to wander around the site, and he even held conversations with his audience as he worked. One eye-witness reported on a visit to Santa Maria delle Grazie:

He sometimes stayed there from dawn to sundown, never putting down his brush, forgetting to eat and drink, painting without pause. He would also sometimes remain two, three or four days without touching his brush, although he spent several hours a day standing in front of his work, arms folded, examining and criticising the figures. I also saw him, driven by some sudden urge, at midday when the sun was at its height, leaving the Corte Vecchia, where he was working on his marvellous clay horse, to come straight to Santa Maria delle Grazie, without seeking shade, and clamber up onto the scaffolding, pick up his brush, put in one or two strokes, and then go away again.[34]

Very much to form, with *The Last Supper* Leonardo produced one of the iconoclastic masterpieces of the age but upset both his employer and patron with his approach. The prior of the monastery soon became exasperated with Leonardo's slowness, and complained that the artist would stare at this work in silence for hours, commit a few brush strokes and then disappear for the rest of the day.

This slowness may be explained in part by Leonardo's familiar considered pace and the distraction created by so many other commitments, but others have claimed Leonardo was so intent upon using 'real' faces for the disciples and for Christ that he spent an inordinate amount of time walking the streets of Milan looking for suitable features he could subject to memory, or trying to find appropriate models he then invited to sit for him at Santa Maria delle Grazie.

The Renaissance poet Giovanbattista Giraldi, whose father witnessed Leonardo painting *The Last Supper*, wrote during the 1550s:

> When Leonardo wished to portray a figure he first considered its quality and nature . . . and when he had decided what it was to be he went to where he knew people of that type would congregate, and observed diligently the faces, manners, clothes and bodily movement . . . noting it down in a little book which he always kept at his belt.[35]

This description is certainly compatible with what we know of the man's exactitude and devotion to research. It is almost certain too that many of the sketches of heads and figures clustered together in his notebooks were drawn upon to be used as a foundation for some of the characters depicted in *The Last Supper*. Leonardo had a huge store of caricatures and intricate drawings he could employ, all taken from two decades of life study.

In 1497, after Leonardo had been working on the project for the best part of two years, the prior, apparently impatient and irritated by the mess the artist had created in his refectory, complained to Ludovico, 'There is only the head of Judas still to do, and for over a year now not only has Leonardo not touched the painting, but he has only come to see it once.'

Angered, Ludovico summoned Leonardo to account for the delay. According to a contemporary account, Leonardo replied:

> Your Excellency is aware that only the head of Judas remains to be done, and he was, as everyone knows, an egregious villain. Therefore he should be given a physiognomy fitting his wickedness. To this end, for about a year if not more, night and morning I have been going every day to the Borghetto where Your Excellency knows that all the ruffians of the city live. But I have

not yet been able to discover a villain's face corresponding to what I have in mind. Once I have found that face, I will finish the painting in a day. But, if my research remains fruitless, I shall take the features of the prior who came to complain about me to Your Excellency and who would fit the requirements perfectly. [36]

This quip so amused Ludovico that in spite of the obvious weakness of Leonardo's claims he sided with the artist against the prior's arguments. As Vasari tells it: 'This thing moved the Duke wondrously to laughter, and said that Leonardo had a thousand reasons on his side. And the poor prior, in confusion, left Leonardo in peace.' [37]

Another of the 'thousand reasons' (which Vasari really should have called 'a thousand distractions'), came in the form of a Franciscan monk named Luca Pacioli, then one of the most widely respected intellectuals in Italy, who arrived to teach in Milan just about the time the prior of Santa Maria delle Grazie started complaining about Leonardo.

Pacioli was renowned for his mathematical ability and had become famous through his masterpiece, *Summa de Arithmetica Geometrica Proportioni et Proportionalita*, which we know Leonardo had already purchased for 119 soldi and begun transcribing wholesale into his notebooks. [38]

Mathematics first attracted Leonardo to the Franciscan, but the two soon became close friends. Leonardo later called Pacioli *maestro Luca* and opened up his notebooks and manuscripts to him. These sentiments were reciprocated by Pacioli who had heard of Leonardo's genius from independent sources. He later described his friend as 'the most worthy of painters, perspectivists, architects, and musicians, the man endowed with all the virtues, Leonardo da Vinci, the Florentine'. [39]

Leonardo was never a skilled mathematician. In fact, if we are to judge him by what we see in his notebooks alone, he was barely competent. He only ever mastered rudimentary geometry and was often inaccurate with his arithmetic. But where he failed in ability he made up for it with enthusiasm, filling page after page of his notebooks with geometric figures, numeric doodles, calculations and mathematical symbols. 'He who does not know the supreme certainty of mathematics is wallowing in confusion,' he wrote.[40] And he realised mathematics was an invaluable tool both for the scientist and the artist, declaring, 'No human investigation can be called true science which has not passed through mathematical demonstrations.'[41] And: 'All the instances of perspective are elucidated by the five terms of the mathematician: point, line, angle, surface and solid.'[42]

Clearly, he gained a good deal from Pacioli, but mathematics remained one of the few areas in which Leonardo did not excel, a fact which for some disbars him from ever being considered a true scientist. However, as we will see in the next chapter, I believe this really reflects upon the limited modern interpretation of what should be considered 'science' or who should be described as 'a scientist'.* As the Renaissance scholar De Lamar Jensen points out, 'We in the twentieth century tend to view science as the increasingly successful search for objective truth and to regard the scientific ideas of the past as mere stepping-stones to our current wisdom.'[43] Perhaps there are more ways in which science may be practised than via applied mathematics.

Leonardo and Pacioli remained lifelong friends, and a few years after their first meeting they composed a treatise together entitled *De Divina Proportione*, published in Venice in 1509.[44] It was a genuine collaboration in which Leonardo contributed a collection of drawings which illustrated the Franciscan's theorems and the ancient authorities he had built upon, including Plato and Euclid.

However, even with his seemingly unending commitments and the constant call of other interests, thanks in large part to pressure applied

---

* Notwithstanding what Leonardo claimed himself in the quote above. This was his opinion at that time, not mine.

by Ludovico Sforza himself, by the summer of 1497, *The Last Supper* finally neared completion.

The Duke had his own reasons for demanding that Leonardo finish his task at least before the year was out. Five months earlier his young bride, Beatrice, who had only just turned twenty-two, had died suddenly. She had been five months pregnant and, ignoring all advice, had attended a ball at which she had danced into the early hours. Over-exerting herself, she miscarried and died.

Although *Il Moro* had recently tired of his wife and had taken a mistress, Lucrezia Crivelli, when Beatrice died he went into deep mourning. Her funeral was a lavish public event and Sforza swiftly arranged for a plot to be laid aside at Santa Maria delle Grazie and for a double tomb to be constructed close to Leonardo's still unfinished work, prompting the rapid completion of the fresco.

But the Duke's mood could change like the wind. Within a year he was once more dangerously cocksure and over-confident. Six months after Beatrice's funeral, Lucrezia Crivelli gave birth to a boy and, encouraged by what he must have seen as a turnaround in his fortunes, *Il Moro* began to set in motion another series of political schemes and

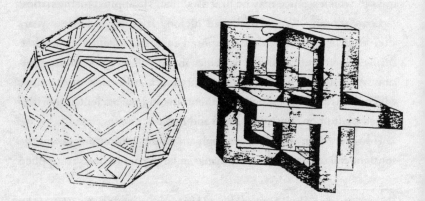

Fig. 6.1: Leonardo's three-dimensional figures.

daring diplomatic manoeuvres which would this time tip the peninsula into bloody war and eventually precipitate his own ruin.

Believing that for his own ends he could unravel the political structure that held in place a precarious peace between Pisa, Florence and Venice, by April 1498 Sforza was again plotting to set his enemies against each other. But once more events rapidly overtook him. The young King of France died suddenly (after banging his head on a lintel) and was succeeded by the Duke of Orléans (Louis XII). As a descendant of the Visconti, who had ruled Milan before the Sforzas, Louis was certainly no friend of *Il Moro*. One of his first actions as monarch was to lay claim to the duchy of Milan.

Within a year, Louis XII was ready to invade and occupy Lombardy. He had already bought off Florence and formed a powerful alliance with Venice. And, as he gathered his armies close to the Alps, Milan was left with no real friends, its coffers drained from the war of 1495; and despite the Duke's personal appetite for conflict, his people had little interest in fighting.

By the summer of 1499, the French were almost on the Duke's doorstep, and at the same time the Venetians were attacking from the east. Realising he was on the verge of total defeat, Sforza secreted away his personal fortune to Germany and the Emperor took in his family. But his own people were now turning against their duke. Ludovico's treasurer was bludgeoned to death during a riot in the heart of the city and effigies of the once glorious ruler were burned in the city's piazza. Days later, the Duke fled and the city fell, without a shot being fired or an arrow being released, on 14 September.

Leonardo appears to have been strangely unconcerned with the unfolding of these traumatic events; at least he makes no reference to them in his surviving notebooks. In April 1499, as Sforza's political world began to fall apart, Leonardo seemed more interested in the fact that he had 218 lire in his bank account. And a little later in the same month he writes of a piece of land '16 perches wide', the Duke has given him, presumably in lieu of payment during a particularly bad cash-flow crisis.[45]

Leonardo did not immediately flee the city along with his patron and most of the ruling elite; he had no more to fear from the occupying forces than any other citizen, perhaps less. He witnessed Louis XII's triumphant entry into Milan on 6 October and simply waited to see how the new Milan would suit him. In fact, ever the magpie, he appears to have made contacts with the French almost immediately and was soon in search of material for his researches. Some snatches of notes, reminders to himself it appears, have survived. 'Get from Gian di Paris [a painter in the service of Louis XII] the method for dry colouring,' he writes, '. . . and the recipe for making white salt and tinted paper.'[46]

But his contact with the French quickly reached the very top. He was aware his fame had spread beyond Italy and that the French King himself and many of his court were admirers of his work, both as artist and engineer. It soon became clear the new rulers valued him every bit as much as Sforza had done. Legend has it Louis was so taken with *The Last Supper* he made enquiries to see if it could be removed from the refectory wall of Santa Maria delle Grazie and transported in sections back to France. Predictably then, not long after the occupation, Leonardo agreed a form of non-exclusive contract with Louis, which resulted in him being treated by the French as 'their' artist.[47]

But Leonardo's calm acceptance of the French was not to last. Along with most of the population, he soon began to regret Sforza's folly and the upheavals that had sent him into exile, recording bitterly: 'The Duke lost his states, his personal fortune, and his freedom,' adding with unintended irony, 'none of his projects came to fruition.'[48] The occupying forces began to abuse the Milanese, looting, raping and murdering almost indiscriminately. Within months, this once proud and wealthy Italian state was reduced to a blanched negative of its former self and Leonardo, along with perhaps many hundreds of others, made preparations to move on.

But he was now in a difficult position. He had been comfortable in Milan and had prospered greatly there. Only six months earlier, *Il Moro* had given him a vineyard outside the city, the piece of land sixteen perches wide he had written about in his notes. But most significantly, he had now become involved with the French.

Then one morning, Leonardo witnessed something that must have sickened him to the heart and negated any remaining indecisiveness. The occupying French archers had positioned themselves twenty paces back from the head of his clay model of 'the Sforza horse' and set themselves up for target practice.

Shocked into action, Leonardo secured his savings with the Monte di Pietà in Florence (the Florentine institution which had traditionally dealt with the Vinci family finances), gathered together all he needed for a long journey through war-ravaged northern Italy, and with Salai at his side, and accompanied by his friend Luca Pacioli, he set forth upon the next stage of his life.

7

THE NOTEBOOKS I
(1484–1500)

He laboured much more by his word than in fact or by deed.
– Vasari, *Lives of the Painters, Sculptors and Architects*

It is difficult to pinpoint the exact date when Leonardo began his notebooks. As we have seen, he had been an avid scribbler since his days in Verrocchio's workshop and we have already considered some of his earliest surviving notes and memoranda. There are the personal references made on the back of drawings, the lists of people to contact and the draft of the letter written in 1482 intended for Ludovico Sforza. But it is not until a few years later we find clear, purposeful accounts including Leonardo's fictitious journey to the East and his detailed ideas for town plans. So, if we ignore the odd surviving scrap, letters, lists and notes to himself, we might safely place the beginning of serious note-keeping at a time just prior to the plague of 1484.

However, for a number of reasons, dating Leonardo's writing after this is problematic. He very rarely assigned dates to anything and because of what may have been an exaggerated fear of plagiarism he only ever used 'mirror-writing' which was often encrypted in codes of his own devising. As well as this, his handwriting remained almost identical throughout his life, a fact that has deprived interpreters of another clue often of great help in deciphering and dating the manuscripts and notes of the great experimenters.* In fact, the surest help in dating Leonardo's work is the fluid nature of his preoccupations. When he fills page after page with set designs and contraptions for theatrical use we can assume they come from the early 1490s when he was absorbed with working for the Duke and Duchess of Milan, and when he covers the manuscript paper with geometric drawings and rudimentary calculations we see the influence of Luca Pacioli whom Leonardo first met in 1496.

Aside from the problems of deciphering what Leonardo has to say, dating and piecing together the lineage of his words is further complicated because of the chequered history of the notebooks and the collection of miscellaneous notes that have come down to us. As we saw in the Introduction, Leonardo's originals have been as mutilated and dissected as one of the corpses over which he often laboured. Pages were torn from bound books and dispersed, damaged, and in some cases lost completely, and this has disrupted further efforts to follow the flow of his thought and the progression of his ideas.

As I have already mentioned, Leonardo was obsessed with discovery, with finding answers to any question through observation and experiment, and this of course is what leaves the greatest impression even when flicking quickly through his writings. He pours out his ideas on to the page in almost random fashion. A sheet of writing on optics might be complemented by a sketch of a face, a brief treatise on the way to prepare a specific type of paint or the recipe for a medical cure.

---

* It is interesting to note that Isaac Newton who also rarely dated his notes went through six distinct phases in which either his handwriting was markedly different or during which time he varied his writing materials, all of which has helped enormously the task of transcribing many of his reports and descriptions.

Ironically, Leonardo was afraid he would contribute little to the canon of human understanding.

> Seeing that I cannot choose a particularly useful or pleasant subject, since the men born before me have taken for themselves all the useful and necessary themes, [he once wrote], I shall do the same as the poor man who arrives last at the fair, and being unable to choose what he wants, has to be content with what others have already seen and rejected because of its small worth. I will load my humble bags with this scorned and disdained merchandise, rejected by many buyers, and go to distribute it not in the great cities, but in poor villages, receiving the price for what I have to offer.[1]

With hindsight this seems rather ridiculous and it is difficult to judge just how much Leonardo really believed it himself. He was never inhibited by any lack of subjects to investigate, nor by his own intellectual ability, but often his ambition and clear-sightedness was hampered by the rudimentary nature of the tools at his disposal. Most restrictive was language itself. But surprisingly perhaps, this realisation came slowly. Early in his researches he wrote: 'I possess so many words in my native language that I ought rather to complain of not understanding things than of lacking for words to express my thoughts properly.'[2]

But he was never a good linguist and knew almost no Latin until he taught himself the language around 1487, when he was already in his mid-thirties. Because of this, Leonardo became the first intellectual of the age to use the vernacular, but in a practical sense it was a serious inhibition to his autodidactic progress and to his ability to express himself. Classical Italian offered Leonardo a rich source for poetic expression but, in spite of his early confidence, many of the words he needed to explain his experiments and to express his analytical conclusions simply did not exist.

Although he made a great show of shunning the idea of learning from past masters, Leonardo knew he had at times to rely upon received wisdom and he read the Classics with determination and attention to detail; but again, language restricted him. Many of the greatest works of antiquity had been translated into Italian, so the ideas of Aristotle, Plato and Socrates were open to him. Along with these, a few volumes by modern masters, including Leon Alberti's *De Familia* and Matteo Palmieri's *Della Vita Civile*, were written and first published in Italian, but within the specialised areas of scientific enquiry, the canon translated into his native language was dominated largely by alchemical treatises and works on astrology and the occult, which were of little use, and indeed of little interest to him.

With his acquisition of rudimentary Latin, from the late 1480s a far wider range of material was made available to him, but it was always hard going. He never mastered the language, and unravelling the complex ideas of the authors he followed was made doubly difficult because of his clumsiness in merely translating their words. Yet persist he did, going on to report his findings in the language he had taught himself and copying tracts of manuscripts and treatises he bought, borrowed or studied in Milanese libraries.

And from his earliest attempts at experiment and recording of his investigations came a surprising realisation and a complete reversal of his former pessimism. Throughout the rich history of humankind, so little, he concluded, had been discovered, so few things invented, so little headway made. More than once he noted this with astonishment: 'So many things have remained unknown or misinterpreted for centuries!' he declared.[3] And with this sense of bewilderment, and armed with an obsessive need to know 'everything', Leonardo set about trying to make amends for what he saw as humanity's sluggish progress.

One of his many lists, this one written in 1489 as he was about to emerge into the spotlight in Milan, illustrates his sense of eclecticism *par excellence*, the sprawling mind of this inveterate intellectual magpie.

'Find out how to install bombards and ramparts by day and by night,' he writes. 'How they built the tower of Ferrara without loopholes, how to square the triangle.' And further down the page he notes that 'a Frenchman' has promised to tell him the dimensions of the Sun. Then he concludes, 'How do they run on the ice in Flanders?'[4]

About this time, as he was first accepted by the Milanese court, Leonardo had already delved into a vast range of studies, put his name to dozens of inventions and conducted hundreds of experiments in almost the entire range of sciences then known and many others previously unknown. The inventions alone included: a crane for emptying ditches,[5] a special octagonal mirror which created a repeat image,[6] a table lamp for which the intensity could be varied,[7] folding furniture[8] and a set of doors which could be made to open and close automatically by the use of counterweights.[9]

But if we go back just six or seven years from this reminder to Leonardo's earliest serious notes, we see he restricted himself in his choice of subjects to investigate two disciplines in particular. One of these was military engineering from which he hoped to earn if not a fortune then at least an entrée into Milanese society. The other was purely a labour of love, the study of acoustics and the design of musical instruments, from which he might also have harboured ideas of earning respect or even much-needed patronage.

We have seen how Leonardo considered approaching the ruler of Milan upon his arrival in the city in 1482, but even at that early stage of his career he had already been interested in military apparatus for some time, and after settling in Milan he continued to find uncharacteristic fascination with the machinery of war and destruction, an interest that remained with him into old age. The most famous product of this line of thought was his 'tank', a vehicle that looks like the modern image of a UFO with a circle of guns protruding from the rim and able to roll along the ground.

The most distinctive aspect of his work as a military designer, and indeed an obsession which showed itself in many of Leonardo's ideas and plans, was his devotion to the notion of automation. This is particularly startling when we recall the world in which he lived, a civilisation in which the fastest speeds were attained on horseback, in which carts and carriages provided the most sophisticated means of transport, a time three centuries before the first steam engine.

Legend has it that Albertus Magnus, the occultist-philosopher of the thirteenth century, had devised automatons and mechanised devices, but there is no evidence to support this. Although, like much of Leonardo's work, his military machines and automated devices were rarely constructed and remained locked in his notebooks, he was clearly thinking in a way that was quite different from almost all his contemporaries. This devotion to automation and labour-replacement manifested itself early in his career in drawings of military drums in which a rolling mechanism powered the beater to pound a drum with half a dozen sticks as the machine rumbled alongside a line of troops. From the same year come drawings of batteries of cannon and mortar that could fire volleys of shells or specially designed projectiles, and multiple bows with which to shower the enemy with a barrage of arrows. Leonardo sketched designs for an aqualung, machines to pump water to siege towers, efficient ways to pour burning oil on enemy heads and techniques for dislodging the ladders of those attacking the battlements of a castle.

Fig. 7.1: Leonardo's scythed car and 'tank'.

Contemporaneously, Leonardo had become preoccupied with the science of acoustics and the engineering problems associated with the design of instruments. His serious research into the nature of sound and its transmission did not come until the mid-1490s, but his fascination with sound and its manipulation, the invention of original ways to produce music and the theory of music itself probably date from before his arrival in Milan in 1482. As we have seen, it is likely Leonardo first travelled to the city as a professional musician or music teacher and we know he had been highly regarded at the Medici court both for his singing voice and his ability as an instrumentalist. It is therefore quite possible he was already designing and building instruments before he left Florence in 1481.

He was aware that many contemporary instruments could be improved, and delighted in drawing designs for completely new instruments and odd hybrid constructions; the instrument he is supposed to have given the Moor may have been just such a thing. Sadly, no model or finished instrument has survived and no score attributable to Leonardo has come down to us, although he was said to have been a talented improviser.

Later, Leonardo was to incorporate his interest in sound and music into a holistic view in which he saw connections between seemingly disparate ideas and thought systems, and during his most productive time as an experimenter he attempted to understand how sound could reach us and to think about how humans interpret sound.

His holistic approach was developing most rapidly during the late 1480s when he was trying to establish himself as an important figure in the world of architecture and to impress the Duke of Milan and his court architects. As we have seen, Leonardo found little real success as an architect but his studies did gain him valuable insights. His universal view at this time linked architecture with the body, but this was only one aspect of his interpretation of Nature and the place of humankind in the greater scheme of things. He saw how the human body had

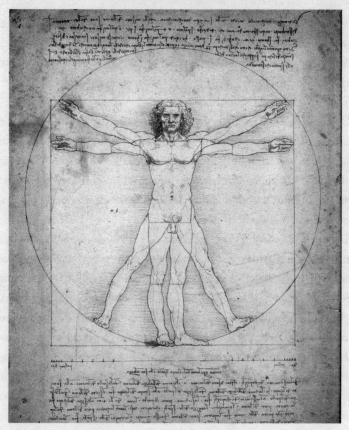

Fig. 7.2: The Vitruvian Man.

observable proportions, a concept he expressed with his now famous drawing of the Vitruvian man from around 1487.

In this, he was leaning heavily on Vitruvius, who wrote:

In the components of a temple there ought to be the greatest harmony in the symmetrical relations of the different parts to the magnitude of the whole. Then again, in the human body the central part is naturally the navel. For if a man be placed flat on his back, with hands and feet extended, and a pair of compasses centred at his navel, the fingers and toes of his two hands and feet will touch the circumference of the circle described therefrom. And just as the human body yields a circular outline, so too it yields a square figure.[10]

Gradually, Leonardo began to see how patterns connecting the structure of the body with the proportions of buildings could also be linked with the harmonic structure found within music. Leonardo could then go on to comment, 'Proportion is found not only in numbers and measurements but also in sounds, landscapes, times and places, and in any form of power at all.'[11]

Taking this even further, he tried to find proportions throughout Nature and even attempted to make connections between the circumference of trees and the length of their branches, but, as one might expect, this time he could find no link.[12] Elsewhere, he makes the succinct pronouncement, 'Man is the model of the world.'[13] And although he could not draw precise links between the structure of the human body and other patterns in Nature, he continued to search for a match.

The culmination of this deliberate blending of ideas and disciplines was the proposal for a treatise to be called *On the Human Body*, a book planned not merely as a collection of anatomical observations but the product of Leonardo's holistic interpretations, honing in on what he saw as the primary forces at work within Nature and in particular the human body. Leonardo was not so concerned with reporting or even interpreting individual parts of the human organism and their function, but was far more interested in elucidating the roots of life, the primal energies and fundamental workings of Nature.

This work must commence with the conception of man [he wrote] . . . and must describe the nature of the womb, and how the baby lives in it, and in what degree it resides there and the way it is enlivened and nourished, and its growth and what interval there will be between one degree of growth and the next, and what it is which pushes it out of the mother and for what reason it sometimes comes out of the mother's womb before the due time. Then I will describe which members grow more than the others when the baby is born, and set out the measurements of a one-year-old baby. Then describe the grown man and woman, and their measurements and the nature of their complexion, colour and physiognomy. Then describe how they are composed of veins, nerves, muscles and bones. This I will do at the end of the book. Then I will show in four expositions the four universal states of man; that is: mirth, with the various acts of laughing and describe the cause of laughter; weeping in various manners with their causes; contention, with various acts of killing, flight, fear, ferocity, boldness, murder and all the things pertaining to similar instances; then show work, with pulling, pushing, carrying, stopping, supporting and similar things. Then describe attitudes and movement; then perspective through the function of the eye, and hearing . . . I speak of music . . . and describing the other senses.[14]

Of particular importance was a study of the nervous system, an attempt to understand how the senses worked and how animals interpreted information gathered by their senses. The ancients had written at length on this subject. In the traditional scheme, the brain contained three chambers or ventricles. The first, the *imprensiva*, gathered information from the five senses. This information was then passed on to the real powerhouse of the brain, the *sensus communis*, where it was interpreted. The *sensus communis* was viewed as the home of reason, imagination and intellect, the very seat of the soul. Information deciphered here could then be stored in the third ventricle, the *memoria*.

This theory had been used since it was first proposed by Aristotle almost two millennia earlier, and initially Leonardo accepted it. He played with the details and was particularly keen to place vision at the top of the sensory hierarchy, describing sight as: 'the chief means of understanding the infinite works of nature'.[15] To be fair, he had very little to go on at this stage in his anatomical studies. He had in his possession just one skull which he drew exquisitely, and used to try to locate the site of the soul, but it was not until around 1508 that he was able to make an independent study of the brain when he set about dissecting dozens of bodies. As we shall see in Chapter 10, this led him to an understanding of how the brain and nervous system might co-ordinate, but of course it told him nothing about the human soul. For Leonardo during the 1480s, as it had been for the ancients, 'The soul apparently resides in the region of judgement located where all the senses run together, which is called the *sensus communis*, and not all throughout the body as many have believed.'[16]

Of course it was no mere coincidence that Leonardo's most productive period as an unpaid researcher and freelance free-ranging explorer coincided with his acceptance by Sforza's court in Milan. Since his arrival in the city some eight years earlier, he had been firing on all cylinders, pushing his way towards ducal acceptance while simultaneously working on his private projects, so that what may be seen as his personal *anni mirabiles*, the decade from 1490 to 1500, was also the time during which his official career blossomed.

His work during this decade is also key to an understanding of Leonardo as a scientist, the period during which he produced his most interesting ideas based upon experience and experiment. In 1491 he began his first notebook dedicated to a single subject. This is now known as *Manuscript C*.* In this notebook Leonardo explores the nature of light and shade and asks questions concerning the behaviour of light,

---

* Even in this manuscript Leonardo started out with the intention of devoting it to one subject but ended up adding notes about the nature of forces and observations concerning the behaviour of water.

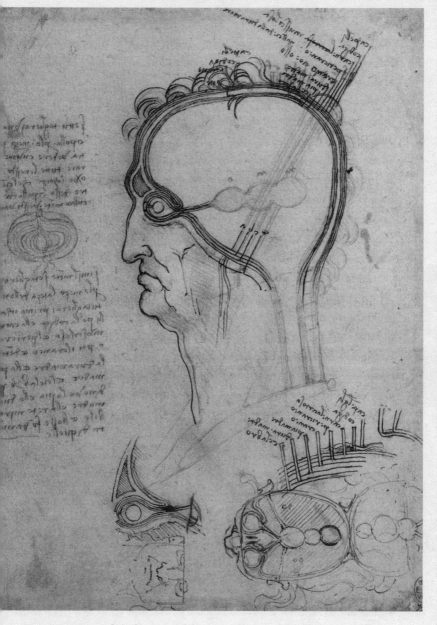

Fig. 7.3: Leonardo's drawing of the brain showing the three ventricles.

before offering suggestions for the construction of optical devices and explorations of the nature of reflection and refraction. Naturally, all of these ideas and descriptions were already close to his heart as both natural philosopher and artist.

His training had taught him much about the nature of light and how it interacts with matter, how shadows appear and how different surfaces cause different degrees of reflection and absorption. He was also familiar with the principles of how primary colours combine, how images are distorted by reflection or magnified by lenses. However, until this time he had come to these ideas as an artist and had been concerned primarily with how light and shade could be employed on the canvas. From around 1490, he began to consider the subject in an abstract sense and tried to formulate rules and hypotheses to explain how the effects he observed came about, as well as to find fundamental principles that could be employed in the construction of optical devices.

The ancients had shown a keen interest in the behaviour and nature of light, and as more was learned and written about the subject, firstly by the Arabic philosopher Alhazen in the eleventh century and later by medieval researchers including Bacon, Magnus and John Pecham, it was realised that optics and geometry were intimately related.

Meanwhile, the Platonists insisted that the philosopher could come closer to God by studying the fundamental mathematical patterns within Nature, and this reinforced the notion that the study of optics also brought the researcher closer to the creator: the simple elegance and beauty of optical phenomena reflected the clean abstract lines of mathematics and therefore the foundations of the Universe. From here, it was a short step to believing, as the Scholastics did, that the study of optics was 'an investigation of the illumination of the world'.

Yet by Leonardo's time understanding of optics was still hampered by misconception and contradiction and many of his contemporaries still clung to false ideas propounded by Aristotle and Plato. The most glaring fallacy was the Platonic idea that humans perceived the

Universe because the eye *projected* particles which were then reflected back to the eye. To us this seems an obvious absurdity, but it would be unfair to criticise our ancestors for such lack of understanding. In his earliest writings on the subject, it is clear Leonardo also subscribed to this popular view, declaring that '. . . the visual power is extended [from the eye] by rays as far as the surfaces of non-transparent bodies.'[17] Only later did he realise this was illogical, and come to the conclusion that if this was indeed how vision worked then we would not see all things equally quickly because the particles from the eye would need different lengths of time to reach their targets and to bounce back to our eyes.

Leonardo believed sight to be the most 'noble' sense (followed by hearing) and spent an enormous amount of time and energy investigating all aspects of light and the mechanism of vision both on a practical and a theoretical level. He began with the daunting task of studying the eye. The eye had been the subject of intense interest to medieval philosophers, but its dissection was extremely difficult. More often than not, after a few cuts the eye collapses into a gelatinous mess and the lens takes on a spherical shape. Leonardo realised the complexity of this study and the failings of his predecessors, commenting: 'The eye, the function of which is so clearly demonstrated by experience, has been defined until the present time by a great many authors in a certain way – but I find it to be completely different.'[18]

And this was no hollow boast, but based upon a unique ingenuity. Leonardo was possibly the first experimenter to realise the role of the lens, even if he did not understand how it operated, and to circumvent the problems he faced dissecting the eye, he first boiled his specimens in egg white and water. But this presented a further difficulty because it distorted the shape of the lens and detached it from the retina, which then led him to make erroneous conclusions about its nature.

But he persisted, and after further experiments he began to make progress. First to go was his adherence to the idea that vision was facilitated by the emission of particles from the eye. This he replaced with a simple description of how light behaved as a wave (what today would be called the wave-like property of light). From this, he went on to describe how light reflected from different surfaces, how the eye perceives reflections and judges distance, how the human eye allows perspective and how light falling on objects generates shadows and shade.

In much of his thinking we can see echoes of the great Arab philosopher Alhazen, who wrote a treatise entitled *Opticae Thesaurus*, together with the innovative experimenter and thinker John Pecham, author of a treatise entitled *Perspectiva Communis*. Both of these important and original works were read widely throughout the Middle Ages and the Renaissance. Pecham's ideas were particularly sophisticated. At the start of *Perspectiva Communis* he comes straight to the point when he observes:

> Among all the studies of natural causes and reasons, light most delights the contemplators; among the great things of mathematics, the certainty of its demonstrations most illustriously elevates the minds of the investigators; perspective must therefore be preferred to all human discourses and disciplines, in the study of which the radiant lines are expounded by means of demonstrations and in which the glory is found not only of mathematics but also physics: it is adorned with the flowers of one and the other.[19]

This passage Leonardo translated from Latin into his notebook and it represents perfectly his own view of optics as both an artist and a scientific investigator. How could he put his own feelings more clearly than Pecham's 'perspective must therefore be preferred to all human discourses and disciplines'?

Pecham and other medieval thinkers, including Roger Bacon, who had devoted a full quarter of his masterpiece, *Opus Majus*, to what was then called the science of *perspectiva* (the fundamentals of optics), had described how the void was filled with images from solid objects. This Leonardo paraphrased as: 'every opaque body fills the surrounding air with infinite images, by which infinite pyramids diffused in the air present this body all in all and all in every part'.[20] In modern terminology this could be restated as: 'Light is reflected from all parts of solid opaque objects in all directions and this light travels in straight lines.'

Pecham's notion of 'pyramids' was later adopted by Alberti and then taken up by Leonardo. The term appears frequently in the notebooks dealing with light, where it is sometimes refined into 'radiant pyramids' or 'visual pyramids'. In each case it refers to the idea that light reaches the eye in the form of a pyramid or cone, light from the edges of an object converging with those from straight ahead to meet at the eye. This was based upon the ancient realisation that light travelled in straight lines, but Alberti rather arbitrarily extended this to explain how an artist gathers information from an object, proposing that rays from some parts of the object give information about texture while others define the size of the object. Alberti may of course be forgiven for misinterpreting what may be learned from observing an object because he knew nothing of the workings of the retina, let alone the cerebral cortex.

Leonardo used some aspects of Alberti's work to reach his own conclusions. He made the distinction between peripheral vision and central vision, at one point commenting: 'The eye has a single central line, and all the things that come to the eye along this line are seen well. There are an infinite number of other lines around this one as their centre, which are of less value the further they are removed from the central line.'[21] He was almost certainly the first to write about the principle of stereoscopic vision and the way a pair of eyes gathers information about an object. He also realised that this information was then passed on to be interpreted by 'the soul', or what we understand today to be the cerebral cortex, the region of the brain responsible for processing sensory information.

From his notebooks it is also clear he knew the reason for farsightedness (a disability he is thought to have himself suffered from from his mid-thirties onwards). It is even possible that from a set of experiments in which he attempted to duplicate the function of the eye with glass instruments, he realised the role played by the cornea (*luce*), reporting: 'In order to see what function the *luce* serves in the pupil, cause a thing resembling the *luce* to be made of glass.'[22] It is also conceivable he worked out the principle of the contact lens, realising that these would be of most use to the elderly.[23] Sadly, like almost everything about which Leonardo theorised, nothing but suggestions in the manuscripts have survived.[24]

Relating the workings of the eye to the *camera obscura* (a device in which light is passed through a pinhole and projected on to a flat surface) he went on to create odd optical devices that could increase the breadth of vision, noting: 'If you take a hemisphere of glass and put your face into it, and close it well around the edge of the face, and fill it with clear water, you will see all the things that are seen from the surface of this globe, so that you will all but see behind your back.'[25]

These then led Leonardo to design projectors,[26] and to prepare a device related to a telescope more than a century before Hans Lippershey's design that by 1609 had inspired Galileo to make his own more powerful model and to observe the Moon and the planets. We will consider the controversial ideas concerning Leonardo's involvement with an early form of telescope in Chapter 10, but for the moment it is important to see how his writings and observations of this period (the 1490s) laid the groundwork for his later experiments and practical applications.

During this time, he wrote page after page about what he believed to be the fundamental principles of optics, a theory of light that took medieval reasoning as its springboard, but tremendously enlarged and extrapolated. Most significant are Leonardo's thoughts concerning the nature of light and the way it travels. He saw light and sound as behaving in a similar fashion. He of course had no idea of the electromagnetic spectrum or concepts such as frequency or amplitude, terms which only came into the language of science some three and half centuries after his death, but he clearly saw that light and sound may travel through a medium by what he described as a 'tremor', a perturbation in one place setting up a corresponding disturbance in the medium close by, a process which is then repeated to propel a signal (or information) from one point to another. He described this beautifully in the following passage:

I say: if you throw two small stones at the same time on a sheet of motionless water at some distance from each other, you will observe that around the two percussions numerous separate circles are formed; these will meet as they increase in size and then penetrate and intersect one another, all the while maintaining as their respective centres the spots struck by the stones. And the reason for this is that the water, although apparently moving, does not leave its original position, because the openings made by the stones close again immediately. Therefore the motion produced by the quick opening and closing of the water has caused only a shock which may be described as tremor rather than movement. In order to understand better what I mean, watch the blades of straw that because of their lightness float on the water, and observe how they do not depart from their original positions in spite of the waves underneath them caused by the occurrence of the circles. The reaction of the water being in the nature of tremor rather than movement, the circles cannot break one another on meeting, and as the water is of the same quality all the way through, its parts transmit the tremor to one another without change of position. Thus the water, although remaining in its

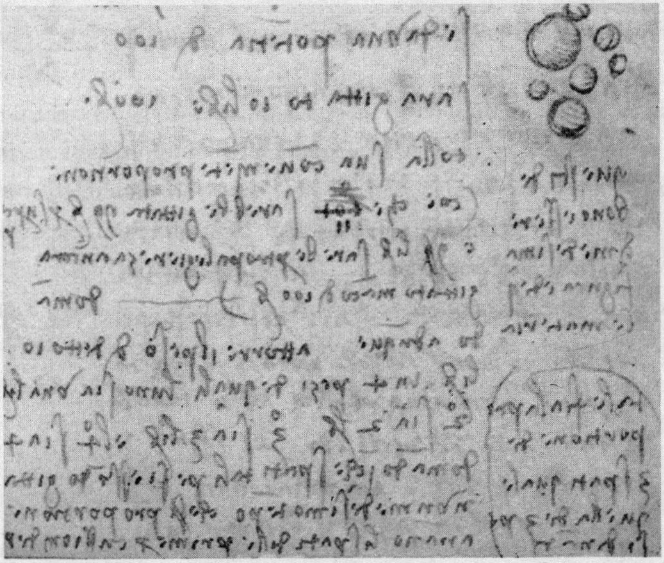

Fig. 7.4: Leonardo's description of wave motion
and the propagation in water of a cast stone.

position, can easily transmit the tremor to the adjacent parts, these transmitting it to other adjacent parts, while its force gradually diminishes until the end.[27]

From this simple but elegantly presented set of observations, Leonardo's increasing absorption with a holistic view of the world led him to see that the fundamental descriptions of what at first appeared to be very different phenomena, sound, light and the ripples on water, were actually inter-related. He saw no distinction between the way waves of water, sound or light might behave and this led him to the statement: 'Everything in the cosmos is propagated by means of waves.'[28] In fact, true to his sometimes over-enthusiastic pursuit of 'unification' in Nature, he went too far and tried, as his new bold assertion demanded, to link smell with light and heat, declaring:

[Invisible radiation] is seen in the sun, which sends out two kinds of *species*, the first luminous, the second of heat . . . That the atmosphere attracts to itself, like a lodestone, all the images of the objects that exist in it, and that not their forms merely but also their nature may be clearly seen in the sun, which is a hot and luminous body. The whole atmosphere of which becomes completely shot through with light and heat and takes on itself the image of the source of that heat and splendour, and the moon and the other planets, without suffering any diminution do the same. Among terrestrial things musk does the same, and other perfumes.[29]

It would be going much too far to suggest that Leonardo had arrived at the concept of the vibratory nature of light-waves as described late in the nineteenth century by the British scientist Thomas Young, but in some respects, with these clear insights, Leonardo was certainly ahead of Christiaan Huygens who published his theory of the wave-like nature of light in 1690. Huygens made no mention of a transverse wave set up by a tremor which is precisely what Leonardo depicts in the above lengthy passage concerning the ripples created by stones thrown into water. Leonardo does not use a precise term like *transverse wave*, but his description is complete and accurate.

And indeed, Huygens may well have been aware of Leonardo's work. Christiaan Huygens, whom Isaac Newton called *summus Huygenius*, first published his great work on optics, *Traité de la Lumière*, in 1690. This established him as one of the most important scientists of the era. In the treatise, he expounds his wave-theory of light which, combined with Newton's *Opticks* of 1704, laid the foundations of optics for the next century and a half. However, in the Preface to the first edition, he comments that he first described the substance of his theory verbally twelve years earlier at a meeting of the Académie Royale des Sciences in Paris in 1678, but did not begin writing his account until some years later.

A few months before the publication of his masterwork, Huygens received a letter, dated 3 March 1690, from his brother Constantine, who was then living in Kensington, London. Constantine relates how he had purchased a manuscript by Leonardo for the princely sum of three and a half guineas.[30] He then gives a brief description of the contents and in particular, Leonardo's descriptions of perspective and his thoughts on light and shade.

What manuscript this could have been is unknown, as this letter is the only reference we have, and Constantine is vague about its contents. It could have been a fragment of a collection now safe in one of the Leonardo repositories scattered around the world, possibly part of the notes that went to comprise his *Trattato della Pittura*, or the letter could perhaps refer to a Da Vinci original since lost. But this must lead us inevitably to the question: in his Preface, did Christiaan Huygens write about his lecture of twelve years earlier so that the reader would know he had come to his own independent conclusions, to pre-empt anybody one day deciding that he had stolen the idea from Leonardo?

It is possible Huygens panicked and added an opening section to his *Traité de la Lumière*, but it is impossible to say for sure how much he was influenced by his brother's find, or indeed by manuscripts of Leonardo's he had perhaps seen in his younger days. The importance Constantine places upon describing his purchase in the letter might be put down to quite natural excitement over the find, or it could be because he knew his brother had a keen interest in the writings of Leonardo. Compare for example, Leonardo's description of how tremors cause the rippling of water with one of Huygens' central statements from *Traité de la lumière*. Leonardo wrote:

And the reason for this is that the water, although apparently moving, does not leave its original position, because the openings made by the stones close again immediately. Therefore the motion produced by the quick opening and closing of the water has caused only a shock which may be described as tremor rather than movement.

Whereas Huygens says:

The propagation does not consist in transportation of these particles but only in a little shock which they cannot but communicate to the particles surrounding them, despite all the movement that perturbs them and causes them to interchange places.[31]

The matter of plagiarism and priority are not so important as the mere fact that Leonardo, working with the most rudimentary equipment and living during an age when most philosophers subscribed to the view that light was produced by the eye and reflected off objects, could create a theory so close to that devised by a scientist living two hundred years later, a man seen as one of the great founders of the Scientific Enlightenment in Europe.

Leonardo was of course a very different scientist to Huygens, but in many ways he was a superior one. Newton, who as we have seen had a tremendous respect for Huygens, nevertheless engaged in often sharp exchanges with the Dutchman because Huygens had no interest in experiment and had done almost no experimental work to verify his ideas, ideas which had sprung almost entirely from reasoning alone. Leonardo could employ little knowledge of mathematics; he did not master more than the rudiments of the subject until the start of his friendship with Luca Pacioli in 1496, but long before then he had conducted dozens of experiments to investigate the nature and behaviour of light.

Furthermore, Leonardo is often criticised by modern scientists as well as philosophers and historians of science because he is perceived to have repeatedly gone too far in his assertions, bringing what is now viewed as mystical and metaphysical ideas into his statements that clouded his reasoning and descriptions.

An example of this is the way he tried to develop his view of an interconnected, holistic cosmos, amalgamating what appear to be very different aspects of the Universe he observed. Taking the behaviour of ripples or waves in water as his starting point, he goes on to say: 'The motion of earth beating against earth moves only slightly the parts struck. Water struck by water makes circles around the spot struck. For a longer distance, the voice within the air. Longer within fire. Further the mind within the Universe: but as it is finite, it cannot embrace the infinite.[32]

These are musings from a little notebook (now called *Manuscript H*) which Leonardo probably carried about with him and in which he jotted down partly resolved ideas. In this example, he starts off with observation and sound reasoning, then extends his ideas into a metaphysical realm unbounded either by convention or physical law. He limits himself with neither verifiable notions nor indeed religious censor. His vision expressed here is that all things are communicated by waves. At the bottom, in an echo of Aristotle, is earth, through which waves can only pass in a limited way; then water; sound through air, followed by light and heat from flame and culminating with the waves of thought produced by the mind, unbounded and capable of 'crossing the Universe', but, he adds, unable to pierce the infinite, as the mind is finite.

To hold the view that such metaphysical wanderings in some way diminish Leonardo's scientific ideas is, I believe, unfair. Although clearly Leonardo does often wander into the realms of metaphysics, he never lets this contaminate his purely scientific stance. Almost always, he states a principle and only then does he go on to what might be considered flights of imagination unsubstantiated by experiment or factual evidence. Even then, we should consider whether this is really a problem; it could be argued that many present-day particle physicists and cosmologists make a living doing precisely that. Furthermore, these ideas were expressed in notebooks, not scientific papers published in a journal.

I have noted how, during Leonardo's time, the accepted notion of light and its behaviour was a blend of Aristotelian and Platonic ideology. With Alhazen and Pecham as notable exceptions, there had been little development in the theory of optics since ancient Greek times. Leonardo realised this, was not content to rely upon ancient inherited wisdom, and set out to formulate a new and detailed theory of light.

His first original conclusion, and one diametrically opposed to the ideas of his contemporaries, was that light had a finite velocity. In *Manuscript F* he states: 'Look at light and consider its beauty. Close and open your eye and then look at it: what you see of it, was not before; and what there was of it, is no more.'[33]

Admittedly this sounds rather vague and contains echoes of Plato, but in a later manuscript, while demolishing the ancient notion that vision is due to particles emitted from the eye, Leonardo clarifies his reasoning concerning the need for light to have time to travel from a source, writing:

It is impossible that the eye should project the visual power from itself by visual rays, since, as soon as it opens, that front portion [of the eye] which would give rise to this emanation would have to go forth to the object, and *this it could not do without time* [author's italics]. And this being so, it could not travel as high as the sun in a month's time when the eye wanted to see it. And if it could reach the sun it would necessarily follow that it would perpetually remain in a continuous line from the eye to the sun and would always diverge in such a way as to form between the sun and the eye the base and the apex of a pyramid. This being the case, if the eye consisted of a million worlds, that would not suffice to prevent its being consumed in the projection of its power; and if this power had to travel through the air as perfumes do, the winds would bend it and carry it into another place. But we do in fact see the mass of the sun with the same rapidity with which we see an object at a distance of an ell [a unit of measurement], and the power of sight is not disturbed by the blowing of the winds nor by any other accident.[34]

This is an amazingly far-sighted observation. During the late seventeenth century, both Descartes and Huygens believed the propagation of light to be instantaneous and this was the view handed down since ancient times (hence the accepted notion that vision was facilitated by particles travelling from the eye). It was not until 1697, while observing the eclipses of the satellites of Jupiter, that the Danish astronomer Olaus Roemer discovered that light had a finite velocity.

From this work, Leonardo was then led to another conclusion predating what we accept as the conventional lineage of scientific discovery. The ancients had subscribed to the vaguely formulated notion that Nature followed the easiest and fastest path to any conclusion. Taking this as a starting point, Leonardo concluded that: 'Every action in nature takes place in the shortest possible way.'[35]

In 1657, the French mathematician Pierre de Fermat restated this as: '*La nature agit toujours par les voies les plus courtes.*' 'Nature always acts by the shortest paths.' But like Descartes, Fermat initially believed the propagation of light was instantaneous. This meant the concept of nature always following the shortest path was in fact a contradiction, and he gave up the idea. But by 1661 Fermat had decided that Descartes had been wrong about the speed of light and went on to reaffirm his statement (which is now known as Fermat's principle) and this was further supported by Roemer's conclusions fifteen years later. So, Leonardo's correct view of a property of light (its finite velocity) led him to another correct outcome: every action in Nature takes place in the shortest possible way, whereas the great minds of later generations were caught up in a sequence of wrong conclusions only disentangled after a great deal of further investigation.

Elsewhere, Leonardo made discoveries in optics and the characteristics of waves that would only find an established place in scientific understanding centuries later. While considering the behaviour of waves in water (the only physical method available to him for actually observing the behaviour of waves), he reports: 'If a stone is flung into motionless water, its circles will be equidistant from their centre. But if the stream is moving, these circles will be elongated, egg-shaped, and will travel with their centre away from the spot where they were created, following the stream.'[36]

This is clearly a description of what was rediscovered in the 1840s by Christian Doppler and Armand Fizeau and is today called the Doppler effect.

The Doppler effect accounts for the fact that as a source of sound moves towards or away from a listener, the pitch, or frequency, of the sound is higher or lower than when the source is at rest. A good example of this is the observed change in pitch as an ambulance or police car comes towards you and then speeds away. The phenomenon applies to all types of waves and is accounted for by the fact that, as a source approaches an observer, the waves in front of the source are bunched together so that the observer receives more waves during the same time than would have been received from a stationary source. As a consequence, the observer (or listener) perceives a rise in pitch. Conversely, if the source is moving away from the listener, the waves are spread out and fewer are received in a given time, resulting in a lower pitch. Compare this to Leonardo's '. . . if the stream is moving, these circles will be elongated, egg-shaped, and will travel with their centre away from the spot where they were created . . .'

And he performed the same trick again and again. A sheet of writing and drawings now in the Royal Library at Windsor shows a Leonardo experiment in which he splits the components of white light into its constituent parts using a prism.

His account of this experiment reads:

If you place a glass full of water on the windowsill so that the sun's rays will strike it from the other side, you will see the aforesaid colours formed in the impression made by the sun's rays that have penetrated through that glass and fallen in the dark at the foot of a window, and since the eye is not used here, we may with full certainty say that these colours are not in any way due to the eye.[37]

Newton famously re-created this experiment during the 1660s. He was almost certainly unaware of Leonardo's own description and we cannot fairly compare the sort of science Leonardo practised with that of Newton. Isaac Newton was the first to utilise the full power of mathematics and to combine mathematical conclusions with experimental findings creating modern deductive science and what has been called the scientific method. Leonardo used little mathematics and almost never combined it with experiment.[*]

Yet Leonardo had the idea of seeing what happened when light was passed through an improvised prism, perhaps by stumbling upon the effect in nature. This is an observation that had been made by many before him and, unlike Newton, Leonardo did not take the experiment very far. When he saw light split into its component parts he did not go on to create a theory to explain how the individual colours behaved, nor did he formulate any general rules to describe his observations in the way Newton did. But unlike the vast majority, who had simply noticed this phenomenon in Nature, Leonardo behaved as a true scientist. He did not merely leave his researches at a simple observational stage but investigated the phenomenon as fully as he deemed necessary. He wrote up his findings, drew an accurate representation of what he saw and then tried to fit his findings into his growing view of optics.

Leonardo also observed the phenomenon of refraction and wrote

---

[*] An exception is when Leonardo uses the concepts of proportion and comparison, such as when he described the results of using his own device for measuring the intensity of light (which some scholars claim is a photometer only rediscovered in the nineteenth century). Comparing intensities observed from the construction of a simple device using a flat card and a pair of candles, Leonardo writes: 'If light source xv is of the same kind as light source vy, the difference between the lights will be proportional to their size.'[38]

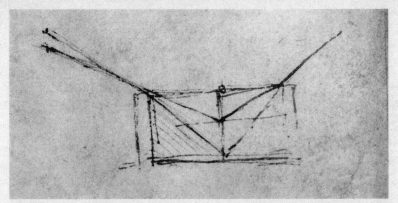

Fig. 7.5: Prism experiment after Alhazen.

about it clearly and concisely. He created no mathematical treatment of the phenomenon, leaving that to René Descartes during the 1630s, but, based upon a series of experiments to repeat the phenomenon, he extended the rudimentary observations made by Alhazen in the eleventh century, observing:

> Have two trays made parallel to each other . . . and let one be ⅕ smaller than the other, and of equal height. Then enclose one in the other and paint the outside, and leave uncovered a spot the size of a lentil, and have a ray of sunlight pass there coming from another opening or window. Then see whether or not the ray passing in the water enclosed between the two rays keeps the straightness it had outside. And form your rule from that.[39]

This is not only an ingenious experiment neatly described, but notice the final line of the account: 'And form your rule from that.' This is nothing short of a statement that Leonardo was proceeding via what would later become known as the scientific method, but minus any sophisticated mathematics. In other words: have your idea, do your experiment, create a hypothesis, develop a rule, repeat the experiment to verify; if not confirmed, then adjust experiment and hypothesis.

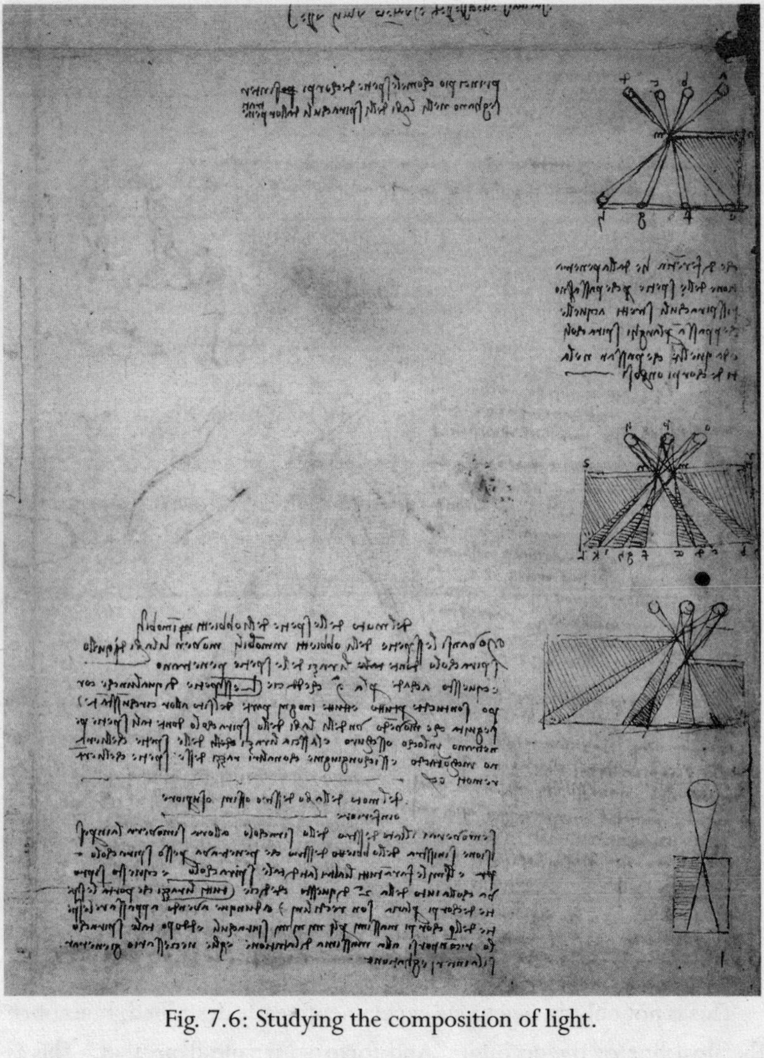

Fig. 7.6: Studying the composition of light.

And Leonardo achieved still more. Centuries before the astronomer Tycho Brahe, he discovered the phenomenon of atmospheric refraction. Brahe concluded that rays of light passing through the Earth's atmosphere travel in straight lines only if they are moving vertically with respect to the Earth's surface. Light waves passing through the atmosphere at any other angle are refracted by the air. Again, Brahe created a mathematical treatment for this phenomenon, but a century earlier and without the advantage of an observatory, Leonardo had described the effect perfectly:

> To see how the sun's rays penetrate this curvature of the sphere of the air, have two glass spheres made, one twice the size of the other, as round as can be. Then cut them in half and put one inside the other and close the fronts and fill with water and have the ray of sunlight pass as you did above [here he is referring to his earlier simpler refraction experiment, described above]. And see whether the ray is bent. *And thus you can make an infinite number of experiments. And form your rule* [my italics].[40]

And here we have further support for the fact that Leonardo regularly applied a form of scientific method. 'And thus you can make an infinite number of experiments,' he says, and with this states one of the key premises of modern scientific undertaking.

The reason why the sky appears blue is another problem explained by a consideration of the principles of optics. This was done by Lord Rayleigh in 1871. He realised the colour was due to the diffraction of sunlight by particles in the air. Staggeringly, Leonardo got there three hundred years before him. In the *Codex Leicester*, he writes:

> I say that the blue which is seen in the atmosphere is not its own colour, but is caused by the heated moisture having evaporated into the most minute and imperceptible particles, which the beams of the solar rays attract and cause to seem luminous against the deep, intense darkness of the region of fire that forms a covering among them.[41]

These findings in optics represent some of Leonardo's finest scientific achievements and are comparable to his discoveries in anatomy (discussed in Chapter 10). The fact that optics was so important to Leonardo and his researches so fruitful should come as no surprise. He was, after all, as much an artist as he was an engineer and scientific experimenter; with the study of optics he was dealing with phenomena he understood instinctively and had been working with almost his entire life.

But of course because of Leonardo's eclectic tastes and free-ranging intellect he could not have been content with these scientific investigations alone. As he researched the behaviour of light, he was also becoming increasingly interested in the principles of mechanics.

It might be argued that he was drawn to this study through his fascination with the human machine. His planned book, *On the Human Body*, was not proposed as a simple analysis of parts; it was to have had a broad overview, in which Leonardo perceived the human body as a single unit. Leonardo's manuscripts of the early 1490s are littered with little figures of humans in motion, each showing an aspect of the human machine in its many contortions. Along with the drawings, some mere matchstick figures, others detailed and intricate, there are passages in which Leonardo notes his findings, demonstrating further the fascination with comparative proportion and the holistic approach so dear to him.

When a man jumps high, the head has three times the velocity of the heel of the foot, before the tip of the foot leaves the ground and twice the velocity of the hips. This is because three angles extend themselves at the same time of which the uppermost is where the torso joins the thighs in front, and the second is where the backs of the thighs join the backs of the legs, and the third is where the fronts of the legs join the bones of the feet.[42]

From these studies he began to see animal physiology as engineering;

the joints and tendons he compared to hinges and winches, the muscles and bones he saw as gears and levers in a mechanical device; and from this he began to think about the fundamental forces of movement and action. All of this then led him to broad overarching statements, such as, 'Motion is the cause of every life.'[43]

Again, this may be viewed as Leonardo taking an idea too far and making a vague, metaphysical statement at the end of an investigation rather than giving the sort of precise but deliberately limited statement of a modern scientist. But then it should be remembered that modern science is hard-pressed to define 'life', and our empirical definitions are no clearer nor more precise than what many today would consider to be often vague statements derived from philosophical considerations. To Leonardo, all living things expressed movement, but of course it is clear that some non-living things do too, so a comment such as 'motion is the cause of every life' is, in the strictest sense, no less 'scientific' than twenty-first century descriptions of the same thing.

Leonardo's successes as a military engineer, his achievements in the Milanese theatre and his designs for such things as a parachute, mechanised vehicles, pumps, irrigation systems and digging machines amply demonstrate his practical genius. Unfortunately this practical mastery was not matched by his understanding of the theoretical principles of the subject.

During the period in which he first committed his ideas to paper, Leonardo's appreciation of such concepts as force, inertia and impetus was almost purely Aristotelian. These were sprinkled with what he had gleaned from medieval thinkers, in particular the work of the fourteenth-century natural philosopher, Jean Buridan, who had made attempts to modernise Aristotle's theories of motion.

Aristotle's mechanics held that all things move according to their nature. This, as we saw in Chapter 2, depended upon the proportions of the four elements in the object; fire rose above the other three, the highest or lightest of these three being air, then water and the heaviest, earth. Aristotle combined this with the idea of the Unmoved Mover, the omnipotent being who controlled the movement of the stars and the planets. Aristotle explained the movement of such things as projectiles using a principle that later became known as antiperistasis. This stated that a stone or any projectile continued its motion through the air because, as it moved, the displaced air in front of the object flowed behind it instantaneously and pushed it forward.

Later thinkers such as Buridan and the fifteenth-century mechanicist Biagio Palacani, both of whom Leonardo studied, suggested that the motion of a body once set in motion was facilitated by a motive power (*virtus motiva*) which remained with it until it ebbed away, a little like the loss of heat from a warm body, or the discharging of an electrical current.

During the 1480s and early 1490s Leonardo toed the Aristotelian line, writing such things as:

Force is . . . an immaterial power, an invisible potency which is created and infused by animated bodies in inanimate ones through acquired violence, giving to these bodies the appearance of life; this life of marvellous efficiency compelling and transmuting all created things from their places. It rushes with fury to its destruction and continues changing in accordance with the causes. Slowness makes it last longer and speed diminishes it. It lives by violence and dies at liberty . . . Great power gives it a great desire for death. It drives away with fury whatever opposes its self-destruction . . . Nothing moves without it.[44]

This, from a notebook of 1492, almost personifies force as though it were a living thing and Leonardo appears to subscribe almost exactly to the medieval adaptation of Aristotelianism, the idea that force is 'an entity' possessed by an object which drains away during an action, the more violent the action the faster the loss: 'Great power gives it a great desire for death'. But gradually he began to formulate an amalgam of Aristotelian and modern ideology, leading him to draw conclusions such as: 'No dissimilar body will ever come to rest within another if it is at liberty to move . . . The thing which is most dissimilar will separate itself from the other with the greatest movement.'[45] This is a significant move away from the traditional Classical principle that all things find their level according to their elemental nature, but it still places the emphasis upon moving the object by its nature rather than via external forces.

But by 1497, a mere five years on, Leonardo had clearly become disillusioned with this halfway house and had begun to struggle to find a new, more accurate path. Realising there was much to be discovered and that philosophers other than Aristotle may hold the key, he wrote another of his notes to himself:

What is the cause of movement; what movement is in itself; what is it that is most adapted to movement; what is impetus; what is the cause of impetus in the medium in which it is created; what is percussion; what is its cause; what is rebound; what is the curve of straight movement and its cause? – Aristotle, 3rd [book] of the *Physics* and Albertus [Magnus] and Thomas [Aquinas] and others on the rebound; in the 7th [book] of the *Physics*, and *De caelo et mundo* [also a work by Aristotle].[46]

Leonardo never did master the theoretical basis of mechanics. Part of the reason for this was his weakness as a mathematician. His understanding of how force and motion operated improved as his mathematical skills developed under the tutelage of Pacioli, but, because he was never a natural mathematician, he never truly grasped the primary concepts of mechanical theory. And so we are presented with the startling irony that such a brilliant practical engineer and a man so capable when it came to designing a vast array of machines and creating engineering techniques never really understood the fundamental theoretical concepts behind many of his creations.[*]

By about 1490 Leonardo had brought together an impressive collection of notes and studies covering a plethora of subjects, and by 1495 he was able to list some forty books in his personal library.[47] These were mostly printed volumes dealing with a range of subjects as eclectic as you would expect from Leonardo. These works covered the intellectual spectrum, from Ovid to Albertus Magnus, including a *Chronicle of St Isidore*, a book about memory, another on surgery, a treatise on rhetoric and many of the great classics, Livy's *Decades*, Pliny's *Natural History* and Aristotle's *Physics*. But for some years he had also enjoyed resources beyond his own growing collection, including the magnificent library at Pavia and the monastic collections at S. Ambrogio and others in Milan. And what he could not discover in institutions, he unravelled by investigation and conversation with those he respected in the various disciplines that interested him. He would then write notes to himself to make enquiries of those within the city and beyond. 'Try to get *Vitolone* [a treatise on perspective by the natural philosopher Witelo] which is in the library of Pavia,' he noted.[48]

And what was Leonardo's ultimate aim at this time? Clearly, he was not pursuing anything that interested him simply for the sake of it, but appears to have been planning to produce an encyclopaedia, a lexicon detailing the sum of human knowledge up to this point. How far he got with this may be seen from his burgeoning collection of notes and manuscripts. Of particular interest is a manuscript now known as *Codex Trivulzianus* which contains a list of nearly a thousand words and terms which Leonardo has defined in different degrees. Some of these words are merely listed while others are explained and illustrated with examples.

---

[*] As we shall see in Chapter 10, an exception to this was his flying machines. Leonardo's understanding of aerodynamics was actually amazingly sophisticated.

During the first half of the twentieth century, some historians tried to analyse Leonardo's character from this list, but their use of dubious Freudian ideas which attempt to imply that within the list and its arrangement may be gleaned insights into the man's sexuality, his obsession with work and his paranoia, are now viewed with justifiable scepticism. It is at least as reasonable to assume Leonardo either wrote lists in the *Codex Trivulzianus* randomly, or that he had some personal reason for collecting them in the way he did.

By his final years in Milan, Leonardo had begun to spread his net still wider. While describing the use of military hardware and designing machines as varied as parachutes and water pumps, he was writing on religion and philosophy and all the while continuing to draw together the threads of his holistic world-view. And by the time he was packing up to leave the city in which he had done his finest work, he had reached a new and original conclusion. Borrowing a little from Aristotle, blending it with neo-Platonic ideology, the exactness of Archimedes and combining all these with his own unique insight, he formulated the concept of 'the four powers', or what he called *potenze*.

The *potenze* were motion, weight, force and percussion and were the key to all action and phenomena in the Universe, hence his declaration that 'Motion is the cause of every life.' This concept was the summation of his years of theorising, and using this concept he found what he believed to be connections between the motion of a river and the proportions of a cathedral, the mechanism of sight and the flight of a bird, the insights of the painter and the analytical power of the engineer, mathematician and logician.

So, more than half a millennium after Leonardo scratched his thoughts into his notebooks, what are we to make of all this effort, these declarations and hypotheses? After studying Leonardo's words and probing his thoughts, we are left with many questions.

First: was this work really science?

The answer to this depends upon how one interprets 'science'. The traditional definition of science is the application of the inductive method credited to the philosopher Francis Bacon, and brought to maturity by Isaac Newton. We saw in Chapter 2 how this definition requires that a scientist must formulate a hypothesis which is elevated to the status of a theory upon experimental verification. A general rule, or law, is then created to describe the process derived from the theory and this may then be applied to a range of situations. If experiment or application of the theory is unrepeatable, the hypothesis remains just that and the scientist has to start again and to rework the original idea. It is because of this definition we now consider the Greeks to have been philosophers rather than true scientists because they based many of their ideas upon *a priori* principles and saw no value in experiment.

Leonardo was a skilled experimenter who attempted to verify his ideas with precise observation and measurement. He recorded his findings with meticulous care and attempted to draw general conclusions from his observations. If he found an experiment did not fit with his original idea then he reworked the idea and started again. Indeed, Leonardo wrote often on the subject of how science should be conducted and what role it should play.

And in fact it happens that whenever reason is wanting [he wrote], men cry out against one another, which does not happen with certainties. For this reason we shall say that where the cry of controversy is heard there is no true science, because the truth has a single end and when this is published, argument is destroyed forever. But true sciences are those which, impelled by hope, have been penetrated by the senses so that the tongues of argument are silenced. They are not nourished on the dreams of investigators, but proceed in orderly sequence from the first true and established principles through successive stages to the end; as is shown by the elements of mathematics. That is to say, number, measure, called arithmetic and geometry, which with complete truth treat of quantities both discontinuous and continuous. In them one does not argue if twice three makes more or less than six, or that the angles of a triangle are less than the sum of two right angles: all argument is reduced to eternal silence, and those who are devoted to them can enjoy them with peace which the lying sciences of the mind can never attain.[49]

The science historian W. C. Dampier has said of Leonardo:

His performance, extraordinary as it was, must be reckoned as small compared with the ground he opened up, the grasp of fundamental principles he displayed, and the insight with which he seized upon the true methods of investigation in each branch of enquiry. Leonardo perceived intuitively and used effectively the right experimental method a century before Francis Bacon philosophised about it inadequately, and Galileo put it into practice.[50]

If science is only science when it is rooted completely in a combination of mathematical analysis and experiment, then many would argue that Leonardo could not be defined as a scientist. However, if we view science in only a slightly broader way and think of it as an approach to unravelling the Universe by experiment and reasoning, then he most certainly was a scientist. Coupled with this is the fact that his science was well in advance of the Classical tradition in that he believed in the over-riding importance of experiment, whereas almost all his contemporaries adhered unquestioningly to Aristotle, Plato and other Greek and Roman philosophers who actively scorned experiment. Leonardo also did use mathematics, albeit in a simplistic way. Perhaps more significantly, he realised the huge importance of mathematics as a means of defining observation and enabling the scientist to draw overarching conclusions that may then be applied to different situations from that explicit in the experiment. We may only wonder what he might have achieved if he had been as talented as a mathematician as he was in so many other areas of human knowledge and understanding.

The second question that presents itself is: was Leonardo original?

Not entirely. In spite of his stated aversion to Classical learning and acquired knowledge, we can see, even in this brief summary of his efforts, that he did rely upon ancient and medieval sources and used ideas offered by his learned friends and acquaintances. Where Leonardo was original was in his remarkable extrapolations upon inherited wisdom. He took his study of optics far further than anyone before him and was indeed hundreds of years ahead of his time in certain aspects of the science. And as we shall see in Chapter 10, he also achieved wonders in anatomical research at the same time as he was making far-reaching discoveries in optics. Furthermore, he developed technology way beyond the ideas of Francis Bacon, the man considered to be the founding father of technology.

What is undeniable is that Leonardo had many of the talents and skills of the scientist, and more importantly a collection of other abilities almost no other scientist in history has been privileged to possess. He had a probing mind, he was determined to unravel the secrets of the Universe, and he was analytical and methodical. But perhaps more important than all these, Leonardo had three great advantages over all others.

First, unlike Copernicus or Galileo, he lived during an age and in a part of Europe temporarily free from over-zealous religious fervour. Second, he had a powerful and free-ranging imagination unshackled by tradition or limited by technique; quite simply he could and did do anything he wanted within the realm of intellectual investigation. And third, he had a unique ability to express his observations and his findings in pictorial form and to accompany this with literary eloquence using a simple style that cut away confusion and obfuscation. Leonardo could give us an overall image of the world (albeit flawed in places), and this makes him not only a great unraveller of what was previously a mystery, but a man exceptionally able to communicate his findings and his vision to the rest of us down through the centuries.

8

THE PERIPATETIC SAGE

I would prefer to lose the power of movement than that of usefulness. I would prefer death to inactivity . . . I never tire of being useful.

— Leonardo

By the beginning of the new century, and as Leonardo was approaching the end of his forty-eighth year, he had spent almost his entire life in only three places: the tiny village of Anchiano and the cities of Florence and Milan. But now, with his patron in exile and the French occupying Milan, he was to enter a period during which he would stay in any one place for no longer than a few years (and more often merely a few months) and begin working for many different people both as painter and engineer.

By this time, Leonardo was famous throughout Italy. This fame had come primarily from his unparalleled artistic genius, but he was also nurturing a growing reputation as an expert on military engineering. It is clear that very few were aware of his devotion to science or even of the existence of his manuscripts. He was seen as a man with two great talents; during peacetime and periods of affluence he could, if pinned down, produce the most beautiful works of art, and during times of war he could advise leaders and develop schemes to solve military conundrums.

Few knew of his scientific researches; those close to him, Salai and Pacioli and perhaps a few friends at the Milanese court, were aware of his private studies, and he may have revealed some of his ideas to the French nobility at some point soon after the occupation of Milan. This is supported by a letter from Charles d'Amboise to the Florentine Signoria written a few years after meeting Leonardo, in which he claimed he had loved the man for his painting before he had met him, but that Leonardo had been ignored for his other excellent gifts including 'drawings, architecture and other things that are required'.[1]

In spite of the general ignorance of his polymathic intellect, Leonardo's famed skills were enough to open doors for him during the following half-decade as he travelled between the great Italian cities with Salai, sometimes accompanied by Pacioli and often with an entourage of assistants and servants.

It is clear Leonardo displayed no loyalty to any particular state or patron. His itinerant lifestyle during the first decade of the new century was forced upon him by the political convolutions of powerful schemers. Besides, the concept of loyalty to a particular state or country would have been quite alien to many people of this time and in particular to a man like Leonardo, who had never displayed the slightest interest in politics and who saw himself as a 'citizen of the world'. If he was to find work with an enemy of Milan or Florence this did not disturb him unduly, and if that work entailed a challenge such as that offered by applying his skills as a military engineer, then any qualms were further appeased. Florence had shown him little loyalty and Milan was now in French hands; beyond this, the kaleidoscope of the Italian political scene was forever shifting, which meant an enemy of one state may be a friend a few years later.

Leonardo now had his own agenda within which he placed his scientific research first, and so he needed an income to support himself and his household as well as to finance his experiments. To this end, he would have preferred work as a military engineer which applied many of his theoretical ideas explored through experiment, but if such work could not be found, he could always paint for a living.

From Milan he travelled, through the hard north Italian winter, 140 kilometres east to the city state of Mantua where he was received personally by Isabella d'Este, the elder sister of *Il Moro*'s dead wife, Beatrice d'Este.

Isabella had met Leonardo at Sforza's court many times and was a great admirer of his work. She was also something of a connoisseur and a keen collector of the work of contemporary artists. Said to be one of the most beautiful women of her time, she was also arrogant and opinionated, and although she paid handsomely for commissions offered to her favourites, she was not content to let them paint as they wished; she invariably dictated their design and layout, the type of background for portraits and the position of the subject, even stipulating the colours the artist should use.

Isabella's interest in art and her dealings with many of the great artists of the era was known throughout the courts of Italy, and she had actively encouraged her image as a patron. Less well advertised, but almost certainly known to Leonardo before his visit, were the way she had interfered with commissions and her appalling behaviour towards at least two of Leonardo's highly regarded contemporaries. She had forced Giovanni Bellini through the courts to get the painting she had demanded of him, and with an exchange of no less than fifty-three letters she had hounded Perugino to change his ideas to suit hers for a painting she had commissioned from him called *Combat of Love and Chastity*.

Until this visit, Leonardo had not painted for Isabella, but for some years she had been trying to get him to accept a commission. Two years earlier she had written to Cecilia Gallerani, Sforza's former mistress whom Leonardo had painted some fifteen years earlier, asking if she could borrow the painting. Cecilia had declined with the diplomatic and perhaps overly modest argument that although she loved the painting, it was no longer a fair likeness.

Why Leonardo had resisted Isabella's approaches is unclear, and is further confused because there seems to have been no apparent reason why he should have travelled to Mantua rather than any other city. He may have been invited there, and most probably saw it as a convenient stepping-stone towards a more permanent place to set up home. It was also close to Milan so that he could return there if circumstances became favourable.

Even so, while at her court, Leonardo did produce a portrait of Isabella, a drawing in profile using black lead and red chalk. Although the artist may have been guided by the lady's instructions, the execution itself is all Leonardo. Now in the Louvre, the drawing has been copied many times. Leonardo must have been pleased with the result because he employed a technique that allowed him to copy it later himself, using a needle to imprint the profile on to another piece of paper. He took this copy with him when he left Mantua with the promise he would present Isabella with a full, completed portrait just as soon as he could. But once again Leonardo was to renege on a promise.

Leonardo tarried in Mantua for no more than two months and his reasons for leaving are as unclear as the intentions with which he arrived there. It is quite probable he become exasperated by Isabella's attitude; she may have tried to interfere with his work, something he could never have tolerated for a moment. But it is also likely he had never intended to stay in the city for long. By late February or early March he was once more on the road, this time heading further east towards Venice.

The choice of Venice was a logical one. It was a rich and powerful city, Pacioli had many contacts there and it would, Leonardo reasoned, offer ample opportunity for a man of his abilities. It is even possible Leonardo and Pacioli had been invited there, but there is no documentary evidence to support this.

The group arrived in San Marco early in March 1500. The exact date is unknown, but Leonardo was certainly there by 13 March because a friend of Pacioli's, the musical instrument maker Lorenzo Gugnasco, sent a lute to Isabella d'Este with a letter in which he tells her he has seen the drawing of her (presumably he meant Leonardo's outline) which he declared, '. . . is in every point a perfect likeness. In fact it is so good that one could not do better. That is all I shall say of it in this letter.'[2]

This was the first time Leonardo had witnessed the glories of Venice first-hand. Unfortunately, we know nothing of his thoughts about the city, the architecture or the countless treasures, for if Leonardo wrote anything on the subject nothing has come down to us. It is inconceivable that he was so absorbed by his work in the city he found no time to sketch St Mark's or the grand sweep of the Doge's palace. He mentions many of the people with whom he came into contact: Alvise Salamon, a Venetian captain;[3] Antonio Frisi, a Council of Justice;[4] and the highly respected Veronese architect Fra Giocondo;[5] but he makes no personal comments, nothing about his feelings or his emotional state.

Venice was a magnet for the greatest artists and thinkers of the day, but the arrival of two of Italy's most famous intellectuals at the same time – Leonardo da Vinci, foremost artist of the age, and Luca Pacioli, the most respected mathematician in Italy – could not have failed to attract the attention of the Council and perhaps even the Doge, Agostino Barbarigo himself. But more important than the fanfare accompanying their arrival would have been the timing of their visit, for at that moment the Venetians were in dire need of a man like Leonardo – the armies of the Ottoman Empire were encamped only fifty miles from the capital itself.

But then, perhaps the timing was no mere coincidence. It would seem unlikely that Leonardo had travelled to Venice merely because Pacioli had contacts there. His fame had preceded him and it is possible he had been invited to Venice by the governing council to help them solve the military crisis they now faced.

Venice had long been the most despised enemy of Milan and when, through his own misreading of the situation, *Il Moro*'s territory had come under threat from French forces, he had made the astute political move of persuading the Turks to attack Venice, thus keeping her armies fully occupied while Milan pitted her forces against the troops of Louis XII.

Actually, the Turks had needed little persuasion. Perpetual enemies of Venice, their ambitions in Dalmatia to the east and Friuli to the north were even more ancient than the enmity between Venice and Milan. By the time Leonardo had arrived in the city, the forces of the Turkish ruler Sultan Bajazet II were at the very walls of Vicenza, two days' march from the Lido. They had taken Venetian prisoners and were at that very moment building forces for what looked ominously like a full-scale attack on the lagoon itself.

The Venetians were close to panic. They had realised the weak point in their frontier defences lay in the Isonzo valley to the north of Venice, where a large army could gather to descend upon the city. Before Leonardo's arrival, some had suggested building fortifications there to resist the advance of the enemy. Nothing had been done about it, but within days of occupying rooms in the city, Leonardo was taken to Friuli to assess the situation.

He came to the immediate conclusion that some form of movable wooden dam should be built across the Isonzo which would re-route its course and allow the build-up of a large body of water. If the Turks launched an attack, the dam could be opened and their armies swept away. In his report to the Council, he said:

Illustrious Sirs, having noted that from whatever part of the mainland the Turks may reach our Italian lands, they must pass by the Isonzo valley. Although I recognise the fact that no lasting defence can be set up at that point, still we must admit that a few men with the help of such a river are worth many without it . . . I have

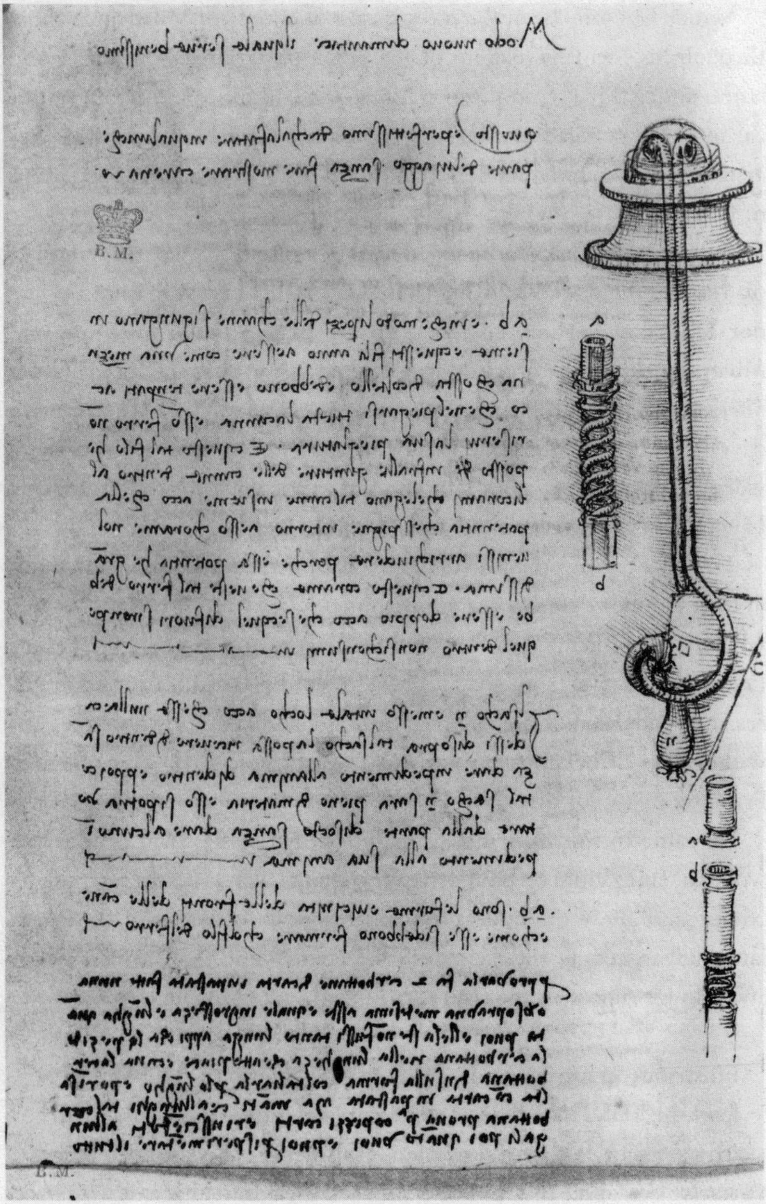

Fig. 8.1: Diving equipment.

concluded that there is no single place where the defence of a site would be of more universal value than at that river.[6]

For reasons still unknown, the Venetians rejected Leonardo's idea. Perhaps they viewed it as practically impossible or absurdly expensive. Yet the situation was worsening by the day. In March, Alvise Manetti, the Secretary of the Venetian Republic entrusted with negotiating with Sultan Bajazet II, returned with an offer of settlement of the conflict, but the terms, which included the handing-over of almost all the Venetian territories in the Peloponnese, were rejected immediately.

In the *Codex Atlanticus*, Leonardo mentions meetings with Manetti immediately after his return from Constantinople during which a new set of ideas was discussed. Leonardo writes these notes beside designs for submarines and diving apparatus that look incredibly modern.

Leonardo worked hard on schemes in which a clandestine attack could be launched against the Turkish invaders. His first new proposal was to send a group of submarines to 'gore the flanks' of the Turkish ships at anchor.[7] He then elaborated this, suggesting that divers could be sent to do the same job and would breathe by means of a tube which ran from a mask to just above the surface. This was not a new idea of Leonardo's; a sketch for this apparatus appeared in one of his earliest manuscripts dating from around 1475 when he was working for Verrocchio in Florence.

But this idea was also soon rejected when it was realised the enemy might see the tubes of the divers. Leonardo then developed an even more adventurous scheme involving a commando-style attack using a small group of volunteers dressed in special diving suits and carrying their own air supply in wineskins strapped to their backs. Walking along the sea-bed and armed with knives, the commandos would position themselves under the ships and gouge holes in the hulls. In his notes, Leonardo describes the diving equipment in intimate detail: 'A diving suit which covers the body from top to toe, with a vent to urinate and a breastplate that contains a tank, which by means of an iron semi-circle is held well away from the chest itself . . .'[8] He even detailed the way the suit could be constructed and fitted: 'Get a simple-minded fellow to do the job and have him sew the suit up for you at home.'[9]

It is unclear whether Leonardo ever showed these schemes to the Venetian authorities. On the one hand, he records how much he hoped to earn from the proposal, maximising his earnings from rewards offered for the release of prisoners held by the Turks.[10] But on the other, he expresses concern about the potential misuse of what he had created, believing that such an invention could be used in what he saw as a future war beneath the sea. Beside one set of notes, he comments: 'How and why is it that I do not describe my method for remaining underwater and how long I can remain there without coming up for air? I do not wish to divulge or publish this because of the evil nature of men, who might use it for murder on the sea-bed.'[11]

Perhaps he placed these fears above his hopes for financial gain. He was certainly no longer poor, despite the fact that he had to support Salai, to maintain his entourage and provide for their travelling expenses and accommodation. However, if he did propose these schemes to the Venetians they must have all been rejected.

Leonardo left Venice almost immediately after he had completed his scheme for a submarine attack. The accepted line considered by many historians is that he had finally grown tired of the rejection of the hard-pressed Venetians and decided to seek employment elsewhere. But this assumes he did in fact offer his proposals to them, an idea which is not supported by any surviving documentary evidence and indeed contradicts the tone of his only known comment on the matter mentioned above. So there may have been other reasons for leaving.

Soon after he arrived in the city, Leonardo learned that *Il Moro* was trying to recapture Milan from the French. It is therefore quite possible he decided to stay in Venice only long enough to see how his former master fared. However, any hopes for the Duke's return were soon dashed. In early March, Sforza mounted a counter-attack using an army comprised of eight thousand Swiss mercenaries. He succeeded in retaking Milan itself but was then overwhelmed at Novara by a superior French force. His mercenary army decided they did not want to fight that day and deserted him. *Il Moro* was forced to disguise himself as a foot soldier but was betrayed by one of his own men and the French took him captive, parading him in the streets of Lyon before incarcerating him in the castle at Loches in Touraine, where he died eight years later.

With the way ahead now clear, Leonardo was quick to move on. By 10 April the French were once more in control of Milan, and according to a brief but enthusiastic note in the *Codex Atlanticus*[12] Leonardo was planning to meet the commander of the French forces, Count Louis de Ligny, whom he had known since the occupation of Milan at the end of the previous year. The note reads: 'Go and find *Ligny* and tell him you will wait for him at *Rome* and that you will go with him to *Naples* to get the *donation*.'

Not only is this an interesting note because it refers to a journey to find what appears to be important work with the French, but it is written in a very odd way. As we know, Leonardo wrote almost everything in his notebooks using reverse or mirror writing. This note is no different except that certain words (in italics) have been written the 'normal' way round. What was the reason for this? Did he think that such a simple device would render the note less readable to prying eyes, or was it for some other, still unresolved, reason?

So once again Leonardo went with the flow of events. Almost exactly at the moment his ideas may have been rejected by the Venetians, he learned of the irredeemable loss of his patron and quickly placed his hopes with another plan. But there could have been other reasons for his leaving Venice so soon after arriving there. Unthinkable as it may seem to most of us, Leonardo may not have liked the place very much. We saw in Chapter 1 how Leonardo's childhood experience of floods and hurricanes may have engendered in him a deep-rooted fear of water. From his own writings about water, it is clear he was acutely aware of its power. Leonardo had lived his entire life in inland cities and his visit to Venice may even have been his first experience of the sea, so it is conceivable he felt extremely uncomfortable there, which might account for the total absence of any personal remarks or observations about the city in his notebooks.

Yet what was Leonardo doing in Venice but working on schemes intimately involved with large volumes of water? Was his obsession with this project not only generated by dreams of financial rewards and the satisfaction of seeing his schemes in action, but subconsciously a way in which he could learn to deal with his anxieties and fears? We see Leonardo's preoccupation with water throughout his notebooks and in particular his detailed plans to tame water, and late in life, a series of drawings of deluges and catastrophes featuring large uncontrollable masses of water. The political flux during his brief sojourn in Venice propelled him to leave and he may have been antagonised by the Venetians' apparent lack of interest, but for subconscious (but nevertheless very powerful reasons) he may have been quite content to depart.

Leonardo did not meet Louis de Ligny in Rome, nor indeed in Naples, and the French commander suddenly left Italy altogether to return to France. Whether or not Leonardo had already packed and made ready to leave Venice when he heard this, we do not know, but it appears he quickly changed his plans again. By the end of April he was back in Florence, the city he had left as a disillusioned and out-of-favour artist almost two decades earlier.

During the time Leonardo had been away, Florence had gone through its own radical transformations. Six years earlier, in 1494, Ludovico Sforza's political scheming had opened up much of Italy to the advancing French who were invited into Florence and promptly expelled the Medici from power. In this confused climate, a Dominican reformer, named Girolamo Savonarola, became virtual dictator. He was a teacher of theology at the Florentine priory of San Marco whose sermons expounded fire, brimstone and impending doom for the pleasure-seekers of the Medici era, and after gaining power he immediately imposed a programme of sweeping moral reforms and began to see himself as ordained for power by God.

His rule was marked by the burning of what he viewed as immoral texts and works of art, a regime that gained the name 'Bonfire of the Vanities'. These actions alienated many, but gained the support of a surprisingly large number who had become disaffected by the Medici. Soon the Borgia Pope, Alexander VI, began to perceive Savonarola as a threat and the Dominican monk was excommunicated. But he ignored this and continued to enforce a fundamentalist theocracy until even his own supporters grew sickened by his fanaticism and he was destroyed by Alexander through clandestine manipulation of the Florentine opposition party. Arrested, tortured and tried for heresy, Savonarola was hanged and then burned.

Many of Leonardo's friends had suffered during Savonarola's dominance. Botticelli's work had been denounced as decadent and he had been unable to secure commissions for almost the entire period between 1494 and the Dominican's execution in 1498. Others had fared better. Approved by Savonarola, the artist who had most prospered was Filippino Lippi, the man who had taken on some of the early projects Leonardo had either ignored or half-finished before leaving Florence. Another was Domenico Ghirlandaio whose reputation had grown with the revolution.

It is difficult to judge how Piero da Vinci's life and career had progressed during the twenty years since his son was last in Florence, and in particular how Savonarola's regime had affected him. There is almost no surviving correspondence between Leonardo and his father, and the only scrap that reveals any personal contact between them comes from an undated fragment most probably from Leonardo's final years in Milan, during which he shows concern for some problem Piero was experiencing:

Dearly beloved father, on the last day of last month, I received the letter that you wrote me and that in the space of an instant gave me pleasure and sadness. I had the pleasure of learning that you are in good health and give thanks to God; and I was unhappy to learn of your trouble.[13]

By the time Leonardo was again in Florence, Ser Piero was living with his fourth wife, another notary's daughter, Lucrezia di Guglielmo, in a new house on the Via Ghibellina with his eleven children who were then aged between two and twenty-four years old. We know of no specific meetings or dealings between Leonardo and Ser Piero during this time, but even if the lawyer's first-born felt little for his father (which may or may not have been the case), it is almost certain he would have dropped into the house in Via Ghibellina to pay his respects and acquaint himself with his new half-siblings.

We actually know very little about Leonardo's day-to-day life in Florence during the following two years. He makes few specific notes relating to his time there and almost everything we have comes from a set of correspondence between Isabella d'Este and her representative in Florence, Fra Pietro da Novellara, through which she kept trying to persuade Leonardo to fulfil his verbal promise of a full portrait. The exchange began with a letter from Isabella, in which she writes:

Most Reverend Father, if Leonardo the Florentine painter is at present in Florence, we pray you to inform us about the life he is leading, that is, whether he has some work in progress, as we have been told, and if so, of what kind, and whether he is likely to remain long in the city. Would you have the goodness to ask him, as if the request came from yourself, if it would be convenient for him to paint a picture for my apartment? If he agrees, we will leave to him the choice of date and subject. If he is reluctant, try at least to persuade him to paint us a little Madonna full of faith and sweetness, as it is in his nature to paint them.[14]

The work Isabella had heard about was a genuine commission, one originally offered Filippino Lippi who, either out of generosity or because he was already overworked, had passed it on to Leonardo. The commission was for an altarpiece for a Servite convent, but once again Leonardo was agreeing to a piece of work he apparently had little intention of working upon with any seriousness. Vasari tells us:

He returned to Florence, where he found that the Servite Friars had entrusted to Filippino the painting of the panel for the high altar of the Nunziata, whereupon Leonardo said that he would willingly have done such a work. Filippino, having heard this, like the amiable fellow he was, retired from the undertaking; and the friars, to the end that Leonardo might paint it, took him into their house, meeting the expenses both of himself and all his household; and thus he kept them in expectation for a long time, but never began anything.[15]

This image of Leonardo is very different from the one with which we are familiar. It is one thing not finishing a project but starting with good intentions; it is quite another to deliberately take expenses and accommodation without ever having any plans to complete one's side of the bargain; and this from Vasari. We learn from the notebooks that Leonardo was spending most of his days on other things, conducting experiments on percussion and acoustics as well as continuing his mathematical investigations under Pacioli's guidance. But, as we will see, Vasari is confused about Leonardo's behaviour and his unusually abrasive comments are uncalled for, because Leonardo did not let the friars down entirely.

How much Isabella d'Este's contact, Fra Pietro da Novellara, was aware of Leonardo's other interests is uncertain, but he seems to have realised the great man was distracted and overworked, claiming in his reply to Isabella: '. . . the existence of Leonardo is so unstable and uncertain that one might say he lives from day to day,' and goes on to describe Leonardo's work for the friars.[16]

Isabella appears unconvinced by this and pushed the monk to find out more. A week later, he wrote to her again, this time after questioning those close to Leonardo. Reporting that the artist was absorbed with mathematics, he added that he was now 'weary of the brush'.[17]

Still undeterred, Isabella next tried to establish a direct link with Leonardo and made the odd move of sending him two antique vases with a request for his opinion concerning their value. There is no record of what Leonardo thought of the vases, but he probably wrote a simple reply to satisfy the demanding Isabella but still offered no comment about a commission, which had of course been the real reason for her correspondence.

Even so, she continued to chase Leonardo for several more years. Two years after her attempt to interest him in antiques, through her agent, Angelo del Tovaglia, she offered Leonardo a substantial reward to paint for her and then even sent him a personal letter:

Master Leonardo, learning that you have settled in Florence, we have formed the hope of achieving our desire . . . When you came to see us, you drew our portrait in chalk and promised one day to paint it in colour; but understanding that it would be hard for you to keep your promise, since it would mean your returning here, we pray you to be good enough to discharge your commitments to us by replacing our portrait by a picture of Christ as a child of about twelve years old, that is, when he disputed with doctors in the Temple, and to execute it with the charm and sweetness which are to such a high degree a feature of your art. If you agree to our desire, as well as the payment, which you may fix yourself, we should be so obliged to you that we shall not know how to repay you.[18]

She wrote again a few months later, and then again a year after that, this time through a contact she had forged with a relative of Ser Piero's first wife. All these attempts failed, and as far as records show Leonardo did not even bother to lift a pen to reply to the woman's pleas. All the other artists Isabella invited to paint for her during her life had complied, including, as we have seen, Perugino and Bellini. Later, Titian and Raphael were also persuaded, but not Leonardo. He never offered her another piece after the little sketch in Mantua, which on the one hand shows us how fervently he must have disliked this woman, once described as the 'heavenly Isabella', but on the other, it illustrates just how much Leonardo was his own man.

It is clear from this exchange that by this time Leonardo felt financially secure. *Il Moro* had rewarded him handsomely during the final years of their relationship (even though it had on occasion taken strenuous efforts on Leonardo's part to actually get the money). We may assume that his stubbornness with Isabella d'Este was in part due to the fact that he was no longer desperate for money. He was of course preoccupied with other interests, but it is nevertheless striking that he did not – as far as we know – even acknowledge Isabella's requests. We might assume then that Leonardo would not have worked for her even if he had been hard-pressed financially. Perhaps he had learned from his relationship with Lorenzo de' Medici that there was little to be gained from creating works of art for a person with whom one shared little empathy.*

---

* Although it should be noted that, to a degree, this unwillingness did not extend to working in other disciplines for people he did not care for. As we have seen, Leonardo was happy to sell his services as a military engineer to anyone who would offer him this kind of work.

Meanwhile, Leonardo had begun to fulfil his promises to the trusting Servite friars. Late in 1501 or during the spring of 1502, he completed the cartoon now known as the *Virgin and Child With St Anne*, which is today in the National Gallery, London, and he began the full-scale painting soon after. According to Vasari, even the cartoon for this masterpiece caused great excitement when it was exhibited in Florence for the first time, and this reaction came not merely from the arts community but from the general populace.

In the end, he made a cartoon containing a Madonna and a St Anne, with a Christ, which not only caused all the craftsmen to marvel, but, when it was finished, men and women, young and old, continued for two days to flock for a sight of it to the room where it was, as if to a solemn festival, in order to gaze at the marvels of Leonardo.[19]

Work on the full painting of the *Virgin and Child With St Anne* (today in the Louvre) did not progress so well as this revolutionary cartoon, and it appears from Leonardo's notes and correspondence that for the following six years the painting would keep pulling him back to Florence when he could afford time away from other projects. The last of these efforts was in 1508, but as with so many of Leonardo's paintings, it was never completed, some detail on the robes and elements of the background remained for ever unfinished. This time, Leonardo's reasons for leaving the painting incomplete are easy to trace, for even as he was beginning the full-scale painting, distracted and 'tired of the brush', he was offered a chance to demonstrate his abilities in a field that was of far greater interest to him and which offered him greater scope than merely working on a religious painting.

During the spring of 1502, as Leonardo approached his fiftieth birthday, he was offered the position of military engineer for a young and ambitious commander he had met soon after the fall of Milan a few years earlier. His name was Cesare Borgia.

History has painted Cesare Borgia as a despot, placing him in the same category as men like Hitler or Pol Pot, and there may be some justification in this comparison. He was the model for Machiavelli's *Prince*, the description of the ideal, emotionless tyrant who could, in theory at least, conquer the world through the application of unalloyed ruthlessness.

Born the illegitimate son of Pope Alexander VI in 1475, he is known to have murdered anyone who stood in his way or who established themselves as potential rivals, including members of his own family. He is said to have had an incestuous relationship with his equally murderous sister, Lucrezia, and persuaded their father to marry her off to a succession of princes for his own political gain before dispatching each of them.

However, as black as Cesare Borgia's soul appears to have been, he committed his crimes for carefully judged purposes. He was not a psychopathic killer in the same way as mass murderers such as Jack the Ripper or Jeffrey Dahmer, who killed because of emotional dysfunction. He worshipped power and did everything to acquire it. He was made a cardinal by his father at the age of sixteen and was defrocked at twenty-two. He then murdered his older brother so he could take on leadership of the papal armed forces. Befriended by Louis XII and rewarded for his help in conquering large parts of Italy in the battles with Sforza and the Holy Roman Empire, Borgia was given French citizenship, a title – the Duke of Valentinois – his own army and a handsome salary.

Cesare Borgia's motto was *Aut Caesar aut nihil* (Caesar or nothing) and his ambition extended to dreams of conquering the entire Italian peninsula. He never came close to succeeding with this, but for a period of some seven years he did hold large parts of northern Italy under his sway. However, this lasted only so long as he was backed by the power of France and Rome. Although Victorian historians and romantic novelists made much of Borgia's evil deeds, he should not be seen as a freak. He was determined and incredibly ambitious and pitted himself against many others with just as much blood on their hands.

At the time Leonardo was invited to work for Cesare Borgia, both men were at the height of their powers. Leonardo was respected throughout Italy as a master artist, and the Duke of Valentinois had acquired a new title, Prince of Romagna. Borgia certainly knew of Leonardo's genius as an artist and probably learned of his interest in military engineering through his master, Louis XII. What Leonardo and Borgia thought of each other is unknown, as neither man left any record of his feelings on the subject.

In some ways, the two were complete opposites. Cesare Borgia was murderous and seemingly driven by only one force – the need for power; Leonardo was a pacifist vegetarian artist who had no interest in acquiring great wealth or domination over others. But there were also striking similarities between them. Both men were born illegitimate, both were very handsome and both were driven by a powerful well-spring of ego and energy. Borgia directed his towards the external world of domination and control over his fellow man, whereas Leonardo turned his will inwards to achieve a peaceful expression and resolution of his desires.

Some historical commentators have seen Leonardo's brief liaison with Cesare Borgia as strange, and wonder how this pacifist could have considered working for a man who was even then renowned for his ruthlessness and hunger for power. But we must remember Leonardo was dependent upon patronage his entire adult life. He could only feed himself by working for rich and powerful people. Lorenzo de' Medici was a relatively peaceful man but he was ruthless in his political ambitions, and for some historians Sforza was every bit as dark and determined as Cesare Borgia. And we must remember that at this stage of his life, Leonardo was as keen to find employment as an engineer as he was 'tired' of painting.

Leonardo did not need much persuading to leave Florence again, and for the following six months he travelled throughout Italy as Cesare Borgia's engineer. The job took him from one city to another where he would suggest improvements that could be made to fortifications and where he developed ideas for defensive systems punctuated by frequent meetings with his new patron in Cesena, Borgia's Romagna capital.

During this time, Leonardo kept an account of his movements and the projects he worked on in a little notebook now known as *Manuscript L*. He had free reign to do as he pleased, to ask whatever he liked wherever he went within Borgia's domain, and was allowed unfettered access to the most secret plans and schemes of his generals. This sanction was given in the form of a 'pass' written by Borgia which Leonardo kept with him at all times during his employment. It read:

To all our lieutenants, castellans, captains, condottieri, officers, soldiers and subjects who read this document: We order and command this: that to our dearly beloved architect and general engineer Leonardo da Vinci, bearer of this pass, charged with inspecting the places and fortresses of our states, so that we may maintain them according to their needs and on his advice, all will allow free passage, without subjecting him to any public tax either on himself or his companions, and to welcome him with amity, and allow him to measure and examine anything he likes. To this effect, provide him with the men he requires and give him any aid, assistance and favour he asks for. We desire that for any work to be executed within our states, each engineer be required to confer with him and to conform to his judgement. Let no man act otherwise unless he wishes to incur our wrath.

It seems to have been an immensely satisfying time for Leonardo; his first period of employment in which he was not required to decorate royal chambers or make toys for a fickle ruler, and his notebooks are filled with pages of designs for defensive devices and odd weapons. He was particularly concerned with the best 'profile' for a buttress or a defensive wall and he made elaborate investigations of how best to build walls that would deflect arrows or protect defenders from projectiles and fire. As well as this, he created movable defences, bridges that could be dismantled and transported long distances, plans for secret escape tunnels and fortresses with self-contained inner chambers that would remain hidden even after the ramparts had been breached. Alongside these are descriptions of such eccentricities as sword-eating shields and schemes to create 'defensive curtains' that could deflect any known weapon. It was also a time during which Leonardo made useful contacts. Most significant of these was Niccolò Machiavelli, with whom he appears to have developed an almost immediate empathy and with whom he formed a lasting friendship.

The most celebrated political writer of his age, Machiavelli was born in Florence in 1469. Although history remembers him for his idiosyncratic political ideas, he was also a renowned playwright, historian, diplomat, and military planner whose most famous work, *The Prince* (first published in1513 and translated into English in1602), remains in print five centuries after it was first conceived. His official position when he met Leonardo was that of Secretary and Second Chancellor to the Florentine Republic, which meant that he was an envoy to Cesare Borgia. Unofficially, he was both diplomat and spy.

The two men may have met during one of Leonardo's visits to Cesare's court where Machiavelli would have been observing the Borgia machinations, or it may have been during a brief visit to Rome. And again with these two men, surface comparisons would lead to the false conclusion that Leonardo and Machiavelli would not have been at all compatible.

By the time they met, sometime in 1502, Machiavelli had already been following a successful political career for some four years, but he

Fig. 8.2: Niccolò Machiavelli.

was a man of many parts whose skills as a diplomat earned him a living and furthered his ambitions, but did not dominate his interests. Machiavelli was an intellectual, but also a man of action, and this combination allowed him to follow a career which took him to the very centre of political power, which he observed in detail and grew to understand thoroughly, providing him with the source material for *The Prince*.

Leonardo may have been attracted to Machiavelli's probing and thorough intellect because it was so different from his own, and Machiavelli probably found Leonardo's freedom of thought, his intensity and drive, inspiring. The two men worked in very different fields, and throughout his life Leonardo appears to have felt nothing but apathy towards politics and the schemes of princes. Nevertheless, he would have appreciated Machiavelli's clearsightedness and his clinical approach to the 'science' of human behaviour as later expressed in *The Prince*, seeing in this a reflection of his own investigations of the inner mechanisms of the human body, viewing it perhaps as another aspect of the Universe to enhance further his holistic ideology.

During those early days working for Cesare Borgia, Leonardo must have felt more content than he had done since the halcyon days a decade earlier at Sforza's Milanese court. Although he was Borgia's military engineer and technical adviser, he appears never to have been close to any form of action and probably never witnessed battle. He worked on defensive systems and spent much of his time devising clever schemes to improve the lot of Borgia's forces and their military efficiency. At the same time, such work gave him freedom to travel and to explore new ideas, and to meet the most powerful and interesting people in Italy. It brought him closer to the French monarchy, which was the real power in the peninsula and presumably afforded him a good salary, although we have no record of his earnings during this time. But once again, this satisfying position did not last long. Little more than nine months after leaving Florence to enter Borgia's payroll, he was once more on the move.

Leonardo leaves no suggestion that he was aware of Borgia's ruthless actions, yet he could hardly have been in his employ and not have had some inside information about what became public knowledge a little later. A few weeks after Leonardo began to work for him, Borgia had ordered one of his generals, Remiro dell'Orco, who was governor of Romagna, to impose order within the region by 'whatever means available'. This naturally led to all forms of excess and barbarism, but in order to divorce himself publicly from these atrocities, Borgia had dell'Orco sliced in two and his body dumped in the centre of the capital with a bloodied knife lying beside him.

Whether or not Leonardo knew the details of these incidents as they were carried out we may never know. They were not connected to his work in any real sense and it would appear unlikely he was made privy to such things; he may even have been working in a different region of Italy at the time. But in the final days of 1502, only nine months after Leonardo had become Borgia's chief engineer, an incident occurred which seems to have precipitated the end of the relationship between the two men.

A group of Borgia's own men, led by a captain whom Leonardo knew personally, Vitellozo Vitelli, had conspired against their ruler. Instead of challenging the renegades to fair combat, Borgia applied the sort of cunning upon which his reputation had been founded. He managed to persuade Vitelli and his men that he had forgiven them and arranged a rendezvous in the town of Senigallia to discuss a reconciliation. Greeting them with open arms, Borgia invited them to his private rooms where they were promptly arrested and strangled.

Leonardo may well have left Borgia's service within days of this treachery. We have no proof of whether his departure was due to this particular atrocity, or because of an accumulation of horrors. Leonardo's whereabouts between October 1502, when the conspiracy began, and March the following year, when he is reported to have taken money from his account in Florence, are unknown, and there is no record of him being close to Senigallia or engaged in any works for Borgia from the autumn of 1502. But it may be more than coincidence that we hear no more of Leonardo's dealings with Borgia. Leonardo departed his company, never to return.

As short as this experience with Cesare Borgia had been, it throws into stark relief the contradictions and apparent conflicts between Leonardo's mild character and his choice of career. A glance at his plans for creating better methods for defensive shields and protective curtains shows he remained a pacifist throughout this period and he tried his best to alleviate the suffering of soldiers on both sides. Yet he had written frequently of the horrors his machines could inflict, most particularly in his letter written to Ludovico Sforza two decades earlier in which he had proclaimed gleefully how he could produce 'mortars that are very practical and easy to transport, with which I can project stones so that they seem to be raining down, and their smoke will plunge the enemy into terror, to his great hurt and confusion'.[20]

Whatever Leonardo's whereabouts during the early part of 1503, there are signs that he was at something of a loose end (which supports the notion he walked out on Borgia on impulse). A clue comes from a Turkish translation of a letter purportedly sent by Leonardo to Sultan Bayezid about this time.* In the letter, Leonardo claims to be familiar with methods of building windmills and silage pumps and proposes a plan to construct for the Sultan a great bridge over the Golden Horn that would link Asia with Europe. The letter was poorly translated by secretaries to the Sultan and may never have reached him. But if contact was made, nothing ever came of it because Leonardo was certainly back in Florence by March 1503 and never visited Asia.

We do not know why he returned to Florence; perhaps it was to continue with his work on *Virgin and Child With St Anne* but, for the moment at least, it appears to have been precisely the right move, for the Florentines now finally seemed to realise that by ignoring Leonardo they had been wasting a vital talent. Suddenly, he found his stock was running high in the city, and offers of work, both as an artist and a military engineer, began to come his way.

We cannot be sure why there was such a sea-change in the attitude of the powerful of Florence, but we might suppose they had been shocked and concerned when Leonardo had entered on to Borgia's payroll, a circumstance that had made them realise they were squandering a remarkable talent from which others were quick to benefit. It is impossible to say whether or not Leonardo had been aware that

---

* This letter was found in the Topkapi archives in Istanbul in 1952.[21]

leaving Florence to work for the Duke of Valentinois would have this effect. I suspect he was not the sort of man who planned such moves (in fact it is difficult to see any form of 'plan' throughout his entire career). He certainly knew what he wanted and how best to impress and inspire the rich and powerful, but he was never a great manipulator or schemer. But he was quick to capitalise on any opportunity that offered itself and he now took full advantage of the change in attitude of the Florentine authorities. He may have returned to spend time on the *Virgin and Child With St Anne*, but he was soon being called away to act as a military engineer for the Signoria.

While Leonardo had been working for Cesare Borgia, Pisa, the former dependency of Florence, had been spurred on by the French to declare its independence. Pisa was too important as a link to the coast for Florence to allow this and they immediately responded to the declaration by laying siege to the city. Within days they had called up young Florentines to join the army. They cut off supplies of food to Pisa by forcibly stopping farmers travelling to the city and sent ships to harass Genoese merchants attempting to break the blockade. But the Pisans showed no sign of capitulation, and months after the dispute began there appeared to be no end to the conflict. It was clear the siege was not working and the Florentines had no stomach to attack the city, a move that would also expose them to their more powerful enemies on all sides.

In June 1503, Leonardo visited the region around Pisa and drew maps of the region. Back in Florence, he put to the Signoria his ideas for resolving the problem. Now with some influence at court and with the encouragement of his friend Machiavelli, Leonardo's ideas were received with interest and all parties sought a peaceful settlement to the dispute.

Leonardo had been thinking about using natural resources in warfare for many years. We have seen how he proposed to the Venetians a method of defending themselves against the Turks by flooding the

Isonzo valley using a dam. To the Pisa problem, he applied similar reasoning and suggested the river Arno be diverted a few miles from Pisa, which would create the double effect of depriving the town of water and cutting it off from its harbour, both of which, he knew, would end the siege far quicker than the moves already instigated and, most importantly to him, without bloodshed.

The scheme was begun in August with all the resources the Signoria could divert from other fronts. It involved building a huge wooden barrier across the Arno and the digging of two enormous channels some eight miles long which would divert the water to a large lake and then on to the sea, cutting it off before it reached Pisa.

The original scheme would probably have worked, but the plan financed by the Signoria was a cheaper expedient and was plagued with problems from the start. The walls of channels kept collapsing, the barrier could not be built properly with the manpower made available, and gradually optimism ebbed away as the weather worsened and the workers were attacked by Pisan raiders. In spite of Machiavelli's continued confidence in the scheme and his attempts to keep the flow of money and men diverted to the Arno project, by the following April, the Florentine government had made an about-turn and abruptly cancelled the effort.

Despite this failure, indirectly many good things came from Leonardo's scheme. First there are his maps. During much of his time with Cesare Borgia and during his travels around Tuscany working for the Signoria, Leonardo had made thorough notes in preparation for a series of detailed maps, which he then completed upon his return to Florence. Pre-eminent among these, and perhaps the most important drawings Leonardo made during this period of his life, are his *Map of Imola* and the *Physical Map of Tuscany, Emilia and Romagna*.

The first of these is an incredibly detailed map of the city of Imola in Emilia-Romagna, northern Italy, that shows the position of roads and includes no fewer than sixty-four surveyor's terms. Its intricacy is quite unique for the time and could only have come from the hand and mind of a man like Leonardo, someone equally well versed as an artist and an engineer. His physical maps of Italian regions show the geography and hydrography in the most incredible detail and with a degree of accuracy far surpassing anything previous generations of cartographers had attempted. Indeed, to me they look strikingly like images beamed to Earth from satellites orbiting at altitudes of several hundred miles.

The plan for diverting the Arno was Leonardo's way of ending the conflict between Florence and Pisa without further bloodshed, but even before the soldiers began to dig, he had started to describe what in his fantasies would have been an industrial corridor along the banks of the Arno linking the two cities. He visualised mills and what we would call factories that could produce silk, paper, pottery, all manner of things, industrial processes all powered by water from the river. Transportation would be facilitated by barge along the river and he devised a scheme for building a series of locks on the main tributaries of the Arno capable of allowing small boats to navigate into the hills and the smaller towns around the main river valley. All this almost three centuries before the Industrial Revolution.

Leonardo saw this as a thoroughly practical scheme, one that would greatly increase the standard of living of people in the region, declaring that it would 'increase the value of the land; the cities of Prato, Pistoia, and Pisa, as well as Florence would gain thereby an annual income of two hundred thousand ducats'.[22] Elsewhere he wrote: 'If one were to divert the course of the Arno from top to bottom, all those who wished to would find a treasure in every plot of land.'[23]

After initiating the proposal to starve Pisa of water, Leonardo had almost nothing further to do with the project to divert the Arno. There are no records of him giving further instructions or even visiting the site. Perhaps he realised early on that the finances would be insufficient for the scheme to work and that the government was only willing to back a half-hearted version of what he had suggested, and so

Fig. 8.3: Map of Imola.

removed himself from a doomed scheme he was powerless to improve. But whatever his feelings, within days of work starting on the project, Leonardo's attention had in any case been drawn elsewhere.

Before his audacious plans for the Arno had crumbled to nothing, and with Machiavelli as his tireless supporter in the Signoria, Leonardo was offered another plum job. On 24 October 1503 he was given a lucrative commission to paint a vast mural of a battle scene to decorate one of the walls of the newly-built Council Chamber in the Palazzo della Signoria, the great meeting hall of the government. On the same day, he was handed the keys to Sala del Papa, the Hall of the Pope, in the church and hospital named Maria Novella in the west of the city. This vast building was to be for his exclusive use to accommodate himself and his entourage and to provide him with a studio in which he could prepare the sketch for the planned painting.

For this mural, the Signoria required a depiction of a heroic battle scene taken from recent Florentine history, and after much debate it was agreed the subject should be the Battle of Anghiari, a great Florentine victory over the Milanese in 1440.

Leonardo was perfectly prepared for the commission. He had almost certainly never witnessed a battle first-hand, but from his recent experiences and from research into warfare both ancient and modern, he was well versed in the customs of battle and his knowledge of the hardware of war was almost without peer. Some thirteen years earlier, long before applying any of his ideas to military engineering, he had described in his notes exactly how a battle scene should be painted:

You will give a reddish tinge to the faces, the figures, the air, the musketeers, and those around them, and this red glow will fade the further it is from its source . . . Arrows will be flying in all directions, falling down, flying straight ahead, filling the air, and the bullets from firearms will leave a trail of smoke behind them . . . If you show a man who has fallen to the ground, reproduce his skid marks in the dust, which has been transformed into bloody mud. And all around on the slippery ground you will show the marks where men and horses have trampled it in passing . . . Make the vanquished look pale and panic-stricken, their eyebrows raised high or knitted in grief . . . The dying will be grinding their teeth, their eyeballs rolling heavenward . . . You could show a warrior disarmed and knocked to the ground, turning on his foe, biting and scratching him in cruel and bitter revenge . . . Several of the victors are leaving the field, they will move away from the mêlée, wiping their hands over their eyes and cheeks to remove the thick layer of mud caused by their eyes watering on account of the dust.[24]

It appears Leonardo took the task seriously and devoted a good deal more of his time to the sketch than he had to any earlier commission. This could be seen as a reflection upon the importance of the piece, or due to his own interest in the subject matter; he was never entirely happy or fulfilled by painting religious themes. But most significantly, for the first time in Leonardo's career this commission had come with a powerful element of rivalry.

Michelangelo Buonarotti was twenty-nine years old when he also was offered a commission by the Signoria to paint a battle scene, *The Battle of Cascina*, on the wall of the Council Chamber in the Palazzo della Signoria directly opposite that against which Leonardo had already built a scaffold in preparation for his *Battle of Anghiari*.

Leonardo was shocked and disappointed by this turn of events, but he should not have been too surprised. Michelangelo was the most esteemed artist in Florence, and although he was primarily recognised as a sculptor of genius, his work as a painter was already highly valued by the Medici and other wealthy families in the city. He was also pro- lific, ambitious and envious of Leonardo. It is almost certain the city fathers played on this competitiveness and engineered their own 'battle' by placing the two men in the same room.

The roots of Michelangelo's dislike for Leonardo are easy to trace. He was born into an upper-middle-class family and had pretensions of nobility. He had been well educated and had established links with the Medici when he was still very young. He was an angst-ridden homosexual who could never come to terms with his sexuality, a man whose body was twisted and hunched and whose face was plain, a man obsessed with religion, who devoted his work to his God, slept on his studio floor and worked twenty hours a day. In almost all respects, he was the very opposite of his rival. Leonardo was not a religious man, and he viewed Michelangelo's fixation with morality, purity and the glory of the Roman Catholic Church as eccentric. As we know, he was handsome, enjoyed company and a comfortable lifestyle. All the two men shared was their genius.

But Michelangelo viewed Leonardo as a dilettante, a man who wasted his talents on dreams and gimmicks, someone who could never hold down a commission and who did not deserve the great talent God had, in his mysterious way, bestowed upon him. The dichotomy between Leonardo's genius and his apparent nonchalance irritated Michelangelo to the point where he despised his rival.

Leonardo hardly knew Michelangelo when he returned to Florence in 1503 but he had seen his work and knew of his reputation. We do not know when they first met or how often they encountered one another before Leonardo was drawn into Cesare Borgia's service, but their first official encounter came in 1504, when Leonardo was asked to join a committee of prominent artists in Florence whose task it was to decide upon the site for Michelangelo's *David*. We know the artist was not happy with their decision to have the statue placed indoors in the Loggia dei Lanzi and had hoped for a more glamorous and public site immediately outside the Signoria. Whether he blamed Leonardo in particular for this is unknown, but according to legend, the beginning of their mutual antagonism stemmed from an encounter which probably dates from a time immediately after the committee had made its decision.

The story relates how Leonardo was stopped in the street by a group of men who were arguing over a detail of Dante's *Inferno* and, believing Leonardo to be an arbiter on all things, they asked him for his opinion. As Leonardo was about to respond, he noticed Michelangelo turning a corner towards them and said, 'Here is Michelangelo, he will solve the argument for you.' At which Michelangelo, who had a reputation for a quick temper, took offence, misinterpreting Leonardo's comment as a sly insult. He whirled on the older artist, yelling,

'Explain it yourself, you, the man who made a model of a horse you could never finish. And the idiots of Milan believed in you!' Stunned, Leonardo could find no words with which to respond and Michelangelo strode off.

The insult dug deep. We can detect this in comments Leonardo made in his notebook lamenting the fact that he had so frequently left projects and schemes unfinished. 'Tell me, tell me if I have ever done anything . . .' he declared at one point.[25]

More poignant are the attacks Leonardo made in his writings against other artists. A good example is this diatribe from his *Trattato della Pittura*:

The sculptor in creating his works does so by the strength of his arm by which he consumes the marble, or other obdurate material in which his subject is enclosed: and this is done by most mechanical exercise, often accompanied by great sweat which mixes with the marble dust and forms a kind of mud daubed all over his face. The marble dust flours him all over so that he looks like a baker; his back is covered with a snowstorm of chips, and his house is made filthy by the flakes and dust of stone. The exact reverse is true of the painter.[26]

And of course, Michelangelo was first and foremost a sculptor.

The rivalry between the two artists was very real and this undoubtedly spurred on Leonardo and kept him at the brush. And it was certainly a rivalry noticed by the commentators of the time. Hoping perhaps to see some sort of clash, people came to see the work-in-progress and the depiction of the two battle scenes. Very soon the matching of the two most famous and respected artists in Florence was aptly dubbed 'the Battle of Battles'.

For three years, Leonardo worked on the sketch for his *Battle of Anghiari*. We know that even under pressure and pursued by the urge to prove his rival wrong, he did not leave behind his other interests completely. He continued to fill his notebooks with ideas for ever more complex mechanical devices, page after page of mathematical studies, and in particular entire notebooks devoted to his study of the flight of birds. It was also a time fraught with personal difficulties.

First, Ser Piero died during the summer of 1504, and although it is believed the relationship between the two men was never a close one, his father's death must have disturbed Leonardo. Ser Piero had really only ever been interested in himself and his career. It is significant that in his notes he made two different references to his father's death, a rare repetition indeed, commenting: 'On 9 July 1504, a Wednesday at seven o'clock, died Ser Piero da Vinci, notary to the Palace of the Podestat, my father – at seven o'clock, aged eighty years, leaving ten sons and two daughters.'[27] And then later he wrote, 'On Wednesday at seven o'clock died Ser Piero da Vinci, on 9 July 1504, a Wednesday at about seven o'clock.[28]

These entries are interesting for several reasons. First, we have the odd repetition each time, dates and times mentioned twice in the same sentence in both passages. But then Leonardo goes on to record his father's age incorrectly; Piero had been seventy-eight when he died. These mistakes and repetitions could be interpreted in diametrically opposite ways. They could indicate that after reaching maturity Leonardo had little to do with his father (even though for many years they lived in the same tiny city), or it could be seen as a sign that he was deeply moved by Ser Piero's death and in his distress made the silly mistake of recording the wrong age.

As Leonardo dealt with this crisis, other personal problems plagued him. Twenty years earlier, he had walked away from the controversial *Virgin of the Rocks* commissioned by the Confraternity of the Immaculate Conception, and the friars had never accepted it as the work they had paid for. Having pursued the matter through the courts for over two decades, they had at last succeeded in bringing litigation against Leonardo, forcing him to travel to Milan to argue his case.[*]

In spite of these problems, by the end of 1504 Leonardo had completed the cartoon within the time limits designated by his contract. In February 1505, the government settled the artist's bills for plaster, oils and other materials required to begin the painting itself and the cartoon was moved from Santa Maria Novella to the Council Chamber where specially designed scaffolding was already erected. Meanwhile, Michelangelo was putting the finishing touches to his sketch of *The Battle of Cascina*.

Excitement among the fraternity of artists in Florence grew as the two master artists approached the next crucial stage of their projects. The sculptor Benvenuto Cellini called the hoped-for outcome 'the school of the world' because it was believed that between them the genius of Michelangelo and Leonardo would keep artists of the world busy for centuries as generations struggled to emulate their masterworks. Sadly, it was not to be. Leonardo records beginning the painting.

On 6 June 1505 . . . a Friday, at the thirteenth hour I began to paint in the palace. I was just picking up my brush when the weather took a turn for the worse and the church-bells rang the alarm, calling people together. And the cartoon [made of paper] began to come apart, water went everywhere for the vessel in which it was being carried broke. Suddenly the weather grew worse still, and it poured with rain until evening; the day had been transformed into night.[29]

---

[*] Eventually the court decided Leonardo and his partner in the commission, Ambrogio de Predis, should be given two years to complete a new version of the painting.

Leonardo began again with new plaster and oils provided by the accountants of the Signoria and the work continued until the following spring. But he was fighting too many battles simultaneously. Aside from the legal dispute with the Milanese friars, he was facing technical problems with the painting (according to one report the linseed oil he was using was of very poor quality),[30] and he had now found himself caught up in a diplomatic dispute between his masters.

King Louis XII of France, to whom Leonardo was contracted, and who showed far more genuine and intense admiration for Leonardo's work than the Florentines ever had, wanted him back in Milan. But the Signoria had already spent a fortune in supplying Leonardo with materials for *The Battle of Anghiari*, and understandably they wanted their Council Chamber finished. However, because Florence was doing its best to maintain a delicate alliance with France, they were actually in no position to clash openly with Louis. At the same time, in order to maintain a semblance of dignity they were obliged to be seen to draw out an inevitable capitulation.

Louis' patience finally drained away. From France, the King's secretary, Florimond Robertet, wrote to the Signoria, declaring: 'We have necessary need of Master Leonardo da Vinci painter of your city of Florence . . . Write to him that he should not leave Milan before our arrival, as I told your ambassador.'[31]

Thus, Leonardo became embroiled in what amounted to a diplomatic tussle between the two powers, adding still more pressure to his already stressful and complex situation. And as a temporary measure, he was obliged to commute between Milan and Florence to appease his rival masters. But it was clear this situation could not continue for long and *The Battle of Anghiari* had to be sacrificed.

Humanity never did get the 'school of the world' from the two greatest artists of the Renaissance, but Leonardo was at least saved the humiliation of seeing his work abandoned while that of his rival came to fruition. The cartoon for Michelangelo's *The Battle of Cascina* was barely finished when he was called away to Rome by Pope Julius II to undertake the most important commission of his life, the frescoes for the ceiling of the Sistine Chapel.

In May 1506, the Florentines finally capitulated to the increasingly angry requests of the French king. Leonardo was awarded a two-month sabbatical from *The Battle of Anghiari* and travelled immediately to Milan to begin work on a collection of small paintings for Louis. But he never did return to the mural, and all that was visible from his efforts was a section close to completion consisting of a central scene since known as *The Struggle for the Banner*.

Even then, Leonardo was forced by circumstance to continue travelling between Milan and Florence. In March 1507, his beloved Uncle Francesco died. Leonardo was made sole heir to the estate, almost as though Ser Piero's brother had tried to make up for Leonardo's exclusion from his father's will. But, meagre as the inheritance was, Leonardo's half-brothers contested it.

It was almost too much to bear, and Leonardo must have made known how much trouble this final problem was causing him, for as soon as the legal battles over the estate began, some of Leonardo's most influential friends involved themselves on his behalf. Both Charles d'Amboise, who was then in Milan, and Florimond Robertet were called upon to help settle the matter quickly and Robertet wrote again to the Signoria of Florence, this time requesting that they resolve the legal wranglings quickly: 'Because it causes the king's painter to interrupt a picture that is very dear to the king,' he pronounced unequivocally.[32] Yet even this did little practical good; the legal system of the time moved with a snail's pace and the dispute dragged on for almost another year.

The fate of *The Battle of Anghiari* was a sad one. The small, nearly completed section survived for a while and was seen and studied by artists who for several years flocked to the building from all over Italy, but this and Leonardo's sketch were allowed to fall into utter ruin within a few decades. In spite of the enthusiasm of artists who came to admire it, no one seems to have had the will or the power to preserve Leonardo's work for posterity.

Many artists made copies of Leonardo's sketch, and these, along with the reams of preliminary drawings Leonardo made in preparation for the sketch, are all we have. In 1560, Vasari was commissioned to remove from the walls all traces of the original and to plaster over Leonardo da Vinci's preparatory work. Attempts have been made using ultrasound techniques to see if anything of the battle scene remains beneath the plaster, but these have produced only disappointing results.

Leonardo sent Salai ahead of him to Milan and wrote in his note-books: 'I am almost at the end of my litigation with my brothers, and . . . I hope to be with you at Easter and carry with me two pictures on which are two Madonnas of different sizes which I began for the most Christian King, or for whomsoever you please.'[33]

By the spring of 1508, the dispute over *The Virgin of the Rocks* settled but the question of Francesco's will still unresolved, Leonardo was back in Milan having made the same journey he had undertaken some quarter of a century earlier. The world had changed beyond recognition in that time, and so had he. Now he was leaving the city that had once again brought him unhappiness and frustration, and entering a period of further change, one in which he would become entangled with the seemingly endless political vicissitudes of the age.

9

THE ARMS OF
THE KING

I want to work miracles!
— Leonardo, *Quaderni, III*

Leonardo was always happiest in Milan, and with the mounting problems he faced with his work on *The Battle of Anghiari* it is easy to believe he was pleased to leave Florence and return to the city which had been his home for so long and where he had been most appreciated. And indeed in Milan he was once again treated with the respect and adulation he deserved.

For Leonardo, free time was a rare luxury. He had been busy with so many different projects and was constantly torn between his need to find work as an artist and his desire to delve into every area of knowledge, but during his first months in Milan he managed to find some relief from his duties at court, perhaps by pleading exhaustion from the chaos of the past few years. And he did not squander the opportunity, but turned to his vast collection of notebooks with grand hopes of collating them into an organised and readable body of work.

When he did, he was immediately horrified by the muddle. His notes had no cohesion and he had never worked to any formula or within any prearranged framework. His method of note-taking had been no real method at all. He had covered page after page with frag-ments on such diverse subjects that to organise them would be, he now realised, a mammoth task.

Aware that he could do little in his lifetime to arrange the entire col-lection into any sensible order, he confined himself to a few subjects, the ones closest to his heart at this time (studies of water, painting, optics and anatomy) with the vain hope of collecting and organising the rest sometime later.

With this more workable target in mind, Leonardo must have been thinking in terms of producing three or perhaps four works for even-tual publication. He certainly visualised treatises on water, painting and anatomy, and wrote in his notes:

> Begun in Florence, in the house of Pietro di Braccio Martelli, on 22 March 1508. This will be a collection without any order made up of numerous sheets that I have copied in the hope of later classifying them in order and in a convenient arrangement relat-ing to the subjects they treat; and I think that before the end of this book, I shall have to repeat the same thing several times; so reader, do not blame me, for the subjects are many and memory cannot hold them all or say 'I shall not write this down because I have already written it'.[1]

This period passed all too quickly and it is intriguing to speculate upon what would have come down to us if he had not had to answer Louis' demands. He had thrown himself heart and soul into the enor-mous task of collating his work, and at the age of fifty-five he was beginning to sense that his abilities and inventiveness might soon begin to wane. Perhaps he believed the time was auspicious to bring a sense of order to three decades of dedication to research and writing. But by the early summer of 1508, Leonardo was obliged to start repaying Louis' patience and help.

Not surprisingly, under his new master Leonardo slipped back into the role he had played at the court of Francesco Sforza a decade earlier. He continued to pursue his private interests (in particular his obsession with anatomical studies) but at the same time he maintained his position in the affections of Louis' court, entertaining them with his mechanical creations, acting as designer and decorator for the more influential courtiers and drawing up plans for extravagant pageants and recreations.

As the governor of Milan and lieutenant to the king, Charles d'Amboise was one of the most powerful men at the French court. Leonardo had been on friendly terms with him since at least the occupation of Milan in 1499 and d'Amboise commissioned Leonardo to design for him a splendid garden for a palace he was planning to have built close to the Porta Venezia in the heart of Milan. Leonardo was allowed free reign with these designs and he came up with an extraordinary confection, including designs for specially contoured miniature lakes with waterfalls to allow wine to be chilled, an area roofed with copper mesh to create an aviary, automatic musical instruments powered by a water mill and '. . . places where water will spray out to drench passers-by, for instance if one wanted to sprinkle the ladies' dresses for fun'.[2]

Leonardo now had a wide and cosmopolitan circle of friends. He and Salai were invited to stay in the Milanese home of the wealthy patron and acclaimed mathematician, Pietro di Braccio Martelli. His house was already home to the eccentric artist and sculptor Giovan Francesco Rustici, who, it is said, kept a menagerie of animals, including a crow that had been taught human speech and a porcupine that behaved like a dog. Leonardo's junior by some twenty years, Rustici had been a pupil of Verrocchio's and had joined his bottega when Leonardo was first living in Milan during the 1490s. He and Leonardo soon became close friends, prompting the latter's initiation into a mock fraternity created by Rustici called the Company of the Cauldron. Members met over copious quantities of wine and designed paintings and sculptures made entirely from food.

Another frequent visitor to Martelli's home was a libertine artist known only as *Il Sodoma*, who, according to some accounts, became a student of Leonardo's. Like Rustici, *Il Sodoma* also kept a large collection of exotic animals, some of which he trained to perform tricks. It was also during these first months back in Milan that Leonardo grew close to a young man who became an inseparable companion (although he may have first met him a year or two earlier). This was Francesco Melzi, the son of a Lombard aristocrat, who was seventeen in 1508.

Francesco's parents owned a large estate at Vaprio, near Milan. Leonardo had probably met the family during one of his frequent sojourns in the Lombardy countryside when he was starting to collate his notes, and it seems that he acquired an instant affection for young Melzi. Vasari tells us of 'Messer Francesco da Melzo [Francesco Melzi, "messer" indicates his social status], a gentleman of Milan, who in the time of Leonardo was a very beautiful boy, and much beloved by him'.[3]

We know well Leonardo's interest in *bellissimo fanciullo* and it is clear from surviving scraps of letters he was soon emotionally involved with the youth. 'Why in God's name have you not replied to any of my letters I sent you?' he writes. 'Just wait till I get back and by God I will make you write till you are almost sick of it.'[4] The tone of this is ambiguous, a blend of affection and a hint of genuine hurt, but sugar-coated with a jesting exaggeration all of which suggests a certain intimacy that must have been established early in their relationship, since this letter was written no more than a couple of months after they met.

Ironically, it would have been Salai who was entrusted with Leonardo's letters to Melzi, and we can only wonder what he would have made of the blossoming relationship between his ageing master and the teenage nobleman. As we have seen, Salai, who by this time had been with Leonardo for some seventeen years, was from peasant stock and we have no record of him showing any exceptional artistic talent or having any interest in his master's other intellectual pursuits. In complete contrast, Melzi, still in the first flush of youth, had from an early age displayed considerable ability as a painter. He was serious-minded, well read and had received an education befitting his class. There can be little doubt Salai felt understandably threatened and intimidated by this new acolyte.

And Leonardo's relationship with Melzi was no short-lived affair. The young man appears to have understood Leonardo almost from their first meeting and, perhaps beguiled by his genius, he soon succeeded in persuading his parents to let him pursue a career as an artist in Leonardo's entourage. This gives us some indication of the esteem with which Leonardo was regarded by all types of people, and also shows that Melzi's parents must have themselves been liberal-minded to allow their eldest son to enter what was then still widely regarded as a slightly insalubrious profession. But Melzi's interest proved to be genuine, for he stayed with Leonardo until the older man's death a dozen years later. And it was he rather than Salai who was entrusted with Leonardo's legacy and who received the lion's share of his friend's property and capital.

As Leonardo concentrated upon collating and organising his notes, his mind again began to ponder the mysteries of the human body. The end of the first decade of the new century marks his return to the study of anatomy and he is known to have conducted a series of post-mortems in Milan which led to his exquisite, and for the most part astonishingly accurate, anatomical drawings. But as always, Leonardo could not give his undivided attention to any one or even any two or three pursuits for long. While satisfying the demands of his masters for courtly trivialities, delving further into the dark mysteries of the human anatomy, attempting to resolve mathematical puzzles and making some sense of the vast collection of his own writings, he found renewed interest in painting. And it was during his second Milan period that Leonardo began a series of paintings including *John the Baptist*, *Leda*, and what has since become his most famous creation, the *Mona Lisa*.*

Almost nothing is known about the genesis of these paintings, nor indeed if any of them were commissioned. It is by no means certain in which order they were painted or even precisely when. It is believed the *Mona Lisa* is the earliest of the three and that *John the Baptist* was the last painting Leonardo began, but not all art historians agree over this.

The *Mona Lisa*, or *La Gioconda* as it is known in Italy, is perhaps the most enigmatic painting in the history of art. Vasari tells us: 'Leonardo undertook to execute, for Francesco del Giocondo, the portrait of Monna Lisa [sic], his wife . . .' But on this occasion Vasari's source is unknown. He almost certainly never saw the painting because it was in France when he wrote about it. This did not stop him waxing lyrical on the subject, reporting:

> In this head, whosoever wished to see how closely art could imi-tate nature, was able to comprehend it with ease; for in it were counterfeited all the minuteness that with subtlety are able to be painted, seeing that the eyes had that lustre and watery sheen which are always seen in life, and around them were all those rosy and pearly hints, as well as lashes, which cannot be represented without the greatest subtlety. The eyebrows, through his having shown the manner in which the hairs spring from the flesh, here more close and here more scanty, and curve according to the pores of the skin, could not be more natural. The nose with its beautiful nostrils, rosy and tender, appeared to be alive.[5]

Yet what he had to say must have been based upon the opinions of others, and copies of the painting produced by lesser artists.

---

* Mona is an abbreviation of Madonna.

Because Vasari is the only source who places the commission with the wealthy Tuscan merchant Francesco del Giocondo, many historians doubt the veracity of his claim. The *Anonimo Gaddiano* makes reference to another portrait Leonardo is supposed to have completed for Del Giocondo, and it has been suggested by some historians that Vasari may have confused the two paintings.

The first reference to the *Mona Lisa* was made in 1517 by Antonio de' Beatis, the only visitor to Leonardo's final home in Cloux to leave us a record of his stay. He wrote about a certain painting he had seen in Leonardo's studio and described it as a portrait of a Florentine lady, but he gave no idea of who she might be and appears not to have questioned Leonardo too deeply about it.

So, who was the woman in the *Mona Lisa*? Many people, not only art historians, but antiquarians, researchers, writers and even conspiracy theorists have offered dozens of possible, often contradictory theories concerning the identity of the woman sitting amid the dark, brooding, almost alien landscape of this extraordinary painting. But the mystery of its creation remains as elusive as the *Mona Lisa*'s smile itself.

If we believe Vasari, then this woman was the third wife of Francesco del Giocondo, a woman named Lisa di Gherardini who would then have been about twenty-five. Alternatively, she may have been the favourite of one of Leonardo's most vocal supporters and admirers, Lorenzo de' Medici's son Giuliano, with whom Leonardo was acquainted by the time the painting was probably begun.

Another theory derives from a poem by an Ischian writer, Enea Irpino, who mentions a great painting produced by Leonardo and suggests his own patroness, the Duchess of Francavilla, Costanza d'Avalos, was the model. But this tale is doubtful because she would have been about forty-five at the time. It is conceivable Leonardo had been persuaded to produce a flattering portrait of this ageing noblewoman but we know how he rebelled against any form of coercion, and at this time he would have been at his most inflexible.

A further suggestion, although one with no material evidence to support it, is that the woman in the *Mona Lisa* is in fact Isabella d'Este and that Leonardo finally succumbed to her persistence and agreed to paint her. But again, she would have been considerably older than the figure in the painting, although from what we know of her character such inconsistencies could have been easily accommodated even if they might not have been accepted by Leonardo.

Other suggestions are pure speculation. Could it have been that with the *Mona Lisa* Leonardo was attempting to represent the 'perfect woman', an idealised fantasy image? This concept led Freud and others to suggest that Leonardo had created a posthumous portrait of his own mother, Caterina, or a vision of his mother drawn from subconscious images. Interestingly, the Marquis de Sade described the *Mona Lisa* as the 'very essence of femininity', implying that the painting is of an imaginary or fantasy figure.

Still more adventurous interpretations attempt to highlight the similarity between the face of the *Mona Lisa* and that of Leonardo himself as it appears in his self-portrait drawn around the same time. This has led to outlandish suggestions that Leonardo and the figure in the painting are one and the same person.

It is tempting to imagine the *Mona Lisa* as a self-portrait, to visualise Leonardo poking fun at posterity. He was always keen on riddles and practical jokes, and loved harmless deception. He also thrived on secrecy and obfuscation. He played up his own mystique and deliberately drew a veil over some of his ideas and creations to endow them with a greater air of mystery. The *Mona Lisa*'s smile is exactly what one would expect of Leonardo, the joker, smiling inwardly. On the surface this would seem a simple piece of mockery, but if we take the idea seriously and push it further we might see how Leonardo could have subconsciously used such a performance to help exorcise his inner demons, his deep hatred for humanity generated by his unfortunate birthright, emotions constantly suppressed and subsumed, bursting out in old age as a harmless jest, just when it no longer really mattered to him what people thought.

There can be little doubt Leonardo would have been delighted by the proliferation of modern theories concerning the identity of his most famous sitter. He would also have been fascinated with the computer enhancement techniques of the investigators, in which the outline of the artist's features are superimposed upon those of the *Mona Lisa* in order to compare points of overlap. But, appealing as it may be to picture Leonardo climbing into a dress and perhaps arranging an ingenious set of mirrors with which he could see himself from the correct angle and paint that vaguely mocking smile, the evidence to support this argument is insubstantial.

There are other mysteries surrounding the execution of the painting, however. If the painting was a commission, why then was it never delivered? If the painting was for Giocondo, the explanation may be straightforward. Leonardo may have felt unhappy with the painting for many years, and did not finish it until after Giocondo died in 1516.

Another possibility is that the woman in the painting became estranged from the man who was to pay for it. Perhaps she was none of the candidates favoured by historians but the wife or lover of another wealthy merchant or nobleman, and by the time Leonardo was satisfied with the work the woman who was the Mona Lisa had fallen out of favour.

This leaves us with the most fascinating aspect of the painting, the enigma of the Mona Lisa's smile. It is not for me to discuss details of the painter's technique or to analyse the painting; this lies within the domain of the art historian, but obviously it is this smile that has bestowed the *Mona Lisa* (and Leonardo) with such a burden of popularity and fascination down the centuries. Through no fault in its execution, nor of Leonardo himself, today the *Mona Lisa* has gone beyond iconography almost to the status of archetype and cliché. It is an over-familiar image, an over-used cultural emblem, like a Beatles song or lines from *Romeo and Juliet*. It has been copied and corrupted so much we no longer see it for what it is, a staggeringly successful representation and a work of art that influenced portraiture for centuries.

The *Mona Lisa* was copied and Da Vinci's conception plagiarised unashamedly almost from the moment it was first seen in public. Raphael, who was on friendly terms with Leonardo, copied the painting, possibly before Leonardo even finished it. The French Dadaist Marcel Duchamp gave the Mona Lisa a moustache and goatee and wrote under it, 'She has a hot ass,' a comment aimed not at Leonardo himself, nor indeed his creation, but at the responses of those who looked upon it. Andy Warhol used her as one of his silk-screen images, awarding the *Mona Lisa* the same cult status as Marilyn Monroe and Elvis.

Oscar Wilde said of the painting:

The painter may have been merely the slave of an archaic smile, as some have fancied, but whenever I pass into the cool galleries of the Palace of the Louvre, and stand before that strange figure 'set in its marble chair in that cirque of fantastic rocks, as in some faint light under sea', I murmur to myself, 'She is older than the rocks among which she sits; like the vampire, she has been dead many times, and learned the secrets of the grave; and has been a diver in deep seas, and keeps their fallen day about her; and trafficked for strange webs with Eastern merchants; and, as Leda, was the mother of Helen of Troy, and, as St Anne, the mother of Mary; and all this has been to her but as the sound of lyres and flutes, and lives only in the delicacy with which it has moulded the changing lineaments, and tinged the eyelids and the hands.' And I say to my friend, 'The presence that thus so strangely rose beside the water is expressive of what in the ways of a thousand years man had come to desire'; and he answers me, 'Hers is the head upon which all "the ends of the world come", and the eyelids are a little weary.' And so the picture becomes more wonderful to us than it really is, and reveals to us a secret of which, in truth, it knows nothing, and the music of the mystical prose is as sweet in our ears as was that flute-player's music that lent to the lips of *La Gioconda* those subtle and poisonous curves.[6]

We will probably never know who the woman in the *Mona Lisa* was, and in fact it matters little. Leonardo left no mention of the painting in his notes and appears to have made no preliminary sketches; at least none have survived, so perhaps he never wanted us to know the truth behind his most famous creation.

As Leonardo was breathing life into his final paintings, the political kaleidoscope of Europe was about to be shaken again, and with this his life was to enter yet another new phase.

Old enemies once again became new allies. This time, Venice joined forces with Pope Julius II and the Holy Roman Emperor and, using Swiss mercenaries, they attacked the French from all sides, driving them from Italy and placing Maximilian Sforza, the legitimate son of Ludovico, upon the ducal throne of Milan. Leonardo gives a hint of this new chaos when he comments in his notebook: 'On 10 December 1511, at the same time, a second fire has been started by the Swiss at a place called Desio [a suburb of Milan].'[7]

Leonardo appears to have stayed in Milan for a while, just as he had done when the French first invaded a dozen years earlier, but he was soon obliged to find peace and safety in the countryside, and retired to the Melzi estate in Vaprio, where he spent at least a year with his group of dependants and pupils. But by the late summer of 1513 he was again planning a move, this time to Rome, and he marked the decision with a typically spartan note that reads: 'On 24 September [1513], I left Milan for Rome, in the company of Giovan Francesco Melzi, Salai, Lorenzo (a pupil) and Il Fanfoia (a servant).'[8]

Although Leonardo was fond of adding little cameos of himself to many of his paintings (most notably as a shadowy figure in his *Adoration of the Magi* of 1481) only one surviving drawing is definitely a Leonardo self-portrait. This is the red chalk drawing now in the Royal Library of Turin, and it was drawn around the time Leonardo travelled to Rome.

This image of Leonardo is the face of the mystic, the wise ancient not so different to our modern vision of Aristotle or Socrates. By this time, Leonardo's hair would have been white, his face we can see lined with the faded years, but time has affected little the strong mouth, the imposing brow and his piercing eyes. How would he have dressed? In a long robe perhaps, sandals in the summer, sturdy leather boots and fur coat in winter. And with him as he travelled, a small group of students and servants and his beautiful younger men: Melzi, now in his early twenties, and Salai (whom it should be noted he had named second in his list of travellers in his note concerning his departure), by this time in his mid-thirties. Their luggage, maybe a trunk of clothes, some fine raiments for special occasions, some treasured painting materials, a lute perhaps, and most precious of all, Leonardo's huge collection of notes and a few special paintings, some half-finished, others nearing completion; these last, items that travelled with him everywhere.

And so Leonardo arrived in Rome in the autumn of 1513. It was a city he had visited many times but in which he had never tarried for longer than a few weeks. This time he had been called to Rome by the Pope's brother, the oldest son of Lorenzo de' Medici, Giuliano, the man some claim commissioned the *Mona Lisa*.

The Medici family were again placed in powerful positions in Italian political life. Julius II, who had instigated the expulsion of the French from Italy in 1512, had died within months of his success and the papacy had fallen to Lorenzo's youngest son, Giovanni. Taking the name Leo X, the new pope was an odd amalgam: lecherous and gluttonous, a man who became incredibly fat in his later years, he was also a great patron of the arts, whose interest in painting, music and literature drew many creative people to Rome.

Giuliano was also a renowned patron and had a keen interest in the natural sciences. Matching his younger brother's interest in women, but less keen on rich foods, he was chief of the Vatican army and the Pope's closest adviser. As a partnership they were highly successful and during this period Rome became prosperous, a city some began to see as a new Florence in the way it cultivated fresh talent. Under the Medicis many new buildings were constructed and commissions for original paintings and sculpture were there to be won by aspiring and gifted young artists.

And in some ways, this demand for the new proved to be a problem for Leonardo. He had been personally invited there by Giuliano de' Medici, an admirer, but the esteemed artist and engineer was no longer fashionable. Now sixty-one, he was regarded as a great genius, a sage even, but a man no longer at the cutting edge of the modern art scene. Younger men had learned great lessons from his creations, from *The Virgin of the Rocks* and the remnants of *The Battle of Anghiari*, but they had also stolen his thunder, catching the eye of rich patrons who were willing to part with their money for innovative, energetic artists who could produce work for them quickly and punctually. At last, Leonardo's reputation for slowness and unreliability was working strongly against him; not only was he seen as yesterday's man, he was simply no longer trusted.

This shift in mood obviously touched and upset him; he could not have failed to notice how Michelangelo was receiving lavish commissions, that Raphael, thirty years his junior and at the time perhaps the most favoured artist in Italy, had been paid no less than twelve thousand ducats by Julius II for decorating *each* of the state rooms (the *stanze*) of the Vatican Palace.[*]

---

[*] It is difficult to give a modern equivalent value to this payment because there were many different types of ducat in circulation at the time. One of the most common and least valuable was approximately equal in value to a 'double florin', worth about ten pence (15 cents). If we take this as the standard ducat, it means Raphael would have been paid the equivalent of at least £1,200 ($1,800) per room.

Leonardo was received in Rome with the respect befitting an elder statesman of the art world and Giuliano had made ready for him a suite of exquisite rooms at the Belvedere inside the Vatican. These had been lavishly decorated at great expense by pupils of Bramante. Leonardo also had many friends in the city, including the singer Atalante Migliorotti, whom he had escorted to Milan some three decades earlier, the great architect Donato Bramante (who died soon after Leonardo's arrival), his old rebel-rousing friend from Milan, *Il Sodoma*, and the young Raphael, whom Leonardo much admired.

In almost all respects, Leonardo could have wanted for nothing. He was living in what was perhaps the most comfortable home he had ever had, he was wealthy from his own endeavours, enjoyed the respect and affection of at least some of the artistic community, his new patron and many of the Roman people, but he was now out of step with modern life, no longer a vital force, and amid the splendour of Rome and the garlands of admiration for past triumphs, he felt lonely and depressed.

In his notes, Leonardo mentions feeling ill during this period. The complaints are not specific but appear to have been true afflictions rather than symptoms of his melancholia. Although his mood could not have helped, his symptoms suggest he may have suffered some sort of stroke soon after arriving in Rome. In places in his notes he mentions the need to keep warm at night,[9] and the fact that he has to wear eye glasses.[10] He had always had little respect for doctors. 'Try to keep in good health, you will do so better if you avoid doctors, for their drugs are a kind of alchemy, which has produced many books as remedies,' he once wrote. And: 'People choose as healers persons who understand nothing about the illnesses they treat,' he claimed.[11] Elsewhere, he called doctors *destruttore di vite*, 'destroyers of lives'.[12] At this time he also wrote in his notebooks: *i medici me crearono edesstrussono*. This is one of Leonardo's most famous statements and has been widely translated as 'the Medici created me and destroyed me'. But although this may have made sense some three decades earlier, the comment tallies little with his actual circumstances at this point in his life, unless we make the improbable assumption that Leonardo blamed his new patron for his depression. It is more likely Leonardo was referring to the plural of *medico*, the Italian for doctor – *medici* – and that he is once more levelling criticism against the medical profession.

For a time at least, Leonardo was free to do what he wanted and he appears to have continued with his usual mosaic of interests. He did no major new painting but filled his notebooks with scientific ideas and anatomical studies, yet although he had the freedom of the city and all the resources he could wish for, his very fame left him open to exploitation and exposed him to deceit.

Soon after his arrival, Giuliano assigned Leonardo two assistants, both Germans, one a master smith named Giorgio, the other a mirror-maker known simply as Master Giovanni of the Mirrors. Within days of their employment in his studio Leonardo began to realise he had made a mistake in allowing them into his household and he was soon in a state of anxiety over their behaviour. This prompted him to write a long rambling letter of complaint to Giuliano, drafted no fewer than six times in his notebooks, each version heavy with re-writings and crossings-out.[13] Among Leonardo's complaints, he speaks of the Germans' idleness and the fact that they went off shooting birds with members of the papal guard, something that would have been particularly offensive to him. But most of all he was angered and anxious because he believed the assistants were spying on him. Once again he was overwhelmed by a fear of plagiarism verging on paranoia and would only entrust the two men with 'width, height, depth and contours of what he was supposed to be making', convinced the Germans were stealing his ideas, 'in order to take them to their own country'.[14] His writings from this time bear further testimony to his anxiety; they are written not only in his usual mirror-writing but heavily encoded, with imagery more at home in alchemical texts than his notebooks.

The relationship between Leonardo and the two Germans finally deteriorated so much that after a few months Giovanni had the temerity to accuse Leonardo of necromancy. Astonishingly, his claims were upheld by the Pope himself, who banned Leonardo from practising his anatomical research at the San Spirito hospital where he had been carrying out autopsies and dissections since almost his first day in Rome. Leonardo notes bitterly in private that the assistant 'hindered me in anatomy, denouncing it before the Pope'.[15]

This time, Leonardo's fears of plagiarism were almost certainly well-founded. It is quite possible the assistants were not only extremely lazy but that they also simply disliked their master. It is possible they disapproved of some half-comprehended aspects of Leonardo's scientific investigations, and it is most probable that, in common with the vast majority of people of the time, they would have been appalled by what they had discovered about his nocturnal anatomical researches.

Yet Leonardo's explosive reaction may also demonstrate his emotional instability during this period, a fact supported by reports of some odd behaviour on his part. One tale relates how he made special wings and horns painted with quicksilver and attached them to a lizard, turning it into a small 'dragon' with which he terrified courtiers at the Vatican. As amusing as some may have considered this to be, it is strangely at odds with Leonardo's usual punctilious treatment of animals, and although he may have done the lizard little permanent harm, it is hardly in keeping with his pronouncements about the wrongs of eating meat or his frequent attempts to improve the lives of animals.

On another occasion, he cleaned the intestines of a bullock and attached them to a blacksmith's bellows. This he placed in the corner of one of his rooms. When a visitor arrived, Leonardo would pump the bellows until the membranous guts apparently filled the room. Vasari relates that Leonardo

. . . formed a paste of a certain kind of wax with which he shaped animals very thin and full of wind, and, by blowing into them, made them fly through the air, but when the wind ceased they fell to the ground. On the back of a most bizarre lizard, found by the vine-dresser of the Belvedere, he fixed with a mixture of quicksilver wings composed of scales stripped from other lizards, which as he walked, quivered with the motion; having given it eyes, horns, and a beard, taming it, and keeping it in a box, he made all his friends, to whom he showed it, fly for fear. He used often to have the guts of a wether [a bull] completely freed of their fat and cleaned, thus made so fine that they could be held in the palm of the hand; and having placed a pair of blacksmith's bellows in another room. He fixed them to one end of these and, blowing into them, filled the room, which was very large, so that whoever was in it was obliged to retreat into a corner.[16]

Perhaps a clearer sign of his mental state in 1514 comes from a collection of drawings and writings which dominate his notebooks of this period. Working again on the problems of geological formation and the way large bodies of water alter landscape, he appears to have become obsessed once more with water and in particular the idea of 'the deluge' which he linked with a morbid fascination with the end of humanity, the *fin de siècle* cataclysm, or re-enactment of the Old Testament flood. In one passage, Leonardo writes:

One will see the dark and nebulous air tormented by contrary winds whirling incessant rain and mingled with hail, and an infinity of broken branches entangled with countless leaves. All around one will see ancient trees uprooted, torn to pieces by the fury of the storm . . . Moreover, on many mountaintops, one will see all kinds of animals, terrified and reduced to a domestic state, as well as men who have taken refuge there with wives and children . . . Some not content with closing their eyes, put their hands over them, one on top of the other, the better to cover them and spare them the sight of the implacable carnage that the wrath of God is visiting on the human race . . .[17]

Leonardo's deluge drawings and writings are paired, almost as though he were producing an illustrated treatise. The drawings are extremely violent, made all the more so by their precision. These are representations derived not just from the skilled hand of the great artist, but carrying echoes of his detailed studies of water and its behaviour, all fuelled by what appears to be a powerful emotional element born, at least in part, from some repressed fear. We know water had always fascinated and scared Leonardo; now, vulnerable, unhealthy and all-too-keenly aware of the rapidly passing years, he was expressing his anxieties in what we can now perceive to be cathartic writings and drawings.

But then, as he seemed to be slipping into a mire of depression, Leonardo's life was to change one final time, a change again precipitated by external factors, another shuffle within the ever-altering political scene. In January 1515, the French King Louis XII died and was succeeded by his twenty-year-old cousin, Francis I.

Energetic, handsome and learned, Francis was a king straight out of Arthurian legend or the chronicles of Charlemagne. Far from the mould of cruel or psychotic leader exemplified by men like Cesare Borgia, Francis did however seek to regain the territory his countrymen had recently lost in Italy, and one of his first political acts as monarch was to turn his attention to a new campaign in the peninsula. By July 1515, less than six months after his coronation, Francis's troops had crossed the Alps and, to the great embarrassment of the Pope and his Roman allies, he had swept aside the Swiss mercenaries and the Milanese army ranked against him, entered Milan in triumph and imprisoned Maximilian Sforza.

Quickly realising the new king was not to be trifled with, Leo X began immediate peace talks with the French at Bologna. It is quite likely Leonardo was there in person because we learn from Vasari that he had been commanded by his patron Giuliano de' Medici to make a suitable centrepiece for the peace talks, something that would symbolise a lasting union between the Italian states and the new French occupiers. For this special occasion, Leonardo fashioned a mechanical lion which apparently walked a few steps before its chest opened to reveal a fleur-de-lis where the heart would have been, symbolising the union of the lion of the Medici and the emblem of the king. Vasari tells us: 'There came to Milan, in his time, the King of France, wherefore Leonardo being asked to devise some bizarre thing, made a lion which walked several steps and then opened its breast, and showed it full of lilies.'[18]

Leonardo had already hinted at such a device in his notebooks. Sounding very much like a simple robot powered perhaps by wound springs or wires, it undoubtedly created something of a sensation and must have impressed the gathered statesmen enormously.

The peace talks would almost certainly have been the first time Leonardo had met the young king, but Francis was already a great admirer. It is conceivable Leonardo was invited to the French court as early as this meeting; the old king Louis had many times offered Leonardo patronage in France, but those offers had always been declined. But if an offer by Francis had been extended on this occasion Leonardo would surely have been very tempted by it.

Yet he did not pack his bags, at least not immediately, almost certainly because of loyalty towards his friend and patron Giuliano. Giuliano de' Medici had married in January that year, an occasion Leonardo had reported with a flourish in his notes: 'Giuliano de' Medici, *Il Magnifico*, left Rome on the ninth day of January 1515, at daybreak, to take wife in Savoy.'[19] But the marriage to Philiberta of Savoy, which had been one of political convenience, turned out to be short-lived; Giuliano died in his late forties in March the following year, 1516.

And even then, Leonardo tarried in Rome. During August 1516 he was making notes about the dimensions of the basilica of St Paul and the earliest he is thought to have set off for his final home in France was the autumn of that year, although considering his age and increasingly frail health, it is quite possible he waited until the following spring.

Cloux is close to Amboise, about a hundred miles south-west of Paris, and it was to here that Leonardo set out upon his final journey. It took him almost three months, and with him went once more his constant companions Salai, Melzi, a group of servants and a collection of large trunks filled with manuscripts and paintings. Leonardo was quite aware this would probably be his last major journey and he took all that he would need in his new home.

The King had arranged for Leonardo what must certainly have been his most salubrious home, a little manor house set in two and a half acres of land which belonged to the Queen Mother and adjoined the King's residence, the Château of Amboise. The ground floor was converted into a studio and the first and second floor provided accommodation for Leonardo and his entourage. Francis also endowed Leonardo with an incredibly generous pension of one thousand écus soleil. Coupled with this, he gave four hundred ordinary écus to Melzi (described in the ledger as 'the Italian gentleman who is with the said Master Lyenard'), and a single payment of one hundred écus for Salai, who was referred to in the same document as a 'servant', a label which probably did not delight him.

The relationship between Francis I and Leonardo exaggerated their respective personalities and characteristics. Like many of his predecessors, Francis was a great patron of the arts, a refined and highly educated man, equal parts knight and scholar, who had been encouraged since early childhood to perceive himself as a great warrior-king in the mould of his revered ancestor, Charlemagne. Six feet tall, he stood some nine inches taller than the average man of the time and he favoured gilded armour. His adviser and intellectual guide, Leonardo, whose face we might recall from the self-portrait drawn only three or four years earlier, possessed more than a hint of Merlin about him, a perfect match for Francis's Arthur.

Even if they did not perceive themselves in these roles, the young king and the elderly polymath were to take on many of the characteristics of these legendary models. Rather than comparing himself and Francis to Merlin and Arthur, Leonardo preferred the model of Aristotle and Alexander, writing in about 1518: 'Alexander and Aristotle were teachers of one another. Alexander possessed the power that allowed him to conquer the world. Aristotle had great learning, which enabled him to embrace all the learning acquired by other philosophers.'[20] And, in spite of a growing awareness of his own mortality, this new, final role of Leonardo's appears to have made him happier than he had ever been in Italy.

There was a tunnel connecting the King's residence to Leonardo's house and Francis would visit him frequently. According to legend, the two spent many long nights deep in conversation, a tale which goes some way to explaining the young monarch's charity. He had a great love for Leonardo's paintings and was of course familiar with those the artist had brought with him to Cloux, his *Mona Lisa*, *John the Baptist* and perhaps the *Virgin and Child With St Anne*. But it was Leonardo's breadth and depth of knowledge, his understanding of science, his documented experiments and his thoughts on almost every aspect of human endeavour that so fascinated Francis. And for his part, Leonardo was fortunate to find a man who did not want him as a servant to decorate his rooms, produce games and *divertimenti* for his court, or to design war machines and to create plans for elaborate fortifications. Francis wished to reach the essence of Leonardo's genius, to get close to him in the hope that something of that genius might rub off. A fellow royal servant, the architect Benvenuto Cellini, wrote of the relationship:

King Francis, being extremely taken with Leonardo's great *virtù*, took so much pleasure in hearing him reason, that he was apart from him but a few days a year . . . I do not wish to neglect repeating the words I heard the King say of him, which he said to me – that he believed there had never been another man born in the world who knew as much as Leonardo, not so much about sculpture, painting and architecture, as that he was a very great philosopher.[21]

In the event, Leonardo was to spend only two full summers at Cloux. In that time he returned to the seemingly hopeless task of collating the thousands of pages of manuscript written and saved for almost forty years. He painted no more masterpieces, at least none that have survived. He continued to probe into a grand mix of subjects simultaneously, drawing up designs for a new palace Francis was planning, conducting further experiments with Melzi's help and probably adding finishing touches to the paintings he treasured.

During those years, his body was failing but his mind remained as sharp as it had ever been. He was suffering from arthritis in one hand (or perhaps both hands) which restricted his ability to paint and to write, but did not stop him completely. He determinedly resisted illness and fatigue, declaring late in 1518: 'I will continue.'[22]

And so he did, writing around this time about a fossil of a fish he had been given, declaring:

How many changes of state and circumstances have succeeded one another since there perished in some deep and sinuous crevice the marvellous form of this fish . . . Now destroyed by time it has been waiting patiently in this cramped space, and with its bones stripped bare, it has become a prop and support for the mountain rising above it.[23]

Here we can discern a distorted reflection of his own fear of death.

Leonardo was quite aware that all life was built upon other life and that one's physical existence was wholly dependent upon the mortality of other organisms.

Later, he reminds himself that he must keep working and thinking if he is to survive, declaring: 'Iron rusts when it is not used . . . stagnant water loses its purity and freezes over when cold; so, too, does inactivity sap the vigour of the mind.'[24] However, for a complex medley of reasons, it is easy to imagine Leonardo becoming increasingly depressed as he entered his final months. He had struggled to succeed all his life and now the failings of his body were robbing him of his future hopes. But more important than this was the agonising realisation that the Universe was a far more complex thing than he had ever dared imagine and that, in spite of all his efforts, he had hardly scratched the surface of reality, made almost no impression, left next to nothing. He had hinted at the enormity of existence a decade earlier when writing about vision and noting with barely repressed hysteria: 'The order of proving how the Earth is a star [meaning planet]: first define the eye; then show how the twinkling of a star arises in the eye.'[25] It was as though he was standing on the rim of discovery, peering down into an orgy of information, experience and the fact upon fact that is the Universe. Centuries before the Age of Reason, and as he approached death, Leonardo began to sense the vastness of life, the grandeur of it all.

There must have been a stream of visitors to the home of the great sage during those final years, but the account of Don Antonio de Beatis, secretary to the Cardinal of Aragon, is the only one to survive. It was De Beatis who reported seeing what was almost certainly the *Mona Lisa* propped up against the wall of Leonardo's studio, along with *John the Baptist*, and the *Virgin and Child With St Anne*, and he went on to describe Leonardo's vast collection of anatomical drawings and the master's ambitious plans for at least three books of scientific studies.

Leonardo, he claimed, had also written 'a quantity of volumes on the nature of waters, on various machines, and on other subjects which he pointed out to us. All of these books, written in Italian, will be a source of pleasure and profit when they appear.'[26]

These were almost certainly collections of notes rather than edited or refined editions ready for the printers. Leonardo most probably never succeeded in drawing together the threads of his intellectual wanderings. As he admitted: 'This will be a collection without order drawn from many pages which I have copied here, hoping to put them in order in their places, according to the subjects with which they will deal, and I believe that before I am at an end of this, I will have to repeat the same thing many times.'[27] Sadly, he had insufficient time to 'repeat the same thing many times'. His *Treatise on Painting* is the only self-contained collection of his ideas; the rest of the material remained in disorganised bundles and confused collections of manuscripts and notes.

Francesco Melzi appears to have taken on the role of Leonardo's assistant and amanuensis. When Leonardo could no longer hold a brush or a quill, Melzi, under his master's instructions, added details to paintings and transcribed notes. Indeed, Melzi had replaced Salai as Leonardo's closest companion some time before they all travelled to France, and soon after arriving in Cloux, Salai left for Milan, never to return. We can only assume he did not care to live under the wing of the French King and, with one hundred écus in his pocket and his role superseded by the 'very beautiful boy' Melzi, he took his leave of Leonardo for the last time.

In April 1519, a few days after his sixty-seventh birthday, Leonardo made his will. He left his half-brothers the not inconsiderable contents of his account at Santa Maria Nuova in Florence (some four hundred écus soleil), as well as the small property once belonging to Uncle Francesco for which Leonardo had fought a court battle a decade earlier. To Salai, he left half the vineyard given to him by Francesco Sforza and half the toll from a canal which King Louis XII had granted him in payment for some consultancy work. The other half of each of these Leonardo left for his servant, one Battista de Villanis. This shows how low Salai had fallen in Leonardo's affections, for he received in the will nothing more than that bestowed upon a trusted servant.

Aside from a few small offerings to other servants and friends, the bulk of Leonardo's legacy went to Melzi, who was entrusted with all Leonardo's manuscripts, paintings and other artefacts, along with his pension, property and personal possessions.

It seems that, as he completed his will, Leonardo knew his life was ebbing away; he died on 2 May 1519, just nine days later. Vasari declares that on his death bed Leonardo offered penitence and desired to return to the bosom of the Catholic Church, telling us:

> Finally having grown old, he remained ill many months, and feeling himself near death, asked to have himself diligently informed of the teaching of the Catholic faith, and of the good way and holy Christian religion; and then, with many moans, he confessed and was penitent; and although he could not raise himself well on his feet, supporting himself on the arms of his friends and servants, he was pleased to take devoutly the most holy Sacrament, out of his bed.[28]

We should not take this account too seriously. Vasari, who was himself a deeply religious man, was fond of placing too much emphasis upon the religiosity of those about whom he wrote. Leonardo may have found some form of solace in conventional religion as he lay dying, but we have no proof of this. His overwhelming attitude towards the approach of death seems to have been resentment and defiance. As his final days approached, he commented in his notebooks, 'It is with the greatest reluctance that it [the soul] leaves the body, and I think that its sorrow and lamentations are not without cause.'[29] Which implies that even at this stage in his life Leonardo saw little evidence to support the idea of any form of afterlife and that he found no comfort in the concept. In fact, he made a point of refusing to make any comment on religion, declaring: 'The definition of the soul . . . to the minds of friars, fathers of the people, who by inspiration possess the secrets. I let be the sacred writings . . .'[30] And, in his most empirical mood, he wrote, 'I do not attempt to write or give information of those things of which the human mind is incapable and which cannot be proved by an instance of nature.'[31]

Even so, he followed convention by including in his will the accepted niceties of the Catholic faith. He wished his body to be interred at the church of Saint-Florentin in Amboise, and gave instructions for a series of high masses to be given by the chaplains of the church, and of course he gave alms to the local poor. But this was only what common good manners dictated; he had, after all, been the guest of a strictly Catholic monarch for almost three years.

Vasari was also the first to claim Leonardo da Vinci died in the arms of the King. Francis, he tells us, had rushed to the sage's bedside and cradled him as he breathed his last:

The King, who was wont often and lovingly to visit him, then came into the room, wherefore he, out of reverence, having raised himself to sit upon the bed, giving him an account of his sickness and the circumstances of it, showed withal how much he had offended God and mankind in having not worked at his art as he should have done. Thereupon he was seized by a paroxysm, the messenger of death; for which reason the King, having risen and having taken his head, in order to assist him and show him favour, to the end that he might alleviate his pain, his spirit, which was divine, knowing that it could not have any greater honour, expired in the arms of the King.[32]

However, Melzi informed Leonardo's brothers of his death, writing movingly, 'It would be impossible for me to be able to express the grief under which I have fallen, and as long as the elements of my body remain conjoined I will be possessed of perpetual sadness.' He made no mention that the King had been at Leonardo's bedside.

Orthodox opinion claims Vasari's version of events to be a work of fiction. The argument revolves around a document, an act of Francis I, dated 3 May 1519 and written at Saint-Germain-en-Laye which was unearthed in 1850 by an historian named Léon de Laborde. Because Saint-Germain-en-Laye is a two-day ride from Amboise, the King could not have reached there in time and Vasari's version of events could not be true. But then, in 1856, another researcher, Aimé Champollion, noted that the document had not in fact been signed by the King himself but by a chancellor in his absence.

So it is possible that on this occasion Vasari was right. Perhaps Leonardo, the illegitimate artist, a man forbidden a formal education, who by his own merits had startled the world of the Renaissance with his brilliance, did indeed die in a manner fit for a king. Such a thing is pleasing to visualise, and actually requires little imagination. Perhaps the man who had inspired monarchs and madmen, fellow artists and men of science, did die resting in the arms of Francis I of France, his final patron and a man who had loved him as he would a long-lost grandfather.

10

THE NOTEBOOKS II (1500–1519)

Science is the Captain, Practice the soldier.
— Leonardo, *Manuscript I*

Leonardo worked without break from the day he arrived in Verrocchio's studio sometime around 1465–66 until his death in 1519, offering over half a century of concentrated effort, first as an artist and then extending himself into a polymathic life in which he studied an enormous variety of subjects.

As we saw in Chapter 7, the first period of his writings unveiled, amid the copying and re-working of others, a few gems of discovery – ideas, experiments and bold statements only reiterated and developed by others sometimes centuries after Leonardo's death. But even so, the first two decades of his scientific investigations were really years of preparation, years during which the groundwork was put in place; to get a fuller picture of his achievement, we should now look at the final twenty years of Leonardo's researches.

Between 1500 and 1519, Leonardo da Vinci was at his most unsettled. This was a time during which he travelled widely and turned his hand to a most varied collection of interests. At the beginning of the sixteenth century he was an artist with a private collection of notes and a desire to be recognised as an engineer and architect. By the end of his life, he had metamorphosed into the stereotypical sage, the 'wise old man', almost the Jungian archetype whose understanding of all facets of the world drew, among many other contemporaries, the King of France, Francis I, to place him above all other geniuses of the age.

I have discussed Leonardo's efforts as a military engineer, as a designer, landscape artist, court inventor and architect, and I have commented upon these interests as they became prominent in his life. Between 1500 and his death he committed to paper sketches of gardens, horses' heads, set designs for plays, trinkets and baubles for the rich and influential, as well as austere designs for military hardware, fortifications, canals, dams and all manner of machinery. But alongside these, and interspersed with them, indeed often on the same page (for Leonardo was always short of paper), we may find notes and drawings covering a small collection of topics which make up the bulk of his writings and constitute what was most dear to Leonardo's intellect, the areas of investigation that fascinated and at times obsessed him. Most important of these were his researches into anatomy, geology and geography, astronomy and the possibility of human flight.

We know Leonardo wanted at least to organise his notes on these particular subjects and perhaps to see them published as individual treatises; if we are to believe the single surviving report of Leonardo's final months at Cloux, it is possible he embarked upon this process. Leonardo's visitor, Antonio de Beatis, noted in his journal:

The gentleman has engaged himself in anatomy so accurately with the display of paintings, of limbs as of muscles, nerves, blood vessels, joints, as much of male bodies as of female ones, in a manner never used by anyone before. This we have seen with our own eyes and he told us he had anatomised more than thirty bodies of men and women of all ages.[1]

But all we have as a finished work is Leonardo's *Trattato della Pittura*, the *Treatise on Painting*; the rest is a patchwork of notes and drawings that appear in a collection of notebooks over a twenty-year period. These observations, experiments, statements and declarations are muddled and scattered, many have been lost and what we have today is perhaps only three-quarters of the original material. Even in this form, though, we can, with effort, trace the workings of Leonardo's mind and piece together his ideas and findings, for with this mélange of creative outpourings Leonardo reached the pinnacle of his achievements. Here lies the essence of Leonardo, 'the first scientist'.

Most important to Leonardo, and perhaps his greatest achievement, is his collection of drawings and observations in the field of anatomy. Little record has come down to us of dissection in ancient times, but we know that the Greeks and Romans were deeply interested in the whole question of the internal workings of the body. Although rare, dissections were certainly conducted between then and Leonardo's time. But during the medieval era, and on into the early Renaissance, human dissection was viewed as unsavoury, a practice obfuscated by taboo and an unwritten ethical haze. A small group of specially licensed doctors were allowed to conduct dissections as a teaching exercise. Yet, for professors themselves, these were rarely interactive; they would merely preside over the process as assistants did the knife-work. The procedure did nothing to further human understanding of the inner workings of the body because invariably the doctor/professor ignored what was displayed and simply trotted out what he and his teachers had been taught, wisdom handed down verbatim from Classical sources, rendering the dissection absolutely pointless.[2]

In 1491, the Renaissance writer and medic De Ketham published a book entitled *Fasciculo de Medicina* which contained illustrations of what the author believed were the inner workings of the human body. Leonardo probably owned a copy of this (it was published in the vernacular in 1493), but the illustrations are almost childlike in their crudeness and would have offered him little guidance.* We know also that Leonardo read some of the ancient authorities before he began his own dissections and made notes based upon these. In the *Codex Trivulzianus*, he states, 'Medicine is the restoration of elements out of equilibrium; illness is the discord of elements infused into the living body.'[3] This is a direct quote based upon the eight-volume *De Re Medica* by the first-century medic Cornelius Celsus, and it is a purely Aristotelian statement which Leonardo later discarded.

So what prompted Leonardo to begin his study of human anatomy? In the final chapter, I will consider the possible psychological reasons for Leonardo's choice. Surprising as it may seem to our twenty-first-century sensibilities, it was not for the benefit or the advancement of medicine. As we have seen, Leonardo had little regard for the medical profession and probably perceived no link between an empirical investigation of the human body and ways to improve the state of health of living human beings. His reason for picking up the blade was probably more prosaic. Quite simply, he wished to follow his intellectual forebears, men such as Alberti and Vitruvius, who had placed great importance upon the study of the physical nature of man. And by doing so Leonardo embarked upon a truly intrepid journey. He probably knew he was the first to attempt a detailed study of human anatomy and must have felt at least a little trepidation at his own boldness. In his early years of scientific investigation he had conducted many dissections of animal cadavers, a practice he would continue into his final years, but the taboo-breaking step of opening up a human body must have taken a certain steeliness of character. This he hinted at years after his first dissections when he wrote:

I have dissected more than ten human bodies, destroying all the

---

* To be fair to De Ketham, his illustrations in *Fasciculo de Medicina* were deliberately simplistic and schematic because they were meant solely for use as a teaching aid.

various members and removing the minutest particles of flesh which surrounded these veins without causing any effusion of blood . . . And as one single body did not suffice for so long a time, it was necessary to proceed by stages with so many bodies as would render my knowledge complete; this I repeated twice in order to achieve the differences. And though you should have no love for such things you may perhaps be deterred by natural repugnance, and if this does not prevent you, you may perhaps be deterred by fear of passing the night hours in the company of these corpses, quartered and flayed and horrible to behold . . . Concerning which things, whether or not they have all been found in me, the hundred and twenty books [chapters] which I have composed will give verdict 'yes' or 'no'.[4]

It was a messy, nocturnal, socially borderline practice. It was messy because, as Leonardo makes clear, dead bodies do not stay preserved for long. Today, chemicals allow medical students to work on a cadaver for perhaps several months. Leonardo did not have this luxury and had to work fast and in extremely uncomfortable conditions. He had to use fresh cadavers and tools he had designed and fashioned himself. To avoid accusations of heresy, he conducted his dissections at night and most probably alone, and he faced the constant danger of infection from the rotting corpses he studied.

We can only assume Leonardo was able to convince the authorities to allow him to conduct post-mortems thanks to his status and recognition at court, and by making it clear his investigations were exclusively to develop his skills as an artist. He could never have even hinted at his scientific interest in the human body. The word 'science' did not exist in Renaissance Europe, and even during this period of religious leniency Leonardo's inquisitiveness was interpreted by some as necromancy. Indeed it is interesting to note how he first obtained a human body for dissection only after becoming a famous and respected figure, and even then he was forced by the Pope to give up his experiments. His German assistants in Rome may have had ulterior motives in probing into Leonardo's activities, but they were nevertheless genuinely horrified by what they discovered.

We are extremely fortunate to have been left a wonderful archive of Leonardo's work as an anatomist, from which it is clear that, more than any other discipline within which he worked, the study of anatomy suited him perfectly. Leonardo was of course a consummate artist as well as a vigorous investigator, so that he could report what he saw in both words and exquisite pictures.

We saw in Chapter 7 how his study of light was so apt for him and how he could represent for us the details of his discoveries in both accurate drawings and with words, but with anatomy this interconnection is even more dramatic. Little surprise then that many Leonardo scholars believe his anatomical drawings to be the finest examples of his artistic brilliance.

Leonardo probably began his anatomical studies during the late 1480s, contemporaneous with his first efforts to construct the Sforza equestrian statue. During his preliminary research, which led to his sketches and plans for this giant bronze edifice, Leonardo was a frequent visitor to stables around Milan; he intended not simply to model the bronze horse on just one favoured beast from the ducal stables but to create an amalgam of all the best features of the finest horses in the city. He studied the proportions of the legs and the ratios of leg to neck and head to back in drawings now in the Windsor collection.

Along with these studies of living animals, during this time Leonardo anatomised cows and oxen, and often used this work to extrapolate his findings to humans, sometimes with erroneous results. An example is his depiction of the human womb, which included flower-like projections, called cotyledons, found in the cow's womb but absent in humans.

Aside from these studies, between the late 1480s and 1507 the only human body-part to which Leonardo had access was a skull he used to study the senses and perception. But a turning point in his anatomical researches came during the final weeks of 1507, when he had the good fortune to conduct a post-mortem on an old man.

> The old man [he tells us], a few hours before his death, told me that he had lived a hundred years, and that he had felt nothing wrong with his body other than weakness. And thus while sitting upon a bed in the hospital of Santa Maria Nuova in Florence, without any movement or other sign of any mishap, he passed out of this life. And I made an anatomy of him in order to see the cause of so sweet a death . . . This anatomy I described very diligently and with great ease owing to the absence of fat and humours which greatly hinder the recognition of the parts.[5]

This single dissection acted as the cornerstone for many of Leonardo's later researches. As he wrote himself, he conducted dissections on more than ten bodies, and according to Antonio de Beatis it was more like thirty. Quite how many is hard to judge, but even if we exclude his interpretations based upon the study of oxen, the sheer range of his findings as described in the hundreds of drawings and thousands of words would at least support his own estimate.

So, what were Leonardo's anatomical findings?

Some of his earliest work during the period immediately following the dissection of the old man in Florence was a continuation of his researches into the senses. In particular, he was fascinated with the workings of the eye and how the eye and brain combined to produce vision; he went on to dedicate an entire manuscript, now known as *Manuscript D*, to this subject. During the 1480s and '90s he was preoccupied with the search for the *sensus communis*, the seat of the soul, and although he continued with this ultimately fruitless enterprise until his death, by the early sixteenth century, armed with practical experience, he had become more interested in the mechanical processes controlling vision and the other senses.

Leonardo was probably the first anatomist in history to observe how the optic nerves left the back of the eye and made connections with the brain, drawing in considerable detail the *chiasm* or intersection of the optic nerves.[6] With this, Leonardo's research marks a distinct

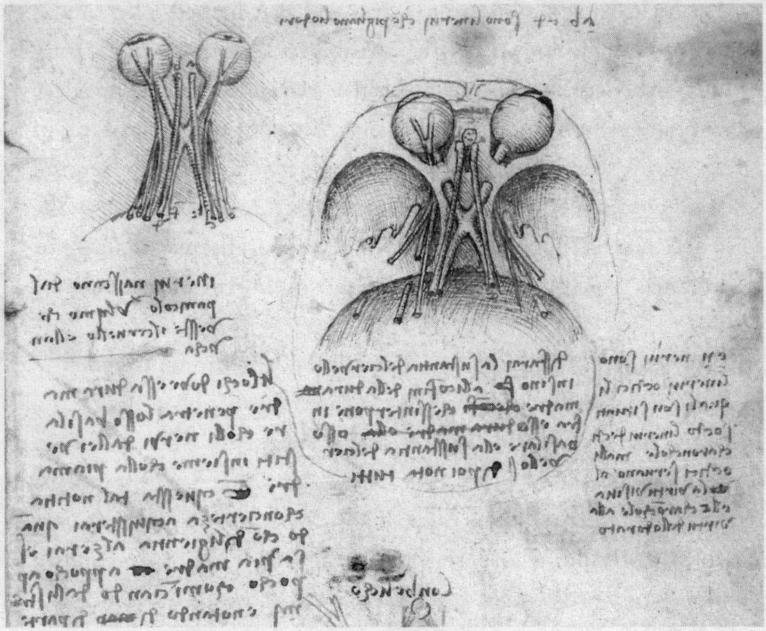

Fig. 10.1: Leonardo's dissection of the eye.

departure from Classical wisdom, which offered no clear explanation for how the eye and brain were connected.

Leonardo also conducted many dissections of animal skulls and concentrated most of his anatomical efforts on the brains of oxen. To obtain more information about the shape of the brain and the configuration of the folds of the cerebral cortex, he developed an ingenious technique involving the injection of wax into the skull cavity. Based

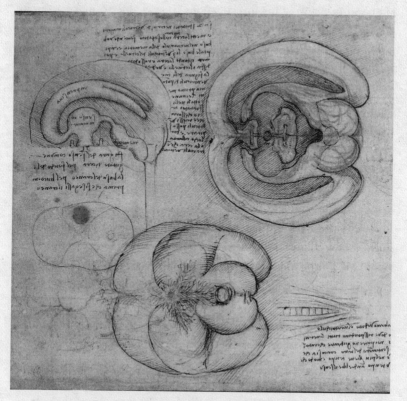

Fig. 10.2: Leonardo's drawing of the brain.

upon these experiments, he drew exquisitely detailed representations of the inside of the skull and the channels and undulations of the brain.[7]

As an artist, Leonardo was fascinated with the structure and inter-relationship of the muscles and, to a lesser extent, the configuration of nerves. As a scientist, he placed great importance upon studying the network of muscles and nerves of the body and investigated how different muscles produced the various movements of the limbs and how the nerves and the brain were linked. The ancients had again offered few clues about the nervous system, and although Leonardo was working blind in many of his investigations he was able to make accurate judgements that were far ahead of his time. 'The nerve branches with their muscles serve the nerve chords as soldiers serve their officers,' he stated, '. . . and the nerve chords serve the *sensus communis* as the officers serve the captain, and the *sensus communis* serves the soul as the captain serves the lord.'[8] If we ignore the anachronistic language, with this neat analogy he laid down the primary neurological structure of the body, that nerves lead to the spinal cord and on to the brain. To reiterate his ideas, he went on to write of 'a tree of nerves that descends from the brain and the nape stretching along the spine and spreading along the arms and legs'.[9]

He compared the muscles of humans with those of other animals and showed how many functions could be matched between species and highlighted those muscles and nerves that played specific roles. One of Leonardo's most inventive contributions to this field was a technique for demonstrating how muscles worked. Replacing the muscles in the arms and legs of cadavers with wires and threads, he pulled them to demonstrate how they operated. In his notes, he writes:

> If you have drawn the bones of the hand and you wish to draw the muscles covering and joining the bones, then draw threads, though not muscles. I say threads and not lines, so that one can see which muscle rests over or under the other given that one would not be able to do so with simple lines. And once this has been done, besides, draw another hand showing the real outline of muscles.[10]

Elsewhere, he observes: '. . . draw threads before muscles; such threads are to indicate the site of muscles and have their ends converging where muscles join bones. This will allow a better understanding when you draw all the muscles, one over the other. Otherwise your drawing will appear confused to the eyes of others.'[11] And in a typical example of how he delighted in finding links within Nature wherever he could, he says: 'No movement of the hand and its fingers is brought about by muscles above the elbow; and thus it is also in birds, and that is why they are so powerful, because all the muscles that lower the wings have their origin on the breast, and have more weight of themselves than all the rest of the bird put together.'[12]

From detailed studies of the muscles of the body, and paying particular attention to the shoulders, arms and legs, Leonardo investigated the musculature of the face and was able to link muscle movements with expressions, writing beside a labelled diagram: '*h* is the muscle of rage, *p* is the muscle of pain, *g* is the muscle of bite, *gnm* is the same muscle, *ot* is the muscle of rage.'[13] This was of course an over-simplification of the complexities of the musculature of the face, but Leonardo was again the first to think seriously about the link between individual muscles and facial expressions and then to qualify his ideas with detailed drawings.

In other places in the notebooks Leonardo drew comparisons between human and animal expressions, a study upon which Darwin was to expend great energy and about which he wrote one of his most famous books, *The Expression of the Emotions in Man and Animals*, first published in 1872. However, as with almost all his studies, Leonardo merely scratched the surface of this vast subject before launching into other areas of anatomy that grabbed his attention.

He spent considerable time studying both male and female reproductive systems and drew many intricate diagrams illustrating the function of the ovaries as well as producing lengthy descriptions of how semen was produced. In his early writings he followed the Classical line that semen was made in the bone marrow of the spine and transported to the testicles, but after conducting his own dissections he changed his mind. Although he could not explain how semen was produced by the body, nor how the ovaries functioned, he was able to detail how hernias form in the scrotum and produced closely

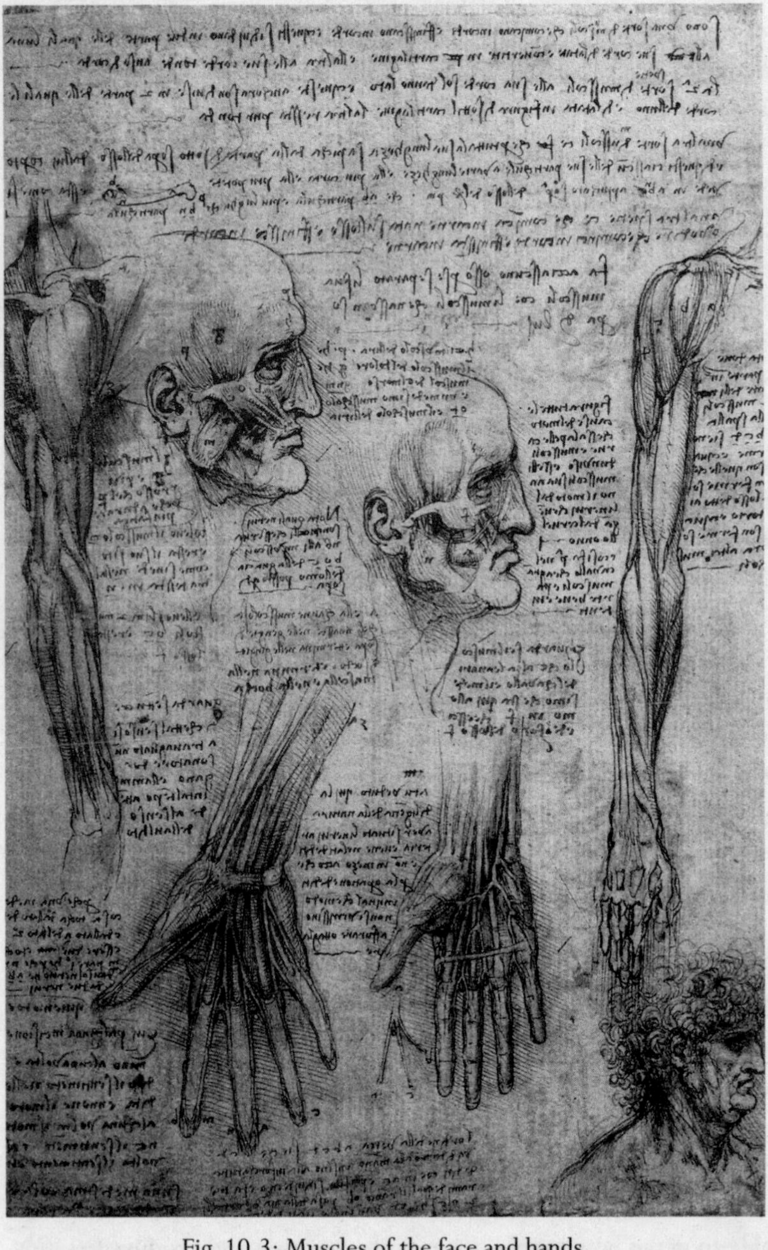

Fig. 10.3: Muscles of the face and hands.

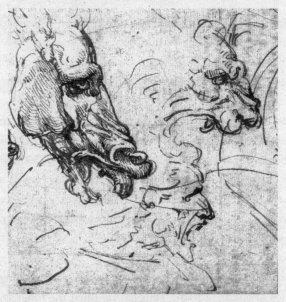

Fig. 10.4: A comparison between the facial expression
in a horse, a lion and a man.

observed drawings of the urinary ducts leading to the bladder and the
ejaculatory canal. However, as we have seen him do before, he went
on to draw conclusions that could only be classified as metaphysical.
One example is the intriguing statement: 'The man who accomplishes
intercourse with reluctance and disdain sires children who are irrita-
ble and unworthy of confidence, but if intercourse is entered upon
with great love and desire on both sides, the children will be of great
intelligence, full of wit, liveliness, and grace.'[14]

Leonardo followed up on his studies of the reproductive system
with an investigation of embryology. Most of his material came from
work with cows, but he is known to have had the rare opportunity of
studying one seven-month-old human foetus. From this dramatic investigation has come what many consider to be the most accomplished of
his anatomical drawings, including his famous image of the foetus in the
womb, possibly the first ever presented in such detail and certainly the

most skilfully rendered. Leonardo said of the foetus: 'The child is in the womb surrounded by water because heavy objects weigh less in water than in air, and more so if the water is slimy and dense. And thus this water distributes its weight and that of the baby on the bottom and on the sides of the matrix.'[15]

Less successful were Leonardo's attempts to explain the functioning of the respiratory system. This was almost certainly because of the unavoidable fact that he had so little time to work with cadavers, and the fabric of the lungs is so easily corrupted, leading him to distorted impressions. However, he was able to reason that the larynx and the trachea were involved in the making of vocal sounds. 'Try to see how sound is produced in the front of the trachea,' he writes.

This may be accomplished by separating the trachea along with the lungs of a human body. Thus having filled the lungs with air and having quickly blocked it one can see immediately how the tracheal pipe produces voice. And this one can see and hear accurately with the throat of a swan or goose, which can be made to sing after its death many a time.[16]

He drew exquisite diagrams of the digestive system and located the various elements of the digestive tract not altogether inaccurately, but he had no inkling of how food was transported through the tract. Unable to witness peristalsis in a dead body, Leonardo followed traditional teaching: that food was moved through the body by the action of breathing.

Elsewhere among his vast collection of some 1,500 anatomical drawings there are superb drawings of the heart, the liver and kidney, the spleen and the stomach, along with what might be called 'the plumbing' of the body, the interconnecting pipes and ducts that constitute the endocrine system, and of course the circulatory system for the blood.

Leonardo's contribution to the understanding of how the cardiovascular system works is fragmentary but at times astonishingly prescient.

Yet it cannot be denied that although his holistic approach was the spur for his anatomical researches, it was also the factor which, to a degree, prevented him making further connections of a truly revolutionary nature. His desire to form over-arching links had been one of the reasons for his initial interest in anatomy. As he wrote in a notebook relatively early in his serious anatomical researches:

Man is said to be the minor world by the ancients and this expression is surely well reckoned, inasmuch as man is made of earth, water, air and fire, his body is the earth's simile. Where man has bone as a support and armour for the flesh, the earth has stones as a support for the soil; where man has a pool of blood, wherein the breathing lung increases and decreases, the earth's body has its ocean sea, that too floods and ebbs every six hours to let the earth breathe; where blood vessels branch out from the mentioned pool of blood through the human body, likewise the ocean fills the earth's body with countless vessels of water.[17]

Much of this is Aristotelian in flavour, and we can see Leonardo still subscribes to the Greek notion of the four elements of nature, a concept he never entirely dismissed. And sometimes his obsession with the holistic ideal combined with a lingering faith in Aristotle led him far astray.

In particular, he expended a great deal of energy and time upon his investigations of both the heart and the circulatory system of blood vessels, only to miss finding a suitable connection between them. He used the term 'circulation' and knew of such detail as capillary veins and the huge importance of the aorta, noting that it 'holds dominion over the life of the animal'.[18] He also made a detailed investigation of the chambers of the heart using again his technique of producing wax models, making such amazing observations as:

Between the cords and threads of the muscles of the right ventricle there are interwoven a quantity of minute threads . . . and these wind themselves round the most minute and imperceptible nerves [here Leonardo is referring to tendons] and weave themselves with them. And these muscles are in themselves very capable of expansion and contraction, and they are situated within the fury of the rush of the blood which passes in and out among the minute cords [parts of tendons] of the muscles before these are converted into the *panniculi* [membranes] of the *uscioli* [cusps of the valves].[19]

Elsewhere he says, 'The heart . . . is a vessel of thick muscle, kept alive and nourished by artery and vein as other muscles are,'[20] noting, 'Of the heart. This moves by itself, and does not stop if not forever.'[21]

He was also aware of the time relationships between the pulse and the heartbeat, observing that '. . . the time of the heart's closing and its beating against the ribs with the apex and of the beating of the pulse and of the entrance into the *antiporto* [the atria] of the heart is one and the same'.[22] By which he meant that the pulse and the heartbeat were intimately linked.

However, in spite of offering these stunningly original observations, Leonardo did not make the proper connection between the heart and the circulation of blood. Amazingly perhaps, for one who knew so much about the heart, including the fact that blood vessels contracted and dilated, he did not make the essential link between the movement of the blood around the body and the pumping or mechanical action of the heart. The reason for this is clearly tied to Leonardo's dedication to a grand holistic view, a rare example of this obsession actually becoming detrimental to his studies and leading him to an entirely false conclusion.

Because Leonardo was so keen to draw comparisons between all areas of nature, he decided, as we saw in the earlier extract from his writings, that the blood of the body was analogous to the water of the oceans, calling it 'a pool of blood, wherein the breathing lung increases and decreases'. Furthermore, he believed the movement of blood in animals was similar to the movement of fluids in plants. Because of this, it would be quite wrong to suggest Leonardo predated Harvey in explaining how the cardiovascular system functions – how the heart pumps blood through a circulatory system which extends around the body.

Leonardo's great achievements as an anatomist and artist of anatomical subjects, however, cannot be fully understood by merely taking individual areas of research in turn. To appreciate fully what he did, we actually need to apply his own cherished holistic approach and to take an overview of his work.

Leonardo's anatomical drawings were not only the most detailed and skilful ever attempted up to his time, but his way of representing his findings was thoroughly modern. In fact working with a form of what we would now call hyper-text and the cutaway, layering technique used in the creation of CD-Roms, his illustrative method was five hundred years ahead of his time. Leonardo frequently drew three-dimensional arrays of muscles or organs of the body from several different perspectives. A good example is his set of drawings of the musculature of the shoulder, found today in the Windsor collection, showing how to represent the shoulder of an old man from half a dozen different angles before stripping away layer after layer of skin, tissue and muscle to reveal the tendons and the sinews, the muscles of the front of the body and then the back.[23]

In his drawings of the bones of the body, he details their appearance from all angles. Showing single unconnected bones and then pairs, he draws them pivoted on joints and contorted into different positions, along with sections of skeletons posed in different ways to illustrate how the joints work together. In his drawings of the skull and the brain, he offers cutaways and sections of the cerebral cortex drawn again in layers as if peeling the skin of an onion.

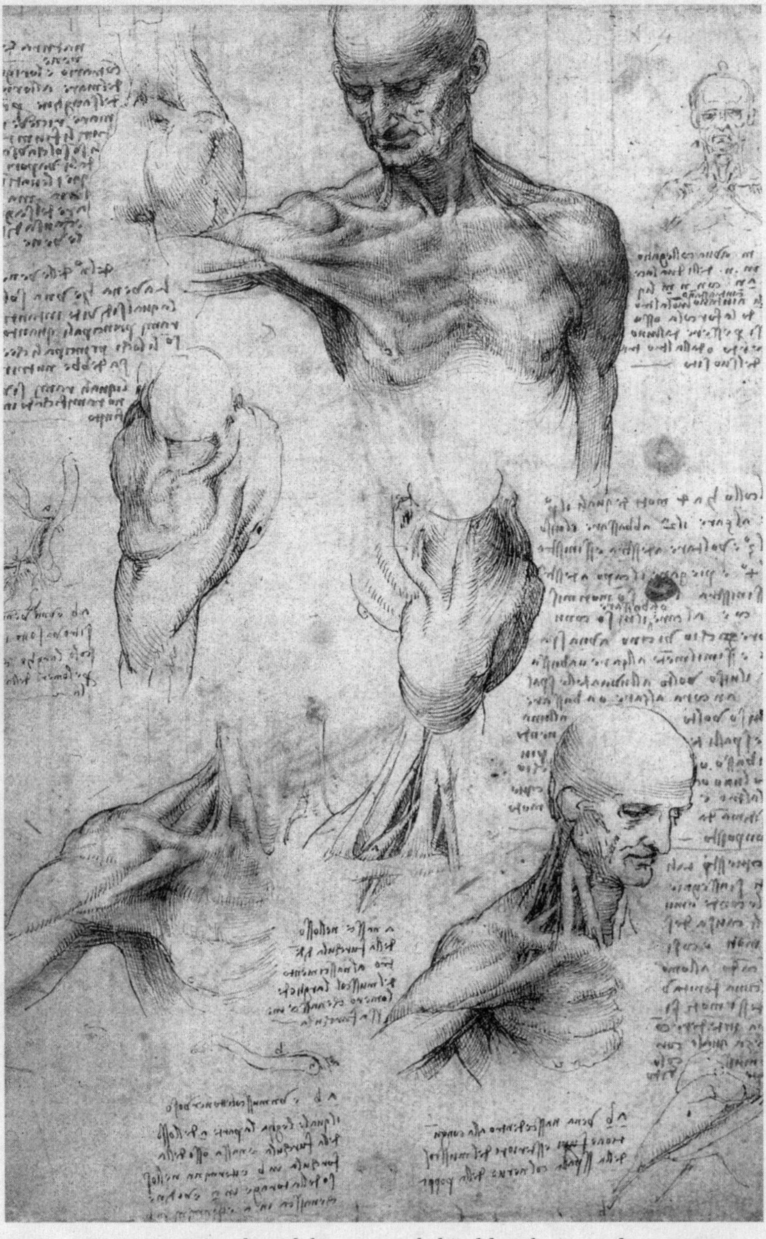

Fig. 10.5: Muscles of the arm and shoulder shown in layers.

Leonardo was aware of the originality of this technique and how useful it was as a way of representing his findings. At one point in his notebooks, when he first applied the idea, he casually sketched an onion sliced in half beside his illustration of a cutaway skull.[24] In another notebook, he described the technique enthusiastically, saying: 'Draw this demonstration sideways, so as to inform that one part is behind the other and then draw one from behind, so as to show the blood vessels filled by the spine and heart and the main blood vessels.'[25]

Clearly, Leonardo had planned a treatise on anatomy and he intended this to be in the form of an encyclopaedia, designed in a way that would be familiar to a modern-day designer of reference material. He saw this treatise as an anatomical partner to Ptolemy's *Cosmography*, in which the author had linked words with images; Leonardo envisaged a similar scheme employing text and drawings with which he would make accessible connections between the different areas of his anatomical findings. Indeed, he valued illustration far beyond the power of words, commenting: 'Writer, which letters will you use to convey with such perfection the whole representation herein displayed by drawing? . . . Do not interfere with matters of the eyes trying to get them through the ears.'[26]

We have seen how anatomy was perfectly suited to Leonardo. He was a careful researcher with great practical skill, he had an unquenchable drive to discover, possessed few qualms about the ethical debate or the physical discomfort of dissecting human beings and, perhaps most importantly, he had unparalleled ability to represent what he had found. But one more skill should not be forgotten. Between Leonardo's first dabblings with simple comparative anatomy and his detailed researches following post-mortems, he had learned a great deal as an engineer. And even if Leonardo was wrong to make so many disparate connections between the human body and the wider perspective of how Nature operated, he was quite correct in perceiving how many of the body's functions could be visualised as mechanical processes.

This is how he could make easy comparisons between threads or wires and muscles, leading him to the development of a useful technique for demonstrating how muscles worked. He could see that the joints were really hinges and he could appreciate how moment and leverage could be applied to the movement of limbs.

But more important to Leonardo was his need to link what he found inside the body of a human with what he observed in the larger world. He saw Man as the model of the Universe. To Leonardo's eyes, Man was indeed a machine, but one which, in an abstract (rather than geographical) sense, occupied a unique position at the epicentre of the Universe; all else was modelled upon this form.

In some ways this is a curious conclusion for him to reach. As we saw in Chapter 7, much of this thinking (especially early in his intellectual explorations) was based upon ancient Classical ideology and had been visualised before Leonardo by men such as Vitruvius. But, as we will see later in this chapter, Leonardo also believed that the Earth is not unique in the Universe and that the stars are suns like our own.

Yet, to him, the human physical form was vitally important. Predating Descartes by over a century, but blending a primitive dualism with his own metaphysical approach, Leonardo took the view that the human body is the *ultimate* machine and model for the Universe, but that God (a nebulous term for Leonardo, who saw God as an abstract force of Nature) had created this wondrous thing called Man as the ultimate product of His 'intellect'. One of the clearest comments Leonardo makes about this – and perhaps, also, a subtle criticism of those who would view his researches as in some way immoral or obscene – is to be found beside a drawing of a human skull: 'Spectator of this human machine, do not sadden for having to make it known through the death of others, but rejoice that our God has devoted his intellect to the perfection of this tool.'[27]

And yet here is an odd conflict in Leonardo's thinking. On the one hand he sees the human body as the ultimate machine, the pinnacle of God's achievement, but on the other, he had little feeling for humankind as an entity. He believed in the supreme nature of the human form, yet, as we have seen, also wrote of people being mere 'fillers of latrines'.[28] Elsewhere, after writing about the reproductive system, he declares sarcastically, 'I expose to men the origin of their first, or perhaps second reason for existing.'[29]

However, for Leonardo there was some resolution to this apparent disparity. He did indeed hold only contempt for humanity as a unit, but this was driven solely by a distaste for what humans did and the way they thought. He believed and stated bluntly that the human form was too wondrous a thing for such unworthy creatures as the men and women he saw each day. 'I do not think that rough men of bad habits and little intelligence', he wrote, '. . . deserve such a fine instrument and such a variety of mechanisms.'[30] A comment written with the passion of one who has seen the splayed remains on the autopsy table.

So what are we to make of Leonardo's accomplishments as an anatomist? It is clear his ideas developed enormously during his second intense spell working within this discipline and that his earlier endeavours in Milan during the late 1480s and early 1490s were merely preparatory. We need only compare two of his anatomical drawings of the internal human form, one drawn in 1490 and the other in 1508–9 (both now in the Windsor collection) to see how much he had discovered and observed.

The earlier drawing is largely accurate but lacking in any fine detail; it is merely an outline providing the framework for the internal organs and their interconnections. The later drawing is a masterpiece of detail and accuracy drawn from years of experience, the product of many nights of messy labour.

Leonardo began his efforts in anatomy as a Classicist adhering to many of the traditional ideas handed down to him, but it took him only a short time to discard most of these shackles, to reach his own conclusions and to re-write the standard texts in his private notebooks. In some areas he remained a Classicist, and he missed the chance of overturning the traditional view of the function of the heart, made little

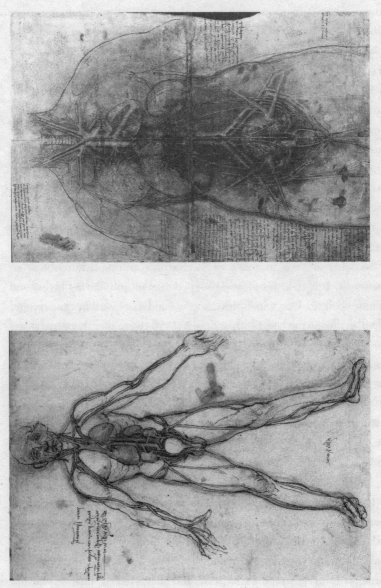

Fig. 10.6: A comparison of Leonardo's anatomical drawings. The first is from 1490, the second from 1508.

headway with his investigation of the respiratory or digestive systems and sometimes drew false conclusions by extrapolating his observations based upon oxen and applying them to human physiology. But he did make some genuinely original discoveries. His investigations of the eye were many years ahead of their time, his understanding of the functions of the muscles and nerves were extraordinarily perceptive, and his technique for investigating the shapes and functions of organs and bodily systems was remarkably inventive.

Leonardo dedicated great effort to his anatomical studies; indeed, it is probably no exaggeration to say that this work was more important to him than any other area of study he ever undertook and it fascinated him more than painting ever had. For Leonardo, anatomy represented a struggle. It was the most difficult subject he could follow. Through his close friendship with Pacioli he had been attracted to mathematics, but probably realised he was not suited to it and would never master it. Painting came almost too easily to him so that he often 'tired of the brush', and for much of his life it provided little challenge.* He had made inroads as an engineer and could have forged a successful career using solely his engineering skills, but anatomy was extraordinarily difficult, and an unploughed field. It was also risqué, barely tolerated, mysterious, seen as heretical by some; and so Leonardo, first and foremost the unconventional explorer, the man who deliberately pursued paths others neglected, found it quite naturally beguiling.

Yet, great as they were, Leonardo's efforts as an anatomist did not yield as much as some observers would like to imagine. Before him,

---

* The exception to this is the series of paintings Leonardo produced during the final decade of his life, the *Mona Lisa*, *Leda and the Swan* and *St John the Baptist*. These may have been painted purely for his own pleasure; they are quite revolutionary in their style and content, they were on themes of his own choosing and appear to have been reflections of deep, often suppressed aspects of his character. They were also works that derived from a lifetime of study, both as artist and scientist, and they stretched his abilities to the limit.

little had been achieved in the field of anatomy since Greek times, and what had been accomplished Leonardo built upon. He drew together strands of ideas already there and pushed just that little bit further, but he made no revelatory discoveries; he produced no revolutionary concepts that were only rediscovered centuries later as he had done with his work in optics, but he pieced together what had until then been muddled and fragmentary investigations, shoddily portrayed.

However, after Leonardo something remarkable happened in the study of anatomy. Within a generation of his death, the subject began to emerge as a genuine intellectual venture. Whereas Leonardo had been living in the shadow of suspected necromancy, later investigators turned the study of human anatomy into a respected science. Most important of these researchers was the Flemish anatomist Andreas Vesalius, who was four years old when Leonardo died. He became physician to the Holy Roman Emperor Charles V and then to Philip II, King of Spain. In 1543 he published his masterpiece *De Humani Corporis Fabrica* (*On the Structure of the Human Body*), an exquisitely illustrated treatise on human anatomy based upon extensive first-hand experience that earned him the title 'father of anatomy'.

Yet of course Vesalius was covering the same ground as Leonardo. As Vesalius was writing his treatise, Leonardo's drawings were in the home of Melzi's son, Orazio, hidden from the world in drawers in a dusty attic in Vaprio. Vesalius gives us slightly more detailed information than Leonardo, but his representations are uniformly inferior, his artistic ability not in the same league as Leonardo's. The twinned genius of Leonardo, both artist and scientific investigator, provided us with illustrations of his observations that were only bettered in terms of accuracy during the nineteenth century, and made clearer visually with the advent of photography, X-rays and, more recently, CAT scans.

And when eventually Leonardo's drawings and anatomical writings became better known, they gradually took their place within the canon of natural philosophy alongside new researches as the subject of human dissection threw off its murky image. Based upon Leonardo's work, artists began to portray dissections as art. Rembrandt's *The Anatomy Lesson of Dr Nicolaes Tulp* (1632) and *The Anatomy Lesson of Dr Joan Deyman* (1656) are the most famous examples. Ironically, the marriage of art and anatomy had come full circle; the artist had originally utilised knowledge of the anatomist to improve his deceits, and little more than a century after Leonardo's death different artists were representing the mechanics of dissection in their paintings. The link between these two was Leonardo da Vinci.

As I have noted many times when describing Leonardo's life and achievements, he only rarely concentrated upon one area of study at a time and fondly mixed his artistic and scientific efforts. Indeed there must have been many days when Leonardo would spend the morning studying some aspect of mechanics, optics or mathematics, the afternoon adding a detail to one of his commissions and then, late at night, he would take up the scalpel, slicing a liver or prising a muscle from a tendon to study its texture. And this pattern changed little, even when he became obsessed with one subject or another. The topic of his devotions would take precedence, but other investigations were never neglected entirely. So, as Leonardo attempted to unravel the secrets of the human form, he continued to observe, experiment and write about many other things that interested him. During the period between the end of the sixteenth century and the final days of his researches, including his itinerant years, Leonardo studied geology and geography, astronomy, the flight of birds and the possibility of human flight, and it is to the first of these we now turn.

Leonardo believed that, 'The knowledge of past times and of the places on the earth is both ornament and nutriment to the human mind.'[31] And he was one of the first to develop the idea that geological and geographical facts could be derived from a study of the physical past; an idea we take for granted today.

We have seen that Leonardo was obsessed with water and its effects, both good and bad, and the properties and importance of water came into almost all aspects of his thinking as a geologist. He considered it the most important element and wrote extensively about it. He made a detailed study of water erosion and composed a 'Book of Rains' in which he wrote about the role of clouds, how they are formed, how they produce rain and the effect of rain upon the environment. 'Clouds,' he said, were, 'mists drawn up by the heat of the sun, and their ascension stops at the point where the weight they have gained is equal to their "motor power".'[32] If we again ignore his odd use of language, what Leonardo is saying is that clouds float at certain heights due to their buoyancy in air and the quantity of moisture they have absorbed. Later he asserts, 'The clouds are formed by the humidity pervading the air; this collects because of the cold, which is brought by the air with various winds.'[33]

He invented a hygrometer, which could be used 'to know the qualities and thickness of the air, and when it is going to rain'.[34] He had clear but controversial ideas about the origin and formation of rivers. The accepted authority on this subject was Pliny, who quite wrongly held that rivers came from the sea. Leonardo instead concurred with the unfashionable but correct descriptions of Vitruvius, claiming: 'The waters of rivers come not from the sea but from the clouds.'[35]

Leonardo's perception of geology and geography, which in places also bordered the study of meteorology and even palaeontology, extended in two directions simultaneously. On the one hand, he was many years ahead of his time in thinking in terms of long epochs, what we now call 'geological time'. He did not name them as such, but hinted at the concept, writing in his notebooks, 'The fossils of Lombardy have *four levels*, and likewise all those that have been made in several stages.'[36]

He was much taken with the concept that geological change appeared to take long periods of time; at various points he returned to a theme that emerged when he was depressed in Florence during the 1470s, applying it here to his observations of Nature, writing such things as 'time, the consumer of things',[37] and 'time, the destroyer of created things'.[38]

Leonardo made a detailed study of fossils three centuries before their formation was fully explained and the true scale of geological time periods realised. He came to the correct conclusion that many fossilised creatures were exposed by the receding of the oceans, which helped him develop a grand theory to describe how the water levels of the planet had been far higher in ancient times and that they were continuing to recede, declaring: 'Within a short time the river Po will cause the Adriatic Sea to dry up in the same way as it has dried up a great part of Lombardy.'[39]

At the same time, he pursued again his holistic ideology and tried to draw parallels between the human body and the Earth – two distinct subjects he was studying simultaneously, but believed were unified on a metaphysical level.

We might say that the earth has a spirit of growth, and its flesh is the soil, its bones the arrangement and connection of the rocks of which the mountains are composed, its cartilage the tufa [porous rock], and its blood the springs of the water. The pool of blood which lies around the heart is the ocean, and its breathing and the increase and decrease of the blood in the pulses, is represented in the earth by the flow and ebb of the sea; and the heat of the spirit of the world is the fire which pervades the earth, and the seat of the vegetative soul is in the fires, which in many parts of the earth find vent in baths and mines of sulphur, and in volcanoes.[40]

As we saw earlier, his obsession with this world-view misled him in his anatomical studies, and in particular lost him the prize of linking the heart with the circulation of the blood, taken as he was by spurious links between what he was seeing in his studies of the Earth and those of the human body, leading him to make odd statements such as, 'Whence we may conclude that the water goes from the rivers to the sea, and from the sea to the rivers, thus constantly circulating and returning.'[41] Such misconceptions obviously did little to help him make accurate and empirically sound judgements about the functions of the human body.

In recent years, Leonardo's ideas about geology have come under particularly close scrutiny. The eminent biologist and author, Professor Stephen Jay Gould, although a great admirer of Leonardo, is highly critical of the idea that Leonardo should be seen as a true scientist. While admitting that Leonardo's observations were remarkably accurate and detailed, he questions the spur, the motivation for his inquisitiveness. Professor Gould quite rightly realises Leonardo was driven to produce a theory for how fossils were created, how strata are formed and how rivers deposit large rocks at high altitudes far from their origins because he wished to tie up the loose ends of his grand holistic vision. But Gould goes on to see this obsession of Leonardo's as a wholly destructive force, removing for ever any scientific credibility Leonardo may have gained from his discoveries.

Professor Gould properly denounces those who proclaim Leonardo to have been 'a modernist among the Medici . . . a futurist in the court of Francis I'.[42] But the fact that Leonardo's drives stemmed from an anachronistic interpretation of the world does not invalidate his findings nor his rightful place in the pantheon of scientific figures. Obviously, Leonardo's ideology was fanciful, he was led to correct conclusions motivated by false premises, but he was certainly not the last scientist for whom this could be said.

In his recent essay, 'The Upwardly Mobile Fossils of Leonardo's Earth', Professor Gould describes how Leonardo tried to reconcile his interpretation of Nature with the observed facts. Leonardo was rooted in his part Aristotelian, part original holistic philosophy, and his central struggle was to show that the microcosm, as represented by the body, and the macrocosm, as represented by the Earth, could be interlinked and that each mirrored the other in detail. To do this, Leonardo wished to demonstrate that the Earth mirrors the body in the way the elements are circulated. In particular, he wished to show that both solid earth and water circulated in the Earth in the same way he thought liquids and nutrients circulated within the body (although, as we have seen, he never did explain how this was facilitated). To this end, he tried to prove that both the rocks and the water of the Earth could rise through air. He succeeded in explaining how rocks could be transported but never managed to fit the movement of water against the air into his scheme.

Professor Gould claims Leonardo's motivation must surely rob him of the mantle of the genuine scientist, but the fact that Leonardo never succeeded in making irrefutable observations to support his vague idea that water circulated within the Earth and that he never once attempted to fudge the matter, merely adds strength to my conviction that he was a true scientist. Many of Leonardo's peers would have failed to understand that facts must fit and support theory or else that theory is invalidated, whereas Leonardo never contemplated forcing the facts to suit his pet hypothesis.

Leonardo's personal interest in geology was also in part derived from a fascination with water and, as we have seen already, this interest may have been stimulated by fears rooted in the experience of his early childhood.

Flying in the face of contemporary opinion, and using clinical scientific arguments, he dismissed utterly the idea that Noah's flood was responsible for creating the deposits of fossils hundreds of miles from their origins. His most lucid argument was based upon the fact that fossils could not have been transported such distances within the forty days stipulated in the Old Testament. Knowing that the movement of a cockle through the flood waters could be measured at six to eight feet per day, he comments dryly: 'With such a rate of motion, it would not have travelled from the Adriatic Sea as far as Monferrato in Lombardy, a distance of 250 miles, in forty days.'[43]

As a scientist, his reasoning about the properties of water and its role in the maintenance of life on Earth was rarely misplaced, and even his metaphysical extrapolations, his attempts to find connections between aspects of nature that are not actually there, were only really damaging to his work as an anatomist. Most importantly, Leonardo knew that just as water was a great shaper of the world, it could also greatly aid civilisation. In an age centuries before the utilisation of steam, when the simple water-wheel and the muscles of beasts provided the only sources of power to aid humans, Leonardo dreamed of ambitious schemes for using water on a grand scale.

We have seen how he drew up plans for redirecting the Arno, and fantasised about what we would now perceive as an 'industrialised zone' following the course of the river across Italy from Pisa to Florence. He was employed to design canals and to devise improvements to waterways. He had offered plans for underwater military strikes and created *divertimenti*, court entertainments and plans for landscaping the gardens of the rich and influential using water to power ingenious contraptions. Leonardo wanted to understand water, to find what he saw as the fundamental essence of the element. By coalescing it with other aspects of Nature, he wanted to neuter it, but most of all he wanted to dominate it, Canute-like, by enslaving it to the service of humanity.

As with so much of Leonardo's work and with so many of his adventurous notions, he only partly succeeded with this task. Once again, he was hamstrung by the fact that he happened to live in an age unable to cradle his genius; he could never fully realise the potential of these ideas. Of course, he never saw even the earliest foundations of any form of industry along the banks of the Arno, and many of his water-driven devices were never built. Yet he was sure such things would be realised one day; that what we call technology would develop using water as a power source. In a note to himself, he wrote, 'When you write of the motions of water, remember to put under each proposition its uses, that this science may not be useless.'[44] The very idea that science could be useful was in itself revolutionary. It would take another two centuries before such a notion would begin to be realised, a step that gave us the Industrial Revolution and the modern world.

If Leonardo's ideas as a geologist and geographer were at times over-ambitious and at others remarkably prophetic, his researches into astronomy displayed an even greater disparity. Almost everything he did in the sphere of astronomical study was based upon his interest in optics and vision. He certainly harboured a deep respect for mathematical astronomy, not least because of exposure to such ideas through his friend Luca Pacioli. Leonardo owned a copy of Ptolemy's *Cosmography*, which he held in high regard; he also possessed a work by the Arabian astronomer Albumasar, a book on the quadrant, and Goro Dati's *La Spera*, but, as far as we are aware, he attempted no investigation of celestial mechanics himself. Instead, he was content to satisfy his fascination with the optical qualities of matter and the interaction of light and the 'physical realm' and to apply his earlier conclusions in optics to what he observed and theorised as an astronomer. 'There is no part of astronomy', he concluded, 'that is not a function of visual lines and perspective.'[45]

As with many of his scientific investigations, he began as an Aristotelian, but gradually many of these traditional ideas were discarded and replaced with his own conclusions and those reached by medieval thinkers. 'Make a discourse on the size of many stars, following the authors,' he reminded himself.[46]

Aristotle held that the 'celestial realm' was entirely different from the 'earthly realm' and that all heavenly bodies were perfect, that the planets and the Moon were unblemished spheres, each self-contained, each producing its own perfect luminosity. Based upon observations of the Moon with the naked eye, Leonardo disputed these ancient, false ideas, sprinkling his notes with contentious statements such as: 'The

Moon is not luminous in itself. It does not shine without the Sun.'[47] And he made the sound judgement that, 'The Moon acts like a spherical mirror.'[48] In this regard, he was influenced by the thinking of the medieval philosopher Albert of Saxony, who had reached similar conclusions a century and a half earlier.

Leonardo believed the Moon was made of similar materials to the Earth and that it was largely covered with water. Unaware of craters, he suggested: 'The skin or surface of water which comprises the sea of the Moon is always ruffled, little or much, more or less, and this roughness is the cause of the proliferation of the innumerable images of the Sun which are reflected in the ridges and concavities and sides and fronts of the innumerable waves.'[49]

As strange as these ideas may seem to us, from them, Leonardo actually reached a conclusion that was both correct and far ahead of his time. He decided that, 'If you were on the Moon or on a star, our Earth would appear to you to make the same effect as does the Moon.'[50] By which he meant it would appear similar as it floated in space. And from this, he went on to speculate: 'The Earth is a star much like the Moon.'[51] A correct statement in spirit, if erroneous in mixing the terms 'star' and 'planet'.

Again, this idea was not entirely original. Half a century earlier, Cardinal Nicholas of Cusa had pondered such ideas in his treatise De Docta Ignorantia. However, this book was no longer widely read by the time Leonardo was studying the Moon and he had almost certainly never seen it. Even if he had, Cusa's was a philosophical work which referred to astronomical phenomena using vague poetic terms, and his writing would have made little impact upon Leonardo's scientific reasoning.

Again, taking many leaps of deduction and making sublime connections between phenomena, Leonardo wrote of our Sun:

There is not to be seen in the Universe a body of greater magnitude and power than the Sun; and its light illuminates all the celestial bodies distributed through the Universe; and the life forces descend from it, because the heat which is in living animals comes from life forces and no other heat is there in the Universe . . .'[52]

We see here once more Leonardo's constant need to inter-relate aspects of Nature. This was of paramount importance to him; the function of the Sun had to be fitted into an orderly universal picture. This time it led him to seek out logical links between energy from the Sun and living things on the Earth.

It would be wholly wrong to suggest Leonardo predated Copernicus' heliocentric view of the Universe propounded in *De Revolutionibus Orbium Coelestrium*, published in 1543. In spite of Leonardo's bold assertions that the Earth is like any other 'star', and his vigorously anti-Aristotelian stance concerning the structure of the Moon, nowhere in the notebooks is there anything close to a heliocentric theory. More intriguing perhaps, Leonardo's work in astronomy leaves us with confusing enigmas still not completely resolved five hundred years on. Most important of these is the idea that he might have invented the telescope.

The argument over whether or not Leonardo was the first person in history to manufacture and use a telescope has raged among scholars for almost a century. He was certainly fascinated by optical devices, and during his time in Rome he experimented with parabolic mirrors and ways to generate energy from the Sun.[53] The primary sources for the dispute over the invention of a form of telescope centre around a collection of statements written by Leonardo between 1508 and 1510, along with a set of drawings to be found in his notebooks. He certainly describes clearly the principle behind the telescope when he writes: 'It is possible to find means by which the eye shall not see remote objects as much diminished as in natural perspective.'[54] And he goes on to describe an instrument containing what is thought by some to be a convex lens inside an extendable tube 'for outside or suitable to keep in the study'.[55]

At other points, he describes how an astronomer might use such an instrument: 'The convex pupil of the eye can take in the whole of our hemisphere, while this method will show only a single star. But where many small stars transmit their images to the surface of the pupil, those stars are extremely small; here only one star is seen, but it will be large. And so the Moon will be seen larger and its spots in a more defined form.'[56]

And again, in another manuscript, Leonardo asserts:

The further you place eyeglasses from the eye, the larger the objects appear in them, when they are for persons fifty years old. And if the eye sees two equal objects in comparison, one outside of the glass and the other within the field, the one in the glass will seem large and the other small. But the things seen could be 200 ells [a little over 200 metres] from the eye.[57]

But most famous of all his statements about a telescope is another of those notes to himself in which he declares, 'Construct glasses to see the Moon magnified.'[58]

But there is more. Considered the most important evidence by those who believe Leonardo did invent the telescope is a drawing found in a pocket-sized notebook now known as *Manuscript F*.[59]

This image was ignored for many years, but in 1938 a scholar named Domenico Argentieri began to realise that it may be a diagram of a telescope. He reached this conclusion by combining the known statements (mentioned above) with other references among Leonardo's notes. Firstly he noted the text written in tiny script in Leonardo's usual mirror-writing on the same page as the drawing. This reads, '*Ochiale di cristallo grosso da' lati un'oncia d'un'oncia*' — 'Eyeglass of

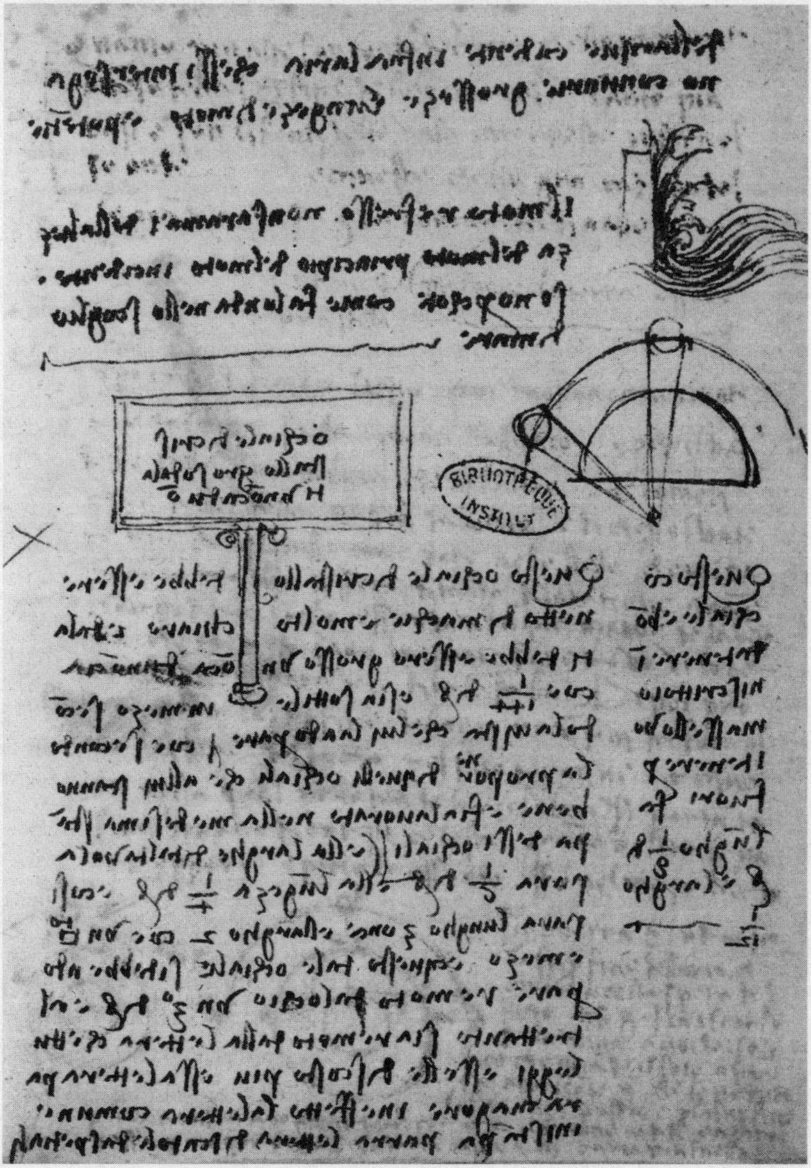

Fig. 10.7: What may be a sketch of a basic telescope.

crystal thick at the sides at ounce of an ounce.' Below this Leonardo has written: 'This glass should be free of spots and very clear, and at the sides it should be an ounce of an ounce thick, that is ¼₄₄ of an ell [a little under 1 centimetre], and let it be thin in the middle.'[60] From these statements, Argentieri concluded that Leonardo had intended fitting a divergent lens in the tube to produce a telescope, and claimed that because the drawing in the tiny notebook was so small, Leonardo could not draw the lens.

Argentieri presented a compelling case for the idea that Leonardo had devised and constructed various telescopes, even concluding that he was experimenting with what later became known as reflecting telescopes which use mirrors to reflect an image on to an eyepiece. And indeed, Leonardo's own statements show clearly that he was aware of some of the principles involved in the construction of a telescope.

However, there are several logical inconsistencies with any assertion that he actually succeeded with this. Most crucially, if he had produced a telescope, then surely he would have used it. He would have made observations of the Moon, of the moons of Jupiter and the stars of the Milky Way precisely as Galileo did a century later. Leonardo would have documented these observations, offering us detailed illustrations of the features of the Moon. These he would have used to support his theories concerning reflection and the nature of the lunar surface, ideas about which he had already written at some considerable length. But there is nothing. In the *Codex Arundel*[61] there is a sketch of the Moon, but this is clearly drawn from naked-eye observations.

But, some have argued, what if we assume the astronomical writings of Leonardo describing the use of the telescope have been lost? Sadly, this conclusion is illogical, for the simple reason that Leonardo would almost certainly have told his close friends about his invention and the discoveries it unfolded. In all probability, he would have tried to capitalise upon the use of the telescope, for it could not possibly have escaped his notice that such a device would have enormous military and civil applications, as well as purely scientific ones. Yet, again, there is no record of Leonardo mentioning the telescope to anyone.

Argentieri's explanation for this is that Leonardo was so hounded by his fear of plagiarism and the possible theft of his work that he could not bring himself to construct many of his inventions and the telescope was a further example of an idea lost. He places the blame squarely at the door of the German assistants, Master Giorgio and Master Giovanni of the Mirrors. At the time they were employed by Leonardo, he was indeed reaching the apotheosis of his experiments into the optical and mechanical requirements for an effective telescope, but there is no irrefutable evidence to suggest he deliberately held back the construction of such a device because of these two characters.

The idea that Leonardo built the first telescope would certainly solve an old mystery. Hans Lippershey is usually credited as the inventor of the simplest device in 1608, a telescope that then found its way to Italy where Galileo made major improvements and used it to make his epoch-changing observations described in his *Sidereus Nuncius*. However, there is evidence to suggest that others had created such a thing earlier. Before Lippershey there was a mysterious figure named Janssen, and before him the story of an anonymous Italian who had engraved *Anno 1590* on a telescope transported from Italy to Holland (although this inscription could well have been a fake). And there are claims that the Italian Mannerist architect Giacomo della Porta, who died in 1602, could have predated all of these, or that he had been the secret engraver.[62]

But evidence for or against Leonardo predating the 'official' invention of the telescope by a century is quite irrelevant. It is simply not feasible to imagine a Leonardo who, having reasoned how such a device could be built, then failed to capitalise on it; this is a scenario that diminishes Leonardo's genius and runs so counter to his character it is hardly worthy of consideration.

The only logical conclusion must be that having deduced many of the theoretical aspects involved in constructing a telescope, Leonardo fell short of actually making one. This failure may have been due to an over-pronounced fear of theft, but even for paranoid Leonardo this seems an exaggerated reaction, especially if we are to assume he understood the potential importance of his finds. It would seem Leonardo was either unable to make a telescope because his tools were not sufficiently sophisticated, or else he saw how only part of the device could be made and merely speculated upon what might one day be possible.

And so we turn to the last of Leonardo's great scientific obsessions, and see how his life-long fascination with birds turned into a determined effort to master the art of human flight. In 1505 he claimed he had in some sense been destined to attempt flight himself, because of the childhood incident in which a bird swooped down into his face as he lay in a cradle. Whatever Leonardo's motivation for attempting this feat, the underlying reason for his love of birds and his wish to fly remains open to speculation, and is a topic discussed in the final chapter.

Leonardo's earliest thoughts on the subject come from his first years in Milan, the early 1480s, but all that has come down to us from this time are vague musings and speculations. However, a few years later, in 1486, Leonardo took a major step forward and was able to make the remarkably mature assertion that:

As much pressure is exerted by the object against the air as by the air against the body. And see how the wings, striking against the air, bear up the heavy eagle in the thin air on high. And see the air as it moves over the sea strike against the swelling sails to make the loaded heavy ship run; so that for those demonstrative reasons that have been given you may know that man, with his great contrived wings, exerting effort against the resisting air, may conquer and subject it, and rise above it.[63]

What is particularly striking about this statement is the first sentence – 'As much pressure is exerted by the object against the air as by the air against the body' – a statement that predates Newton's third law of motion by almost precisely two hundred years.*

Leonardo was not studying conventional mechanics when he stumbled upon this conclusion and he did not apply the concept to a range of situations, nor did he create a mathematical framework to support the idea, all of which Newton accomplished with brilliance. Nevertheless, this is a fine illustration of how Leonardo was no Icarus, donning a pair of wings and diving off the nearest tall building. He approached what would then have been one of the most far-sighted and adventurous concepts of his time, the mastery of the air, with the same empirical vigour and attention to detail he applied to all his undertakings as an inventor, scientist, engineer or artist.

Leonardo spent many years studying the bodies of birds and the mechanism by which they remained in and travelled through the air. He filled notebook after notebook with drawings, both sketches and intricately-drawn annotated illustrations on the subject. He wrote thousands of words describing his observations and conducted endless experiments to replicate specific motions of wings and the effects of a shifting centre of gravity, and he used a range of different materials to replicate bird and bat wings. 'First determine the motion of the wind,' he wrote, 'and then describe how the birds stay poised in it, merely by balancing of their wings and tails.'[64]

Through experiment and careful observation, Leonardo was able to understand how a bird maintains stability in the air, how it alters its pitch and compensates for fluctuations in the force of the wind, as well as how it glides. His conclusion was: 'The bird is an instrument

---

* Newton's third law, often known as the principle of action and reaction, states that every action gives rise to a reaction of equal strength but opposite direction. An example is the movement of a rocket in the opposite direction to that in which the exhaust gases are expelled; another is the recoil of a fired rifle.

operating through mathematical laws, which instrument is in the capacity of man to be able to make with all its motions.'[65] Clearly then, he believed it would be possible to re-create the way birds fly on a larger scale using a machine that could carry a man.

Others had already attempted to fly and were working on their own methods contemporaneously with Leonardo. The Italian engineer Giovan Battista Danti crashed on to a church roof in 1503, and Leonardo must have been familiar with discourses on the subject of human flight. These ranged from the thirteenth-century natural philosopher Roger Bacon, who described 'a flying machine in the middle of which a man could be seated and make an engine turn to activate artificial wings that would beat the air like those of a bird',[66] to the drawings of giant birds by the medieval engineer Villard de Honnecourt.

Convinced the mechanics of bird flight could be extended to practical human flight by using movable wings and muscle power, Leonardo wrote:

If you should say that the sinews and muscles of a bird are incomparably more powerful than those of man, because all the flesh of the big muscles and fleshy part of the breast goes to increase the power of the wing's motion, and the bone of the breast is one piece which affords the bird's very great power, while the wings are all compact of big sinews and other very strong ligaments of cartilages, and the skin is very strong, with various muscles: then reply to this is that all this strength is the purpose of enabling it, over and above the ordinary action of wings in keeping it up, to double and triple its power in its claws and moreover carry as much weight through the air as it itself weighs; thus we see a falcon carry off a duck and an eagle a hare. This sufficiently proves the purpose of such an excess of power; but they need little power to keep themselves up in the air and balance on their wings and flap them on the currents of air and steer along their paths, a little movement of the wings sufficing, and the larger the bird, the slower.[67]

To satisfy himself this was a correct conclusion, he reported a simple experiment. 'A man also has a greater amount of power in his legs than is needed for his weight,' he declared.

To show that this is true, have a man stand on the shore and consider how deep his footprints are. Then put another man on his back and you will see how much deeper his feet sink in. Then take the second man off his back and have him leap straight up in the air as high as he can; you will find that the impressions of his feet have been sunk in deeper by the jump than with the man on his back. Hence, we have proved in two ways that man has more than twice the power that he needs to support himself.[68]

Leonardo called his vision of a flying machine 'a ship of the air', and in one of its incarnations he pictured a device with four wings, the operator positioned vertically and moving the wings by pushing his head on to a pole, turning two cranks with his hands and pressing down two pedals with his own body weight. From a long series of calculations he deduced that in this way a man could generate a power of 600 Florentine pounds (about 200 kilograms).

And there were other designs. Most famous is what has since been called an 'aerial screw', or 'Leonardo's helicopter'; a framework with a spiral of fabric above it that whirls round to create lift.[69]

These are marvellously inventive designs and many are based upon sound aerodynamic principles. Yet none of them could have come close to flying, simply because the human occupant could never have generated enough power to propel the machine fast enough to gain the lift it required. Leonardo lived during an age in which sufficient energy to power a flying machine was simply not available, and once again he was thwarted by the absence of any form of infrastructure upon which he could build.

Yet Leonardo's efforts were not entirely wasted. That he actually

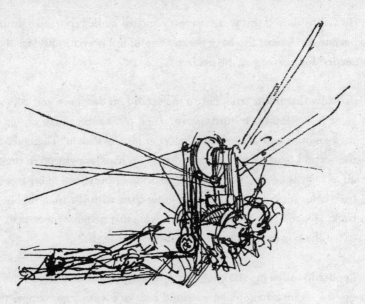

Fig. 10.8: One of Leonardo's many flying machines.

attempted to fly himself is doubtful. He dreamed of creating what he called the 'giant bird' and launching it from Monte Ceceri near Florence, reporting in his notebook: 'From the mountain bearing the name of the great bird, the famous bird will take flight that shall fill the world with its great renown.'[70] But there is little evidence to suggest he ever conducted a test flight, although one reference made after Leonardo's death comes from a descendant of a friend, one Fazio Cardano, who in 1550 wrote, '*Vincius tentavit et frustra*' – 'Vinci tried in vain.'[71] At first glance this would suggest that Leonardo might have attempted to fly, but even this is ambiguous, as it could have been a remark made simply to encompass Leonardo's entire approach to life and work: that he tried in vain to achieve so many wondrous things.

Even so, important ideas did emerge from Leonardo's dream of

Fig. 10.9: Leonardo's 'helicopter'.

human flight. He drew designs for parachutes, although it should not be ignored that at least one other researcher, Villard de Honnecourt, had created similar designs two centuries earlier. Leonardo also devised safety systems for use in his flying machine, some of which are not dissimilar to modern-day life-buoys. These he imagined would be used to rescue his aeronaut if the 'giant bird' happened to land on water.

The destruction of these machines may occur in two ways, the first being rupture of the machine, and the second being the turning of the machine edgewise or almost edgewise; for it always should descend at a long slant and virtually along the line of equilibrium. With respect to guarding against the machine's breaking, this can be effected by making it as strong as possible in whatever direction it may turn . . . As for the turning toward any aspect of the edge [losing equilibrium and rolling] this must be prevented beforehand by constructing the machine in such a way that in descending in any manner the remedy may be inherent, and this will occur if the centre of its gravity is always in a straight line above the centre of the heavy body carried by it . . .'[72]

He also drew illustrations and wrote about 'bags with which a man, falling from a height of 6 ells [7 metres], will not be hurt either into water or to earth; and these bags, tied together like the beads of a rosary, surround each other'.[73] And then, 'If you fall, see that you strike the earth with the double bag you have under your rump.'[74]

Leonardo's parachute was probably designed originally as a toy, as were some of his simplest designs for flying machines. These devices would have worked well because of their lightness. It was only when he tried extending the application of these ideas to full-size models with human occupants that resources failed him.

It is unclear whether Leonardo ever gave up theorising about manned flight. He certainly overhauled his thinking on the subject at least once. Sometime during the early 1500s he realised that his attempts to impose the mechanics of bird flight on to a man-made flying machine would never succeed. Turning to alternatives, he embarked upon the series of designs that include the 'aerial screw' or 'helicopter'. These projects almost certainly never went further than sketches in Leonardo's notebooks dating from his Rome period, and by this time, Leonardo himself would have been too old to try manned flight. Besides, it is by no means certain he had the necessary resources or support to fulfil his ambitions using a human volunteer. No records of test flights using these devices have come down to us.

So were Leonardo's tremendous efforts to build flying machines wholly in vain? The answer to this is a definite 'no'. Leonardo did not even come close to succeeding as an aviator, but his work on the anatomy and the flight of birds is one of his finest achievements, both as scientist and artist. Mirroring his studies of human anatomy, this work is another example of how Leonardo could uniquely combine his great skills as an artist, an observer and an experimenter. He planned a *Treatise on Birds* which was supposed to consist of four 'books' (chapters). These were to include a discourse on the resistance of the air, the anatomy of the bird and its feathers, the feather movements during flight and the behaviour of the tail and the wings. Like so much of what Leonardo attempted, this project was never fully realised, but he did produce a *Codex on the Flight of Birds*. This is a short manuscript consisting of eighteen sheets (recto and verso) about 8 inches by 6 in which he details his findings from over a decade of study.

The *Codex* is beautifully illustrated with technical drawings and elegant images of birds in flight, and offers a selection of wonderful insights that had never been brought together in one study before and have been little bettered by modern ornithologists or anatomists. Breaking down the subject into separate studies of the anatomy of birds, the mechanism via which the wings and tail operate and coordinate, and the conclusions he had reached about the dynamics of flight, Leonardo provides many important and quite original details: 'When the bird wishes to rise by beating its wings,' he writes, '. . . it raises its shoulders and beats the tips of its wings towards itself and condenses the air between the points of the wings and the bird's breast, and the tension thereof lifts the bird up.'[75] And:

When the wind strikes the bird under its course from the centre of its gravity towards this wind, then the bird will turn with its spine towards the wind; and if the wind were stronger from below than from above, then the bird would turn upside down, unless it were alert and immediately drew the lower wing in and extended the upper wing, and in this way it rights itself and returns to a position of equilibrium.[76]

These are wonderfully accurate observations derived from endless hours watching his beloved birds soaring and swooping above the Tuscan and Lombardy countryside.

Leonardo was aware of how his thinking was quite unconventional, and also of how important his work was, writing in his notes:

Study me, reader, if you find delight in me, because on very few occasions shall I return to the world, and because the patience for this profession is found in very few, and only in those who wish to compose things anew. Come, oh men, to see the miracles that such studies will disclose in nature.[77]

He was equally well aware that only a few would understand him or care about his efforts. Indeed, the Victorians, who more or less ignored Leonardo's scientific writing, passed over such splendid work as the *Codex on the Flight of Birds*, failing entirely to see its quality because they were blinkered by the idea that Leonardo had been chasing sunbeams.

Some may argue that Leonardo himself reached for the sky but achieved little of any substance, but this is a most unfair assessment. He produced genuine results, including remarkable conclusions from his study of optics, his findings concerning the anatomy of the eye and his unparalleled brilliance as an anatomical illustrator. He worked methodically and with scientific precision centuries ahead of his time in the areas of geology and geography, and he took the idea of applied science (or technology) far further than the wildest dreams of Francis Bacon, the man usually awarded the title 'father of technology'. Quite simply, if Leonardo had chosen to concentrate upon only one of the areas of research he tackled and had even then come up with the results he did, he would still be remembered today for his genius and imagination. That he derived even a small collection of important results in a wide range of disciplines places Leonardo da Vinci in a league of his own.

11

THE SCIENCE OF ART

True sciences are those which have penetrated through the senses as a result of experience and thus silencing the tongues of disputants, not feeding investigators on dreams but always proceeding successively from primary truths and established principles, in a proper order towards the conclusion.

— Leonardo, *Codex Urbinas Latinus*

And so this is Leonardo the pure scientist, but what of another aspect of his many-faceted intellect, the artist-scientist? By this I mean the Leonardo who blended an understanding of the scientific principles governing the Universe with those that guide the hand of the artist as he represents what the eye beholds.

This amalgam developed slowly and only reached full maturity in Leonardo's old age, the final decade of his working life, during which he produced his most sublime artistic work and went as far as he possibly could within the realm of science. But we can see the evolution of Leonardo's thought in the single work published under his name, the *Trattato della Pittura*, the *Treatise on Painting*.

Leonardo's treatise was most probably started in Milan during the early 1480s. In the introduction to his *Divina Proportione*, written in 1498, his friend Luca Pacioli tells us that Leonardo had '. . . finished with great diligence an admirable book on the depiction and movements of men'.[1] But this would have only constituted what we would call a chapter of Leonardo's treatise, and he continued to refine his ideas until almost the day he died.

The bulk of his writings may be found scattered throughout a series of notebooks. Most important of these are *Manuscript C*, which deals with light and shade; *Manuscript E*, concerned with the structure of trees and plants and how they should be represented; a manuscript in the Bibliothèque Nationale known as *2038 Italien*, which contains a vast collection of tips and advice concerning the practical aspects of painting; and the *Codex Atlanticus*. These notes were collected together at the end of the nineteenth century by a Leonardo scholar named J. P. Richter and published under the odd title, *The Literary Works of Leonardo*.

Leonardo's original concept for the treatise was to produce a collection totalling eight 'books' which together covered all the major principles with which he was concerned. These included what we would call the 'scientific aspects' of painting; the importance of understanding anatomy, the study of optics and perspective, the nature of trees and plants, the behaviour of water and the study of proportion. As well as these, Leonardo wrote in detail about the ethics of painting, the lifestyle of the artist, the relative merits of different types of art, matters we might refer to broadly as the 'philosophy of art'. In his vision, all of these would be encompassed within almost one thousand sub-headings, each beginning with a question followed by an attempt at resolution. Some of these expositions would be merely a few lines, others several pages in length.

He had high hopes for his treatise, and not without reason. With typical cheek, he declared in the Preface:

I know that many will say that this is a useless work, and these people will be those of whom Demetrius said that he took no more account of the wind from their mouths which caused these words, than of the wind which issued from their lower regions. These men possess a desire only for material wealth and are entirely devoid of the desire for wisdom, which is the sustenance and truly dependable wealth of the mind.[2]

For the serious scholar, he added:

> These rules will enable you to possess a free and good judgement, since good judgement is born of good understanding, and good understanding derives from reason expounded through good rules, and good rules are the daughters of good experience – the common mother of all the sciences and arts.[3]

As I have noted elsewhere, Leonardo's book was finally published in 1651, but this version was based upon at least a second-generation copy of his original collection of notes made fairly soon after his death that found its way to the Vatican library. The original *Trattato della Pittura* was the only collection of Leonardo's notes that were collated in any form during his lifetime, and even these were in a muddled and confused state when he died. During the following decades the manuscript changed hands many times and Vasari describes a copy of the treatise he had heard about:

> There are in the hands of . . . [the name is missing in the original], a painter of Milan, certain writings of Leonardo likewise in characters written with the left hand, backward, which treat of painting, and of the methods of drawing and colouring. This man not long ago came to Florence to see me, wishing to print his work, and he took it to Rome, in order to put it into effect, but I do not know what may afterwards have become of it.[4]

During the sixteenth and early seventeenth centuries *Trattato della Pittura* was copied and rewritten so much, many versions contained little of the original, and it was only with the discovery of Leonardo's seminal text on the subjects in the treatise towards the end of the nineteenth century that this gradual degradation was halted.

The treatise is not an easy book to read in any of the forms into which it evolved, but the original notes offer an invaluable insight into the way Leonardo thought, the way he loved to draw endless parallels between disciplines, and how he evolved as a thinker within the realms of both science and art. As well as this, it also gives us rare glimpses into his personal thoughts.

So, let us consider in turn Leonardo's primary concerns dealt with in his *Trattato della Pittura* and how these reflected in his life and work in all the many arenas he mastered during his career.

First there are the notes on optics, perspective and the workings of the eye. We saw in Chapter 7 how Leonardo had stepped beyond many of the suspect ideas of Aristotelian philosophy, including Greek notions of how vision was facilitated. He had then gone on to incorporate the ideas of Alberti and medieval researchers such as Pecham and Bacon, fusing them with some of his own discoveries. But at this time (the 1480s and early 1490s) he still maintained a rather simplistic notion of how our senses recorded the world. During the 1490s, he took the line that what the eye perceived via the *sensus communis* was a true representation of the world, but after returning to optics he began to realise this was actually far from the truth.

Medieval thinkers believed the image of an object appeared on a surface inside the eye and was an exact representation of that object. John Pecham had written in *Perspectiva Communis*: 'Vision takes place by the arrangement of the image on the glacial humour exactly corresponding to the object outside.'[5] Following a series of experiments probably conducted in Rome during late 1513, Leonardo came to see this as a false premise. First, he believed instead that every part of the pupil was able to support images of external objects, writing, 'Every part of the pupil possesses the *virtù visiva*.'[6] Second, he reasoned that the way light from an object was used by the eye was a complex process and that it did not, as the medievalists would have it, simply fall upon a receptive surface and then become interpreted via the *sensus communis*.

To prove his ideas he conducted three separate, elegant experiments.

With the first, he demonstrated that the entire pupil receives an image. He did this by holding a needle close to one eye and observing a distant object. 'The thing in front of the eye which is smaller than the pupil will not', he found, 'interrupt in the eye any other distant object and although it is dense it has the effect of a transparent thing.'[7] In other words, light rays from the distant object are not blocked by the needle and the eye receives impulses from all directions and can build a picture of the distant object.

In the second experiment, he satisfied himself that, 'The eye does not know the edge of any body.'[8] To demonstrate this, he held an object close to the eye with an edge adjacent to the line of sight.

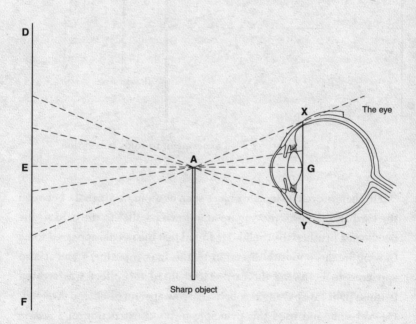

Fig. 11.1: A schematic representation of Leonardo's experiment to show that 'the eye does not know the edge of any body'.

The top edge of this (point A), he believed, cannot be interpreted properly by the eye because the receptive surface of the eye (XY) will perceive the edge against a varying backdrop (different points along the entire background field of vision, DF). Instead, the eye will create the clearest image along the central line of vision (GE).

In his third experiment, Leonardo placed a card with a small hole about six inches in front of his eye.

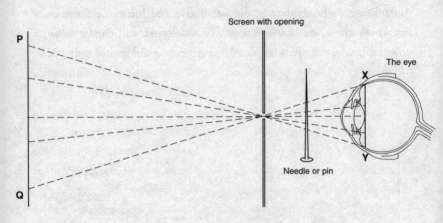

Fig. 11.2: Leonardo's third experiment to study perception.

He then moved a slender object such as a pin or a needle between the card and the eye, moving up and down parallel to the card so the needle just brushed the eyelid. He found that the needle appeared to be moving in the opposite direction to the true movement and it also appeared to be *behind* the card. He realised this effect was created because light rays passing through a narrow aperture become inverted. He had seen and used this principle in his construction of a *camera obscura* during the 1490s and it was an effect already witnessed and recorded many times by medieval researchers.

What this last experiment confirmed was that the entire inner surface of the eye (XY in the diagram) was used to receive impulses from the external world, because, as the needle is moved downwards, it appears to be passing in front of successively higher parts of the background field of vision, PQ, and viewing this background employs the entire receptive surface of the eye.

Early on in the *Trattato della Pittura*, Leonardo wrote:

> Painting embraces all the ten functions of the eye; that is to say, darkness, light, body and colour, shape and location, distance and closeness, motion and rest. My little work will comprise an interweaving of these functions, reminding the painter of the rules and methods by which he may imitate with his art all these things – the works by which nature adorns the world.[9]

But these experiments did not lead him to a full and modern interpretation of the workings of the eye. He realised there was a surface inside the eye, what he referred to as 'every part of the pupil', that received images, but not directly as they appeared in the world. However, he could not accept that these images were inverted in the eye, as we now know they are.

Light passes through the lens and forms an inverted image on the retina, this is then inverted again by the brain so that we see the world 'the right way up'. Bypassing this concept, Leonardo went to extraordinary lengths to describe a 'double inversion process' within the eye itself in which impulses are inverted by the lens and then inverted again inside what we now term the aqueous humour.[10]

Leonardo's realisation that all was not as it might seem went further. What he called 'the perspectivist who believes that the visual rays come straight into the eye'[11] had to be wrong because, as his experiments had shown him, light could be received from the entire visual field and then refracted into the eye where an image is created. Leonardo also found that: 'The eye judges the size of an object

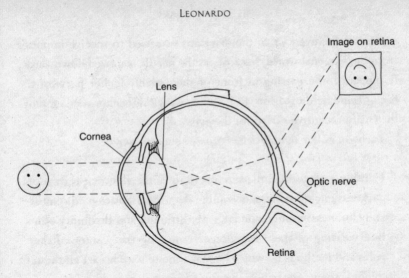

Fig. 11.3: Modern interpretation of how the image is inverted on the retina.

as being larger than that which is shown in the painter's perspective.'[12]

Elsewhere, he writes about the way light is reflected and refracted endlessly in Nature so that no object is seen as it really is. This realisation led him to make startling and original comments that only a man equally well versed in science and art could produce. 'The eye will often be deceived,' he remarks.[13] And: 'Every object will at a distance appear to be spherical.'[14]

This confusion of optical purity he saw at its most poignant in the way the 'true' colour of anything was always affected by other objects. An illuminated object 'is never seen entirely in its true colour', Leonardo observed, and reported seeing alien hues in many objects, 'yellowish' reflections in faces, 'reddish' lights and 'greenish' shadows in white objects.[15] He was also fully aware that the mere act of representing three-dimensional objects in two dimensions upon the canvas required of the artist a certain element of deceit and that this transference from three to two dimensions could never be made perfect.

It is easy to underestimate what a shock these ideas must have been for Leonardo. Based upon his earliest researches, the world must have seemed a far simpler place. He must have believed (with some justification, given the information available to him) that the world operated by a simple series of rules, and that observation and reality were identical. For an artist to conclude that the eye deceives, that the world is full of false images, and that our interpretation of the external world is complicated by phenomena such as reflection, refraction and interference must have rocked the very foundations of his worldview. Again, we can only wonder at the strength and flexibility of his intellect and his hardiness of spirit, for he managed to accommodate these realisations and, as a true scientist, he built them into his model of the Universe.

As a great artist, he also used these discoveries to clarify further the way he could represent with the brush the world of light and shade, colour and contrast. This is most captivating in his final set of paintings, including perhaps his best use of *chiaroscuro*, his peerless management of light and shade in his *St John*.

Very great charm of shadow and light [he wrote about the same time as he was working on this masterpiece] . . . is to be found in the faces of those who sit in the doors of dark houses. The eye of the spectator sees that part of the face which is in shadow lost in the darkness of the house, and that part of the face which is lit draws its brilliancy from the splendour of the sky. From this intensification of light and shade the face gains greatly in relief . . . and in beauty.[16]

And in his treatise, Leonardo wrote some ten thousand words on the subject of shadow and shade, how the artist should best use shadows, how shadows differ according to the position of an object or the nature of the source of light. This attention to detail has prompted some authorities to claim he became too much of an academician, that his drawings and paintings became stilted, artificial. But this is far from the mark. Leonardo never lost sight of the primary purpose of the artist; to represent the 'soul', to depict the inner essence of a thing, whatever that may be.

Leonardo's findings in the field of optics and the function of the eye undoubtedly played an important role in developing the quality of his artistic representations, but of equal importance was his understanding of anatomy. I considered Leonardo's anatomical studies in Chapter 10, but in order to understand how this research influenced his work as an artist we need to ascertain what value Leonardo placed upon an understanding of anatomical form and how it could be incorporated into his paintings.

Alberti believed the artist should be aware of three stages of anatomical study as they should be applied to painting. First, the artist should know how bones are arranged within the human superstructure. Second, he should be aware of the layout of nerves and muscles, and finally and most importantly, the artist should understand how to depict what Alberti described as 'flesh and skin', the outer, visible layer surrounding the framework of bone, nerves and muscles.

Leonardo was certainly familiar with Alberti's advice, and Verrocchio had also been extremely interested in anatomy as it applied to the representation of human and animal form. And there were other artists before Leonardo who showed much more than a passing interest in anatomy. Donatello, Giotto, and most especially Antonio Pollaiuolo, had each honoured basic anatomical principles and placed great emphasis upon the importance of understanding how the human body was organised internally and how this influenced its visible, exterior form and therefore how they should represent it upon the canvas.

Before Leonardo, the artist who took these ideas most seriously

Fig. 11.4: Left, a study of light intensities upon the face, and right, the end result, an angel from *Virgin of the Rocks*.

was Pollaiuolo, who had been inspired particularly by the writings and descriptions of the Roman writer, Pliny. Pollaiuolo's fascination with the internal organisation of the body is most clear in his famous work, *The Battle of Nude Men* from around 1465.

As Pollaiuolo was engaged upon this painting, Leonardo was twenty-three and acting as Verrocchio's assistant, honing the skills that would serve him well not only as an artist but in his preliminary studies as an anatomist. It was common during the Renaissance for artists to take casts of parts of cadavers as well as to produce casts of their own bodies. Verrocchio's workshop is known to have contained many casts of limbs and torsos, and in one of Leonardo's first sets of notes he comments that his works so far include 'several whole nude figures, arms, legs, feet and postures'.[17]

But what distinguishes Leonardo from all other thinkers and artists of the Renaissance is that he was not content merely to accept inherited wisdom, nor simply to apply the word of the ancients. He was almost

Fig. 11.5: Antonio Pollaiuolo, *The Battle of Nude Men* (*c.* 1465).

certainly the first to carry out detailed anatomical studies with the joint intentions of refining his art and scientific enquiry; beyond that, he perceived anatomical revelation through dissection as an essential ingredient in the development of his most treasured intellectual precept, his holistic vision.

We have already seen how Leonardo spent a great deal of time studying comparative anatomy, drawing links between the physiology of different animals and man. In his notes he writes: 'Here make a note to demonstrate the difference there is between man and the horse, and in the same way with other animals.'[18] And again, in another set of notes, he declares his intention to investigate 'how close the arrangement of the bones and muscles of animals is to the bones and muscles of man'.[19] Elsewhere, following in the footsteps of Vitruvius and others, he made copious notes describing relative proportions both within the human body and as comparisons between species. But, whereas a pure anatomist might be primarily concerned with the form of an animal as an academic exercise, Leonardo the artist took the work of Leonardo the scientist and applied what he had discovered to help him represent human and animal morphology in his paintings and drawings.

Leonardo then took his understanding of anatomic form even further, believing he could project deep psychological features into his portrayal of physical form. This was a skill he considered the highest form of artistic expression, leading him on many occasions to describe art as 'silent poetry'.

From his anatomical studies of human beings, Leonardo also appreciated the importance of representing the most accurate physiology of different types of people, writing:

> Knowledge of the structure of the body is only a preparation for knowledge of the form. Even though a given structure, apart from the organic differences between the sexes, is roughly the

same in every individual, individuals nonetheless always differ from one another. This disparity of form is a result of the variation above or below the norm, with respect to the bulk and amount and hence to the relationships and proportions of the various tissues and parts of the body. We shall have more or less fat according to age, sex and individual constitution.[20]

At another point in his notebooks, he observes, 'The superficial venous system will stand out to a different extent in young and in old men, in a person exerting effort, and in one at rest.'[21]

From these conclusions, he went on to formulate rules for the best way to draw and paint humans in different postures, noting, 'Then describe the attitudes and movements.'[22] This is an idea he refers to repeatedly at different times and in different collections of notes, remarking, 'After the demonstration of all the parts of the limbs of man and of the other animals, you will represent the proper method of action of these limbs.'[23]

The next natural step from here was for Leonardo to investigate mimicry. To truly represent a human or any other animal in fluid motion, the artist needs to understand how the muscles of the face and the rest of the body generate expression. We have seen how Leonardo identified and studied the muscles of the face and how these related to the many expressions we see in those around us, a vast range of ways to display our feelings and emotions. Leonardo spent long hours studying the face, and often took forays into some of the shadier districts of Milan or Florence to find interesting examples – 'variations from the norm', as he would have put it. His notebooks are filled with caricatures of ordinary folk accompanied by sketches of grotesques, some of whom may have been real characters, others amalgamations created with a stretch here, an enlargement of a feature there.

Leonardo's thoughts on the subject of how an artist should represent human and animal figures is almost evangelical in its intensity. He was particularly concerned that artists should cover a range of subjects, saying that the artist must use as much variety as possible in the representation of 'women, children, dogs, horses, buildings, fields and hills'.[24] Artists should also, he believed, resist the temptation to make their background figures look too alike, declaring, 'Differentiate between the actions of humans according to their age and worth, and vary them according to type, that is male types and those of women.'[25] Just as important to him was his feeling that his contemporaries were too keen to project their own looks into characters in their paintings.

> And know that you must fight your utmost against this vice, [he wrote] . . . since it is a shortcoming which is born in company with judgement, because the soul, the mistress of your body, is that which makes your individual judgement; and she naturally delights in works similar to that which she made in the composition of your body.[26]

Leonardo's personal search for information about the anatomy of humans and other animals could give him the confidence to announce that 'the measurement of parts and their thicknesses vary greatly in nature, and you should vary them yourself [in your work]'.[27] At other times, his stern line on this subject offers valuable insights into how he perceived some of his artistic rivals and friends. With a particular flourish, he writes:

> Oh, anatomical painter, beware that the overly strong indication of the bones, tendons and muscles does not cause you to become a wooden painter, with your wish that all your nudes should display their feelings. Therefore, wishing to rectify this, observe in what manner the muscles in old or lean persons cover or clothe the bones, and in addition to this note the rule concerning the

same muscles filling the spaces interposed between them, and which are the muscles that never lose their appearance in any amount of fatness, and which are the muscles which lose the signs of their terminations with the least plumpness.[28]

There can be no mistake about the identity of the artist to whom Leonardo is referring. He had been critical of Perugino and Botticelli for their laziness in portraying unsuitable figures in their paintings, but his clearest criticism was for his great rival, Michelangelo. When Leonardo arrived in Rome in the autumn of 1513 there can be no doubt that one of the first things he did was to visit the Sistine Chapel, a short walk from his rooms at the Belvedere. Michelangelo's work had been widely admired, but Leonardo was critical of the way the younger artist had painted only Herculean figures, even when they were entirely inappropriate. He reserved his most serious criticism for Michelangelo's depiction of the sea and the earth in the *Deluge*, claiming it to be entirely unrealistic. As well as this, he believed Michelangelo's figures demonstrated a musculature bearing little relation to the types they were meant to represent. Michelangelo, he knew, had concerned himself little with studying Nature and had shown absolutely no interest in science. For Leonardo this was a cardinal sin.

Leonardo's amalgamation of art and biology extended far beyond the dissection table. His innate affinity with Nature, a quality with its origins in his childhood, had always guided and inspired him. Positive influences were the wind, the soil and the sunlight of his native Anchiano, the memory of Uncle Francesco's weathered hands and his wise words. A negative counterbalance to this was the deep impression created by the natural disasters that had struck the region of his birth during his formative years.

Both the positive and the negative forces informed Leonardo's depictions of Nature and combined with his scientific investigations. Most crucially, he always sought to represent accurately but without losing the essence of the thing he was portraying. 'You imitator of nature, be careful to attend to the variety of configurations of things,' he declared with genuine passion.[29]

Trees and plants were a particular favourite for showing attention to detail. Whereas most artists gave insufficient consideration to the intricate structure of trees and, with the eyes of the artist, 'saw' them only in part, Leonardo knew how trees and plants were constructed and how they fitted into the greater scheme of Nature. 'Nature has placed the leaves of the latest shoots of many plants', Leonardo observed, '. . . so that the sixth is always above the first and follows successively in that manner.'[30]

At another point, he noted how trees could be fitted into groups according to their shape: 'The top of the outermost shoots form a pyramid from the middle upwards,' he says. 'And the walnut and the oak from the middle will make a hemisphere.'[31]

Leonardo's studies of water in turmoil offer us the flip side of this coin. The energy behind these drawings comes from the negative force as expressed through Leonardo's own subconscious. As we have seen, he turned to these depictions late in life as his health was failing, and they appear to be the outward manifestation of his childhood fears blended with the anxieties of his last days. In them, deep-rooted terror of water merges with the horror of death. But again, the power of these pictures comes not merely from Leonardo's passion but from information, from knowledge, from experience and experiment.

Leonardo understood water, he had *needed* to understand it. In the end, he knew he could not master it and that the civilisation of which he was a part could not master it, and although he may have harboured dreams that one day humans could manipulate water to serve them, the best he could do was to demythologise it by representing it on paper.

So, Leonardo's scientific investigations clearly added to his abilities as an artist. In him, art plus science equals transcendence. But strikingly, and pleasingly, the origin of this union had come when he began to realise the importance of science as a way to improve his abilities as an artist.

Although he had little natural ability as a mathematician, there can be no doubt Leonardo was naturally inclined towards science. He was also aware of the latest scientific ideas from the philosophers and thinkers who visited the bottega. But Leonardo first experimented with optical effects simply to gain greater insight as an artist. It was only later he realised the potential of these enquiries; that experiments with lenses and mirrors, dissection and researches into the properties of water, could be an end in themselves.

During thirty-five years of scientific investigation, Leonardo learned more about science and its use for him as an artist than any other person of his time. Much of this found its way into his paintings and drawings in subtle ways. He certainly did not show off his knowledge and never attracted the focus of his art away from representation. He never lost sight of the fact that science was there to aid him as an artist rather than allowing it to overwhelm the spirit or the substance of his work. '. . . Love of anything is the offspring of knowledge,' he remarked, '. . . love being more fervent in proportion as knowledge is more certain, and this certainty springs from a thorough knowledge of all the parts which compose the whole.'[32]

The researches of Leonardo the scientist working within the fields of optics, anatomy, geology and hydrology helped Leonardo the artist; but others who followed him also gained insights from his work. The *Trattato della Pittura* has long been a standard text for all young artists. In his later paintings, Rembrandt demonstrated how he had gained much from Leonardo's ideas about light and shade, and Impressionism was constructed upon altering the relative importance upon the canvas of highlights, lowlights and stray reflections. Perhaps Renoir and Cézanne found guidance from Leonardo's comment that: 'In the streets when night is falling in bad weather observe what delicacy and grace appear in the faces of men and women.'[33]

Fig. 11.6: One of Leonardo's drawings of the deluge.

And again, in Leonardo's deluge paintings we might glimpse the progenitor of Cubism or abstract art. And in the photographs of Robert Mapplethorpe might there be caught echoes of Leonardo's words on the subject of shadows and his emphasis upon chiaroscuro? 'Very great charm of shadow and light is to be found in the faces of those who sit in the doors of dark houses. The eye of the spectator sees that part of the face which is in shadow lost in the darkness of the house, and that part of the face which is lit draws its brilliancy from the splendour of the sky.'

327

12

PLANET LEONARDO

It should not be hard for you to stop sometimes and look into the stains of walls, or ashes of a fire, or clouds, or mud or like places, in which . . . you may find really marvellous ideas.

— Leonardo, *Codex Atlanticus*

What then may we conclude about Leonardo the man, and the products of his mind? For it seems to me, the more one probes into Leonardo's life and tries to prise a way into the enigma of his mind, the more mysterious he becomes, the more questions arise that resist answers.

Five hundred years on from Leonardo's prime, the facts of his life remain sparse. The last insight came in 1965, when a manuscript, since named the *Madrid Codex*, was found in the National Library in the Spanish capital. This includes a little information about Leonardo's life in Milan as well as a set of maps, astonishingly detailed drawings of mechanical devices, and designs for the equestrian bronze. And although nothing of substance has been unearthed since then, we can only hope there will be other finds in the coming years to shed more light upon Leonardo's life and ideas.

In spite of the fact that so much that Leonardo produced has been lost and that he shared so little of his feelings with us, I hope I have managed to present a clear picture of Leonardo's personality and activities. But just as important, for the purposes of this book, is the need to clarify Leonardo's position in the history of science.

As I have emphasised, I believe Leonardo was certainly a scientist, but to accept this one must allow for a broader interpretation of what the word 'science' means, and many are unwilling to do so. To me, science is exploration, it is questioning, it is the application of imagination, it is analysis. And so, without doubt, Leonardo was a practitioner of science because he fulfils all these criteria. What he lacked in mathematical skills he made up for with his genius as an artist. For although mathematics is a tool for the scientist and used to manipulate information, it is also employed as a means to express ideas, to portray concepts, to illustrate principles. But many modern scientists have also used pictorial representations to support their mathematical descriptions. A particularly good example are 'Feynman Diagrams' created by the late Nobel laureate, Richard Feynman. Although his work is highly mathematical and he used the regular equations of nuclear physics, he also pioneered a method for demonstrating the exchange of particles in sub-nuclear processes using simple line diagrams.[1] So, if we can accept the idea that scientific ideas might be expressed pictorially as well as mathematically, we are again led to conclude Leonardo was indeed a true scientist.

And what of Leonardo, the man? Do we have answers for some of the fundamental questions about his character? What, for example, motivated him? What drove him in his lifelong quest to find ultimate answers? Why did he *have* to do what he did? Why was he so obsessed with the inner workings of the human body? Why the constant search for unification, his unyielding attachment to a holistic vision?

Sigmund Freud held the view that Leonardo was motivated by two impulses. First, he believed, there was a great dearth of love in Leonardo's life and he replaced love with a quest for knowledge. Second, Leonardo had sublimated sex with art. Freud was convinced Leonardo created his works of art because he was sexually unfulfilled.

In recent years, Freud's work in all areas of psychology has been subjected to plentiful criticism, and his essay about Leonardo based upon often fragmentary accounts is, without doubt, highly suspect.[2] Leonardo was certainly loved as a child. The source of that love, at least during his first two or three years, may have been his mother, Caterina, but she then grew to represent confusion by leaving him and living close by with a new set of young children. But then Leonardo's grandparents appear to have been caring and affectionate people who prized their family above all things. As well as them, Leonardo's Uncle Francesco became a key figure in his early development and a person for whom Leonardo held a life-long affection.

Today, most psychologists dismiss the notion that by creating art, the artist is sublimating his sexual impulses. To me, it seems more likely Leonardo's motivation came first from a natural desire to learn. This was a factor dependent upon straightforward influences from early childhood, a time during which he gained pleasure from learning, combined certainly with a genetic predisposition towards such things. To find another impetus, need we look further than the condition of Leonardo's social life as a youth? Shunned as a bastard, he could, as we have seen, find little outlet for his intelligence through the traditional professions and was directed by his father into a career as an artist. But as a painter, success came naturally. The fact that he began an autodidactic course and the search for universal answers precisely when he scored his first major successes as an artist can be no coincidence. Quite simply, scientific research and the development of his analytical powers, along with his construction of experimental knowledge, was an enormous challenge, a challenge that, in part at least, drove him on into candle-lit mortuaries, endless repetition of experiments and tortured nights attempting to resolve convoluted engineering puzzles.

Leonardo was of course a polymath *par excellence*, but even from a brief perusal of his notebooks it is clear there was a small collection of subjects which for him went beyond mere interest to obsession: his studies of water, the flight of birds and human anatomy.

His fascination with water punctuated all his writings from his earliest notes to his final jottings at Cloux, and elsewhere I have speculated that this may have come from a fear of water created by bitter childhood experience. But what of the flight of birds?

As we know, Leonardo loved birds and studied their behaviour with great intensity. He freed them in marketplaces, never ate them and appears to have maintained a special interest in them throughout his life. But may we read more into his quest for flight? Is it too obvious to suggest that the reason Leonardo expended so much energy in attempting to fly came from some convoluted wish to escape?

I do not think this is an unreasonable assertion. Leonardo almost certainly never analysed the fact that he was bound by the restrictions of his age. At one point in his notes he declares with amazement how little he believed had been learned by humanity and how much remained to be discovered, but nowhere in his writings does he imply a wish to live in a future world, or that he felt frustrated by the infrastructure of his era.*
Yet perhaps subconsciously he did. I would not be surprised to learn that some part of Leonardo knew greater things were possible than those he might achieve with the resources at his disposal: wood, stone, sweat and muscle. Neither would it surprise me to learn that it was this aspect of his personality that drove him to design flying machines. He could empathise with birds because they were free of all shackles, they could soar unhindered, restricted only by their own strength.

And what of his anatomical studies? Of course, delving into human flesh was all part of the search, part of the escape, but could there be more to this also? At times, Leonardo expressed a strangely twisted

---

* Some might argue such obtuse ideas were completely alien to the Renaissance mind and that such a concept is too modern. To those people, I would simply say: remember to whom we are referring!

view of Man. Could he perhaps have been searching for an inner spark, a 'core of gold', that might somehow confound the prejudices that had formed in his mind as a result of his rejection as a bastard?

We know Leonardo spent a great deal of time and energy following the path others had trodden in search of a physical manifestation of the 'soul'. This was one of the primary forces that drove him to dissect 'more than ten bodies'. And perhaps to Leonardo this search for the soul and the quest for some hidden 'core of gold' were one and the same thing. Leonardo wanted evidence, clear and meaningful, in the palm of his hand, that we humans are not merely 'fillers of latrines'.

Of course he found no seat of the soul, nor did he unravel physical evidence of the divine stamp, and it may be argued that instead he fell back upon his unshakable belief that humans are the ultimate expression of the divine. If he could not find the soul, then perhaps the soul of Man and Nature were the same thing and lay all around us. His was then a form of pantheism backed up by what he believed to be evidence from scientific investigation, a conclusion motivated by a need to find some good within the human condition.

And so in this light we should consider Leonardo's religious stance. Vasari has it that Leonardo was a heretic who reformed during his last living moments, but he offers no evidence to support this and Leonardo says almost nothing about religion anywhere in his notebooks. Is this because he gave the matter little thought? Is it because he could not express his religious feelings just as he so often failed to record his emotions? Or did he not wish to declare what may well have been views considered heretical by his contemporaries?

As we know, he certainly roused the suspicions of those around him. A generation after his death, a friend of Vasari noted with barely disguised outrage that Leonardo 'dissected the corpses of criminals in the medical schools, remaining impassive in the face of this inhuman and repulsive work'.[3] And Leonardo was almost certainly aware of the attitudes of those around him towards his work. He knew he was perceived as a heretic and a necromancer, and it is conceivable the German assistants were not the only ones to complain of his activities. It may even be that the peripatetic nature of his later years was in part influenced by a constant need to avoid prying eyes and suspicious minds. Perhaps he was perpetually 'on the run'.

But he was lucky to live during a brief interlude free from extreme religious persecution in Europe. This was a luxury not afforded many other great thinkers. Yet even during a time of tolerance, the vast majority of people living in the fifteenth and early sixteenth centuries were devoutly religious, and the writers and philosophers of the age were no different, imbuing their work with copious references to what they saw as the prime mover of all things, their personalised, omnipotent God. The fact that Leonardo makes almost no reference to the divine in all his reports suggests he saw little use for a traditional deity.

It may also be argued that after growing up within the bosom of the Catholic Church and maintaining an orthodox faith as a young man, he lost this when faced with his own profound discoveries. Of course, there are many modern scientists who, having somehow reconciled science with religion, continue to cherish a profound faith. But we must remember that Leonardo lived in very different age from the modern philosopher-scientist. Religious people today have long managed to maintain a faith in the divine while simultaneously accepting the fact that we are made of flesh and blood, atoms and electrical impulses. For Leonardo, one of the first to discard taboos and to slice into organs and blood vessels, a man who failed utterly to find a 'soul', a man who had little respect for humanity but boundless enthusiasm for the beauty of the body and the place of humankind in the greater structure of a pantheist vision, there simply could be no personal God.

And how has Leonardo fared across half a millennium? Reputation is a nebulous quality. Across the years, the efforts of creative individuals can often be damaged by capricious human nature and the whims of fashion as well as justifiable re-evaluation. Consider once globally esteemed figures such as Sigmund Freud and Karl Marx. In their cases, a mere hundred years was enough to take them to a giddy pinnacle and on to their present cultural nadir. Such cannot be said of Leonardo da Vinci. He has his detractors, and some have tried to diminish his achievement, almost as a reaction against those who would have us believe he discovered and invented almost everything worth consideration.

But today, Leonardo's reputation as an artist is as profound as it ever was. And, as we charge on to create a world ever more dominated by advanced technology and scientific refinement, his status as an engineer and an original scientific thinker is growing rather than diminishing. Yet, in present-day Florence, tourists flock to Michelangelo's former home and workshop, whereas Via de Agnolo, close to the city centre, cannot even boast a plaque to commemorate the location of Verrocchio's workshop, the place where Leonardo learned his trade. But then the Florentines do have a vast array of Michelangelo's works to display, and he was always beloved by the city fathers, whereas Leonardo clashed with them constantly.

Michelangelo's tomb, designed by Vasari, is positioned close to that of Machiavelli in the Church of Santa Croce in Florence. In stark contrast, Leonardo's physical remains have been lost and even the location of his grave is uncertain. He was buried in the little church of Saint-Florentin in Amboise, but this was vandalised during the French Revolution and later, under Napoleon's instruction, it was demolished and the bones buried there scattered. During the 1860s a poet named Arsène Houssaye excavated the area and found a tomb containing a skeleton beside which he found a slab bearing the partial inscription: 'EO DUC VINC[——-]', which might possibly have once said 'LEONARDUS VINCIUS'.

Leonardo was without doubt an aberration, a man who has been described as a 'freakish genius' and by one biographer as 'abnormal'.[4]

But he was very human and lived his life desiring to remain in touch with Nature, to live by his intellectual conviction that, as a human being, he was merely an element in the greater scheme of things.

Leonardo da Vinci became a legend during his lifetime, and to many of his contemporaries he accrued almost magical powers. Yet he was a flesh and blood mortal, although indisputably imbued with extraordinary talent, a man interested in everything around him and possessed of enough energy to investigate all he encountered. He was an experimenter who eschewed magic and the occult, he worked with flesh and blood, metal and wood, mind and will. But what he left us transcends this lumpen material world and has, in some magical way, found a home both in our brute physical Universe and in a realm sublime.

APPENDIX I:

THE MAJOR
CHARACTERS IN
LEONARDO'S LIFE

The Borgia Family: Cesare Borgia's father and sponsor, Pope Alexander VI, died the year after Leonardo left Borgia's company. Almost immediately, Cesare Borgia was captured and imprisoned by the new pope, Julius II. He was killed in an ambush near Viana, Spain in 1507. Cesare's sister, Lucrezia Borgia, enjoyed a reputation almost as infamous as her brother, but she was also recognised as a great patron of the arts. She married Alfonso d'Este (her third husband), who became Duke of Ferrara in 1505. There she attracted the greatest artists and poets of the time to her court, including Titian. This was the high point of the family's fortunes, for within a century and a half the dynasty had all but vanished.

King Francis I of France: Declared war on the Holy Roman Empire but was roundly defeated at the Battle of Pavia in 1525, where he was captured. Freed a year later, he went on to build a wonderful château at Fontainebleau. However, as he grew older he became increasingly intolerant of Protestantism. He continued to patronise the arts, but grew equally fond of military campaigning and waged a number of largely futile wars with neighbours, draining the royal coffers almost completely. He died in 1547.

Niccolò Machiavelli: When the Medicis returned to power in Florence in 1512, Machiavelli was imprisoned and tortured. A year later he was released and retired to his family estate, where he turned to writing. He returned to politics briefly in 1525, but is best remembered as an historian and writer. He wrote *The Prince* (1513), *Discourses on the First Ten Books of Titus Livius* (1513–21), *The Art of War* (1521), a play, *Mandragola* (1524), and *A History of Florence* (1532).

The Medici Family: Lorenzo the Magnificent's grandson, also named Lorenzo, died at the age of twenty-seven in the same year as Leonardo. Several of the Medici line became popes, including Lorenzo's uncle, Giovanni, who was installed as Leo X in 1513, and Giulio Medici, named Pope Clement VII in 1523. The family were expelled from Florence in 1527, but returned three years later to establish a dynasty which ruled by hereditary right, a system very different from the approach of previous generations. The first of these new-style rulers was Cosimo I, born two months after Leonardo's death. He took the title of Grand Duke of Tuscany in 1569. Two Medici women married into the French monarchy. Catherine de Medici married Henry II in 1533 and Marie de Medici became the second wife of Henry IV. The family's power waned during the seventeenth century, and by 1734 they had been superseded by the Habsburgs.

Francesco Melzi: After Leonardo's death, Melzi lived out his days on the family estate at Vaprio. He made a concerted effort to catalogue and organise Leonardo's notebooks but made little real headway. He married and had a son, Orazio. He died in 1570.

Michelangelo: Masterminded the Medici Chapel in Florence which was completed in 1534. His religious zeal became ever stronger as he aged and his late works, in particular the *Last Judgement* (1536–41) and the *Conversion of St Paul* (1542–45), demonstrate an edgy religiosity bordering on fanaticism. In old age he was widely adored, and although he had spent most of his life in Rome, when he died in 1564 he was buried with great ceremony in Florence.

Luca Pacioli: Lectured on mathematics throughout Italy. As a Franciscan friar he did not need patronage but worked for many of the Italian nobility. He died in 1509.

Salai: Leonardo's erstwhile companion returned to Lombardy shortly before Leonardo's death. Nothing is known of his activities after the two men parted except that he was killed by a bolt from a crossbow in 1523; all other circumstances of his death remain a mystery.

Ludovico Sforza (The Moor): In 1500, he was imprisoned by the French in the castle of Loches in Touraine, France. He attempted to escape but failed. Unrepentant for his actions, he died there in May 1508

APPENDIX II:

LEONARDO AND HIS PLACE IN THE HISTORY OF SCIENCE

BC

c. 580–500	Pythagoras
c. 460–370	Democritus
428–348	Plato
384	Aristotle born
287–212	Archimedes
c. 250	First records of the library at Alexandria

AD

23–79	Pliny
129–c. 200	Galen
125–51	Ptolemy teaches at Alexandria
c. 450	The Fall of Rome
c. 450	Venice founded
c. 500	Arabic science becomes organised
c. 1000	Florence founded
1206–80	Albertus Magnus

1225–74	Thomas Aquinas
c. 1210–92	Roger Bacon
1389–1464	Cosimo de' Medici
c. 1440	First printing press
1449–92	Lorenzo de' Medici
1451	Francesco Sforza born
1452	Leonardo da Vinci born
1465–6	Leonardo joins artist workshop in Florence
1473	Copernicus born
1475	Cesare Borgia born
1482	Leonardo moves to Milan
1485	Plague in Milan
1490s	Leonardo conducts experiments in optics
1492	Columbus discovers the New World
1499	Leonardo leaves Milan
1502	Leonardo works for Cesare Borgia
1504	Ser Piero da Vinci dies
1508	Leonardo settles again in Milan
1509	Coronation of Henry VIII of England
1508–19	Leonardo conducts his most important anatomical work
1513	Leonardo moves to Rome
1517	Leonardo leaves Rome for Cloux
1519	Leonardo dies
1543	Copernicus' *De revolutionibus orbium coelestium* published
1561–1626	Francis Bacon
1564–1642	Galileo Galilei
1571–1630	Johannes Kepler
1596–1650	René Descartes
1609	Galileo first uses telescope to observe the Moon and the satellites of Jupiter
1628	William Harvey's *Exercitatio anatomica de motu cordis et sanguinis* published

1629–95	Christiaan Huygens
1642–1727	Isaac Newton
1662	Royal Society officially formed in London
1666	Calculus devised by Newton
1687	Newton's *Principia mathematica* published
1690	Huygens' *Traité de la lumière* published
1704	Newton's *Opticks* published

PICTURE CREDITS

The author and publisher gratefully acknowledge the following institutions and agencies for permission to reproduce illustrations in the text: AKG Photo (pp. 84, 89, 163, 165, 219, 304, 305); the British Museum, London (pp. 185, 204, 320); the Institut de France/Photographie Bulloz, Paris (pp. 176, 297); the Louvre Museum, Paris (p. 21); the National Gallery, London (p. 319 *top*); and the Royal Collection at Windsor © Her Majesty the Queen (pp. 76, 117, 169, 186, 226, 270, 271, 274, 275, 280, 284, 319 *bottom*, 327). The photographs on pp. 11, 13 and 59 were taken by the author.

NOTES

ABBREVIATIONS OF WORKS BY LEONARDO DA VINCI

CAr	*Codex Arundel* (283pp), British Museum, London
CAt	*Codex Atlanticus* (403pp), Ambrosiana Library, Milan
CF	*Codex Forster* (1,000+pp), Victoria & Albert Museum, London
CFB	*Codex on the Flight of Birds* (18pp), Biblioteca Reale, Turin
CM	*Codex Madrid* I & II (330pp), National Library, Madrid
CT	*Codex Trivulzianus* (51pp), Castello Sforzesco, Milan
CUL	*Codex Urbinus Latinus* (243pp), Vatican Library, The Vatican
Ms. A	*Manuscript A*, Institut de France, Paris (also *Ms. B* to *Ms. M*, numbering over 1,000 pages in total)
Ms. 2037/8	*Ashburnham* I & II (34pp), Bibliothèque Nationale, Paris
RLW	Anatomical studies from *Codex Leicester* (36pp), Royal Library, Windsor

The remainder of Leonardo's works are in private collections, the most famous of which is *Codex Hammer* (sometimes known as *Codex Leicester*), which is owned by Bill Gates of Microsoft. There are also individual pages and miscellaneous fragments to be found in Christ

Church Library, Oxford; the Accademia, Venice; the Uffizi, Florence; the Louvre, Paris; the Metropolitan Museum, New York; and the Schloss Museum, Weimar.

INTRODUCTION

1. Giorgio Vasari, *Lives of the Painters, Sculptors and Architects*, Random House, London, 1996.
2. Giorgio Nicodemi, 'The Life and Works of Leonardo', in *Leonardo da Vinci*, Morrow & Co., New York, 1938.
3. Alexander Moszkowski, *Conversations With Einstein*, Sidgwick & Jackson, London, 1972, pp. 51–2.

1: SINS OF THE FATHER

1. Discovered in 1939 by Emile Möller, the original document is now in the Florence City Archives.
2. *CAt*, folio 117r b.
3. See Note 1.
4. Quoted in Ludwig, *Das Buch von der Malerei*, Berlin, 1882, paragraph 404.
5. *CAt*, 71r a.
6. Ibid., 202v a. Although there were reasons for Leonardo's distaste for reproduction and children, this note does seem out of character and unnecessarily blunt. It may be that this letter was never actually sent, but was more of a note to himself about his half-brother's news.
7. *CF*, III, 74v.
8. *CAt*, 370r a.
9. Ibid., 145r a.
10. *CAr*, 212v.
11. *CF*, II, 9v.
12. See Michael White, *Isaac Newton: The Last Sorcerer*, Fourth Estate, London, 1997.
13. Letter from Freud to Jung, 17 October 1909.
14. It was first published in Vienna in 1910.

15. Giorgio Vasari, *Lives of the Painters, Sculptors and Architects*, Random House, London, 1996, pp. 627–8.

16. *CAt*, 66*v* b.

17. Quoted in Kenneth Clark, *Leonardo da Vinci*, Penguin, London, 1989, p. 18.

18. Ibid.

2: LEONARDO'S INTELLECTUAL INHERITANCE

1. De Lamar Jensen, *Renaissance Europe: Age of Recovery and Reconciliation*, D. C. Heath & Co., New York, 1992, Chapter 6.

2. Arthur Koestler, *The Sleepwalkers: A History of Man's Changing Vision of the Universe*, Penguin, London, 1979, p. 111.

3. Morris Bishop, *Petrarch and His World*, Bloomington, New York, 1963, p. 23.

4. *CUL*, folio 13*r*.

5. A. Wear *et al.*, *The Medical Renaissance of the Sixteenth Century*, Cambridge University Press, Cambridge, 1985.

6. This remedy appears in a letter to Lorenzo de' Medici from Petrus Bonus Avogarius, dated 11 February 1488.

7. Coluccio Salutati, *Tractatus de nobilitate legum et medicinae*, 1399.

8. See the 'Life of Alberti' in *Rerum italicarum scriptores*, XXV, Milan, 1751.

9. Leoni Alberti, *Treatise on Painting*, Florence, 1436.

10. See Lisa Jardine, *Worldly Goods: A New History of the Renaissance*, Macmillan, London, 1996.

3: A NEW BEGINNING

1. Giorgio Vasari, *Lives of the Painters, Sculptors and Architects*, Random House, London, 1996, p. 549.

2. A. H. R. Martindale, *Verrocchio*, 1992.

3. Ugolino Verino, *De illustratione urbis fiorentiae*, Book II.

4. Cennino Cennini, *Le Livre de l'art: Ou traité de la peinture*, edited by Chevalier G. Tambroni, Paris.

5. *CF*, I, folio 43*r*.

6. *Ms. 2038*, 23*r*.

7. *CAt*, 119*v* a.

8. *Ms. 2038*, 25*r*.

9. Martindale, op. cit., p. 628.

10. Giovanni Lomazzo, *Trattato dell'arte della pittura*, 1560.

11. See Anonimo Gaddiano in *Codice Magliabecchiano*, edited by Carl Frey, Berlin, 1892.

12. Vasari, op. cit., p. 629.

13. *CAt*, 181*r* a.

14. Ibid.

15. *CF*, III, 55*r*.

16. *CAt*, 119*v* a.

17. Ibid., 199*v* a.

18. Ibid., 154*r* b.

19. Ibid., 181*r* a.

20. *CAr*, 155*a*.

21. *Ms. H*, 118 25*r*.

22. *Ms. A*, 10*r*.

23. RLW, 19101*r*.

24. *CAt*, 175*v*.

4: SHATTERED DREAMS, NEW AWAKENINGS

1. However, the final Lippi painting now in the Uffizi bears little resemblance to a Leonardo.

2. Giorgio Vasari, *Lives of the Painters, Sculptors and Architects*, Random House, London, 1996, p. 626.

3. *CAt*, folios 11*b*, 37*b*.

4. Martin Kemp, *Leonardo da Vinci: The Marvellous Works of Nature and Man*, J. M. Dent & Sons, London, 1989, p. 86.

5. *CAt*, 11*b*.

6. Ibid., 71*r* a.

7. Kemp, op. cit., p. 88.

8. Ovid, *Metamorphoses*, XV, I, pp. 232–6.

9. Leonardo's emotional description of the passing of time appears on the same sheet as his list of people with whom he wanted to communicate.

10. *CT*, I, a.

11. *CAt*, 120r d.

12. From *Studies of Heads and Machines*, Uffizi, Florence, 1478.

13. *CAt*, 4v a.

14. Ibid., 71r a.

15. Vasari, op. cit., pp. 627–8.

16. Kenneth Clark, *Leonardo da Vinci*, Penguin, London, 1976, p. 42.

17. Nello Tarchiani, *Leonardo in Florence and Tuscany*, Reynal & Co., New York, p. 97.

5: RECOGNITION

1. *CUL*, folio 6v.

2. RLW, 12697.

3. See Anonimo Gaddiano in *Codice Magliabecchiano*, edited by Carl Frey, Berlin, 1892.

4. *CAt*, 324r.

5. Giorgio Vasari, *Lives of the Painters, Sculptors and Architects*, Random House, London, 1996, p. 631.

6. For further details of this argument, see Nello Tarchiani, *Leonardo in Florence and Tuscany*, Reynal & Co., New York, pp. 97–9.

7. *Ms. H*, 40b.

8. Quoted in Alessandro Visconti, 'Leonardo in Milan and Lombardy', in *Leonardo da Vinci*, Reynal & Co., New York, pp. 109–26.

9. *CAt*, 391r a.

10. Ibid.

11. Sabba de Castiglione, *Ricordi*, Venice, 1555.

12. Vasari, op. cit., p. 633.

13. This may be the piece Vasari misunderstood as being commissioned by the Duke.

14. *CAt*, 287r a.

15. Ibid., 76r.

16. Ibid., 65v b.

17. Quoted in Jean-Claude Frère, *Leonardo*, Terrail, Paris, 1994, p. 106.

18. Ibid., p. 108.

19. Ibid., p. 109.

20. *CAt*, 270*r* c.

21. Ibid.

22. Quoted in Visconti, op. cit., pp. 109–26.

6: TRIUMPH AND TURMOIL

1. RLW, folio 19060*r*.

2. *Ms. H*, 60-12*r*.

3. *Ms. I*, 15*r*.

4. *CAt*, 76*r* a.

5. Ibid., 76*v* a.

6. Ibid., 76*v* b.

7. Ibid., 182*v* c.

8. *Ms. H*, 16*v*.

9. *Ms. H*, III, 89*a*.

10. *CAt*, 380*a*, 1179*b*.

11. *Ms. C*, 15.

12. Giorgio Vasari, *Lives of the Painters, Sculptors and Architects*, Random House, London, 1996, pp. 634–5.

13. These comments and lists are scattered throughout *Ms. C*.

14. *CM*, II, 4b.

15. *CAt*, 312b; 949b; RLW, 32.

16. *Ms. F*, 2*r*.

17. *Ms. L*, 94*r*.

18. *CF*, II, 60*c*.

19. Kenneth Clark, *Leonardo da Vinci*, Penguin, London, 1976, p. 58.

20. Ibid.

21. Letter to Lorenzo de' Medici, dated 22 July 1489.

22. Windsor, 12345.

23. Donato Bramante, *Antiquarie prospetiche romane*, Casanatense Library, Rome.

24. *CAt*, 335*v*.

25. *CF*, III, 88*r*.

26. *CAr*, 272*r* a.

27. K. R. Eissler, *Léonard de Vinci*, Paris, 1980.

28. *CAt*, 71r a.

29. Fiscal declaration for Vinci, 1490.

30. *Ms. H*, 264b.

31. *Ms. M*, II, 95a.

32. *CAt*, 308b, 939a.

33. Matteo Bandello, *Lucca*, 1554.

34. R. Marcolonga, *Studi Vinciani. Memorie sulla geometrica e sulla meccanica di Leonardo da Vinci*, Naples, 1937.

35. Marcolonga, *Leonardo da Vinci, artista, scienzato*, Milan, 1950.

36. See Note 34.

37. Vasari, op. cit., p. 632.

38. *CAt*, 104r a.

39. Luca Pacioli, preface to *De divina proportione*, Venice, 1509.

40. *Quaderni*, II, 14r.

41. *CUL*, IV.

42. *CAt*, 132r.

43. De Lamar Jensen, *Renaissance Europe: Age of Recovery and Reconciliation*, D. C. Heath & Co., New York, p. 195.

44. Although a richly produced manuscript version was presented to Ludovico Sforza in 1498.

45. *CAt*, 248r.

46. Ibid., 251v.

47. In *CAt* (203v a) there is a brief mention (not in Leonardo's handwriting) of a request for him to help design fortifications for the French in Tuscany, but there is no evidence that he acted as a consultant for Louis.

48. *Ms. L*, 10r.

7: THE NOTEBOOKS I (1484–1500)

1. *CAt*, folio 393v a.

2. *Quaderni*, II, 16r.

3. *CAt*, 119v.

4. Ibid., 22r b.

5. *Ms. B*, 65v.

6. *CAt*, 292v a.

7. RLW, 12675v.

8. *CM*, I, 172r.

9. *Ms. B*, 23v.

10. Vitruvius, *Ten Books*, III, 1.

11. *Ms. K*, 49r.

12. *CUL*, 246r; *Ms. M*, 78v.

13. *CAr*, 156v.

14. RLW, 19037v.

15. *CUL*, 8r, 9r.

16. RLW, 19019r.

17. *CAt*, 270v b.

18. Ibid., 361v.

19. Ibid., 203r a, from the introduction to John Pecham, *Perspectiva communis*.

20. *Ms. A*, II, 6v.

21. *Quaderni*, IV, 12v.

22. *Ms. K*, 118v.

23. *CAt*, 83v b.

24. *Ms. D*, 3v.

25. *CAt*, 222r a.

26. Ibid., 10r a.

27. *Ms. A*, 61r.

28. *Ms. H*, 67r.

29. *CAt*, 138v b.

30. M. Nijhoff (ed.), *Oeuvres complètes*, Société Hollandaise des Sciences, The Hague, 1901, p. 380.

31. Christiaan Huygens, *Traité de la lumière*, 1690.

32. *Ms. H*, 67.

33. *Ms. F*, 49.

34. *Ms. 2038*, 1.

35. *Quaderni*, IV, 16r.

36. *Ms. I*, 87.

37. RLW, 19149r.

38. *Ms. C*, 22r.

39. *Ms. F*, 33v.

40. Ibid.

41. RLW, 4r.

42. *CUL*, 130r.

43. *Ms. H*, 141r.

44. *Ms. A*, 34v.

45. *CT*, 10r.

46. *Ms. I*, 130v.

47. *CAt*, 201r a.

48. Ibid., 225r b.

49. Leonardo da Vinci, *Trattato della pittura* (*Treatise on Painting*), edited by A. P. McMahon, Princeton University Press, 1956.

50. W. C. Dampier, *A History of Science*, Cambridge University Press, Cambridge, 1984, p. 103.

8: THE PERIPATETIC SAGE

1. Letter from Charles d'Amboise to the Signoria of Florence, 16 December 1506.

2. Letter from Lorenzo Gugnasco to Isabella d'Este, 13 March 1500.

3. Unpublished papers in RLW, XVI, folio 28a.

4. *Ms. I*, 135r.

5. *Ms. K*, 100r.

6. *CAt*, 234a b.

7. Ibid., 333v a.

8. Ibid.

9. Ibid.

10. Ibid.

11. RLW, 22b.

12. *CAt*, 247r a.

13. Ibid., 62v a.

14. Letter from Isabella d'Este to Fra Pietro da Novellara, 16 March 1501.

15. Giorgio Vasari, *Lives of the Painters, Sculptors and Architects*, Random House, London, 1996, p. 635.

16. Letter from Fra Pietro da Novellara to Isabella d'Este, 8 April 1501.

17. Letter from Fra Pietro da Novellara to Isabella d'Este, 14 April 1501.

18. Letter from Isabella d'Este to Leonardo da Vinci, 14 May 1504.

19. Vasari, op. cit.

20. *CAt*, 391r a.

21. This letter was published by F. Babingher in the *Nachrichten der Akademie der Wissenschaften* in Göttingen in 1952.

22. *CAt*, 45r.

23. Ibid., 284r.

24. *Ms. 2038*, 30v, 31r.

25. *CAt*, 368v b.

26. Leonardo da Vinci, *Trattato della pittura* (*Treatise on Painting*), edited by A. P. McMahon, Princeton University Press, 1956.

27. *CAr*, 272a.

28. *CAt*, 70b, 208b.

29. *CM*, II, 2a.

30. Anonimo Gaddiano, *Codice Magliabecchiano*, edited by Carl Frey, Berlin, 1892, p. 2.

31. Florimond Robertet to Florentine Signoria, January 1507.

32. Florimond Robertet to Florentine Signoria, May 1507.

33. *CAt*, 310a.

9: The Arms of the King

1. *CAr*, folio 1r.

2. *CAt*, 217v a, 231r b.

3. Giorgio Vasari, *Lives of the Painters, Sculptors and Architects*, Random House, London, 1996, p. 634.

4. *CAt*, 141v b.

5. Vasari, op. cit., p. 635.

6. Oscar Wilde, *The Critic as Artist*, 1890.

7. RLW, 12416.

8. *Ms. E*, 1a.

9. *Ms. L*, 1b.

10. *CAt*, 83r a.

11. *Ms. A*, 2r.

12. *Ms. F*, 96b.

13. *CAt*, 179b, 243b, 278a, 541b, 729b, 850a.

14. *Ms. G*, 46v.

15. *CAt*, 182v c.

16. Vasari, op. cit., p. 638.

17. RLW, 12665v.

18. Vasari, op. cit., p. 634.

19. *Ms. G*, verso of cover.

20. *CM*, II, 24a.

21. Benvenuto Cellini, *Treatise on Architecture*.

22. *CAt*, 249r.

23. Ibid., 244r.

24. Ibid., 289v c.

25. Don Antonio Beatis, *Voyage du cardinal d'Aragon*, Paris, 1913.

26. *Ms. F*, 25v.

27. *CAr*, 1r.

28. Vasari, op. cit., p. 639.

29. *Ms. A*, 2r.

30. RLW, 19115r.

31. Ibid., 19084r.

32. Vasari, op. cit., p. 639.

10: THE NOTEBOOKS II (1500–1519)

1. Don Antonio Beatis, *Voyage du cardinal d'Aragon*, Paris, 1913.

2. For more details, see Roy Porter, *The Greatest Benefit to Mankind: A Medical History of Humanity from Antiquity to the Present*, HarperCollins, London, 1998.

3. *CT*, folio 4r.

4. *Quaderni*, I, 6r.

5. RLW, 19027v.

6. Ibid., 19052r.

7. Ibid., 19027r.

8. Ibid., 19019r.

9. *Ms. B*, 17*v*.

10. RLW, 19017*r*.

11. Ibid., 19003*v*.

12. *Ms. A*, 15*v*.

13. RLW, 19012*v*.

14. Quoted in Ludwig, *Das Buch von der Malerei*, Berlin, 1882, paragraph 404.

15. RLW, 19102*r*.

16. Ibid., 19054*v*.

17. *Ms. A*, 55*v*.

18. *Quaderni*, IV, 14*v*.

19. Ibid., 13*r*.

20. *Ms. G*, 1*v*.

21. *Ms. B*, 13*r*.

22. *Quaderni*, IV, 11*r*.

23. RLW, 19001.

24. Ibid., 12603.

25. Ibid., 12281*r*.

26. Ibid., 12326*r*.

27. Ibid., 19075*v*.

28. *CF*, III, 74*v*.

29. RLW, 19097*v*.

30. Ibid., 19060*r*.

31. *CAt*, 373*v* a.

32. Treatise II, paragraph 926, p. 320.

33. Ibid., paragraph 928, p. 322.

34. *CAt*, 241, 242.

35. Ibid., 60.

36. RLW, 36 (author's italics).

37. *CAt*, 71.

38. *Ms. B*, 156.

39. RLW, 27*v*.

40. Ibid., 34*r*.

41. *Ms. A*, 56*v*.

42. Stephen Jay Gould, *Leonardo's Mountain of Clams and the Diet of Worms*, Jonathan Cape, London, 1998, pp. 17–45.

43. *CAt*, 18*v*.

44. *Ms. F*, 2.

45. Leonardo da Vinci, *Trattato della pittura* (*Treatise on Painting*), edited by A. P. McMahon, Princeton University Press, 1956.

46. *Ms. F*, 56*r*.

47. *CAr*, 94*v*.

48. Ibid., 28*r*.

49. Ibid., 94*v*.

50. *Ms. F*, 93*r*.

51. Ibid., 56*r*.

52. Ibid., 4*v*.

53. *CAt*, 185*v* b.

54. *Ms. E*, 15*v*.

55. *Ms. F*, 25*r*.

56. *CAr*, 94*v*.

57. *Ms. A*, 12*v*.

58. *CAt*, 190*r* a.

59. *Ms. F*, 25*r*.

60. Ibid.

61. *CAr*, 4*r*.

62. Domenico Argentieri, 'Leonardo's Optics', in *The Life and Works of Leonardo da Vinci*, Morrow & Co., New York, 1938.

63. *CAt*, 381.

64. *Ms. E*, 23*v*.

65. *CAt*, 161*r* a.

66. Roger Bacon, *Epistola de secretis operibus*.

67. *CFB*, 16*r*.

68. Ibid.

69. *Ms. B*, 83*v*.

70. *CFB*, 18*v*.

71. Girolamo Cardano, *De subtiliate*, 1550.

72. *CFB*, 12*v*.

73. Ibid., 16r.

74. Ibid.

75. Ibid., 6r.

76. Ibid., 9r.

77. *CM*, I, 6r.

11: THE SCIENCE OF ART

1. Luca Pacioli, *Divina proportione*, 1498, Introduction.

2. *CAt*, folio 119v a.

3. Ibid., 221v.

4. Giorgio Vasari, *Lives of the Painters, Sculptors and Architects*, Random House, London, 1996, p. 634.

5. John Pecham, *Perspectiva communis*, I, 37.

6. *Ms. D*, 4v.

7. Ibid., 6v.

8. Ibid., 10v.

9. *CUL*, 160v.

10. *Ms. D*, 10v.

11. Ibid., 2r.

12. Ibid.

13. *Ms. G*, 12v.

14. Ibid., 26v.

15. *CUL*, 193r, 207v, 75r.

16. Leonardo, *Trattato della pittura* (*Treatise on Painting*), edited by A. P. McMahon, Princeton University Press, 1956, Chapter 90.

17. *CAt*, 324r.

18. *Ms. K*, 109v.

19. *Quaderni*, 22r v.

20. *Ms. E*, 20r.

21. *CAt*, 345v.

22. *Ms. B*, 20v.

23. *Ms. A*, 11v.

24. *CUL*, 61r.

25. Ibid., 115v.

26. Ibid., 44*v*, 45*r*.

27. Ibid., 104*r* v.

28. *Ms. E*, 19*v*, 20*r*.

29. *CUL*, 104*r*.

30. *Ms. G*, 16*v*.

31. Ibid., 51*r*.

32. RLW, 19048*r*.

33. *Ms. A*, 110*v*.

12: PLANET LEONARDO

1. Richard Feynman, *Six Easy Pieces*, Addison-Wesley, New York, 1995.

2. Sigmund Freud, *Ein Kindheitserinnerung des Leonardo da Vinci* (*A Childhood Memory of Leonardo da Vinci*), Vienna, 1910.

3. Paolo Giovio in *Storia della letteratura italiana*, edited by Tiraboschi, Rome, 1781.

4. Kenneth Clark, *Leonardo da Vinci*, Penguin, London, 1989, p. 43.

INDEX

Page numbers in *italics* refer to the illustrations.